The Other Side of the Couch

The Other Side of the Couch

THE HEALING BOND IN PSYCHIATRY

Gail Albert

Faber and Faber
Boston · London

Excerpts from *The Standard Edition of the Complete Psychological Works of Sigmund Freud*, translated and edited by James Strachey, used by permission of Sigmund Freud Copyrights, The Institute of Psycho-Analysis, The Hogarth Press, and W. W. Norton.

Library of Congress Cataloging-in-Publication Data

Albert, Gail, 1942–
The other side of the couch
Gail Albert.
p. cm.
Includes bibliographical references
ISBN 0–571–19869–4
1. Psychiatry. 2. Psychiatrists. 3. Psychotherapist and patient.
I. Title.
RC454.4.A42 1995
616.89'023—dc20
94–48391
CIP

Jacket design by Adrian Morgan at Red Letter Design
Jacket photograph courtesy of the Image Club
Printed in the United States of America

to the memory of Harry Dean Albert,
and to our sons, Jared and Eric

Contents

Acknowledgments

I wish to thank first the psychiatrists who gave so freely of themselves in the interviews that form the backbone of this book; I hope they are pleased with the outcome. I am also intensely grateful to my parents and to all the friends who have encouraged and supported me in what has often seemed to be an overwhelming project. In particular, I wish to thank Louise Passick for invaluable editorial advice from the first step to the very last; Joanna Fancy, for our many conversations about the book and her thoughtful readings of the manuscript; Katherine Falk, M.D., for her continuing mentoring and the sharing of her deep psychiatric understanding; Richard Glass M.D., whose enthusiastic support, careful reading of the manuscript, and psychiatric wisdom were essential to the book's completion; and Barbara and Peter Leary, without whom it might never have reached publication. I also wish to thank my agent, Gloria Loomis, for her unflagging encouragement and sensitivity, Betsy Uhrig, my editor at Faber and Faber, for her unfailingly helpful suggestions, and Maggie Carr, for her remarkably careful copy editing.

Above all, my thanks to my children, Jared and Eric, for their love and support through many difficult years.

INTRODUCTION

The Healing Bond

By definition, half the people in any line of work are below average.[1] While this fact may not matter in most circumstances, it's one to remember when you need a surgeon or a cardiologist—or a psychiatrist. For the harsh reality is that poor psychiatrists waste their patients' lives, while good psychiatrists help change the rules that define life's possibilities.

This book explores an ideal, the landscape of psychiatry at its best. I stand as a guide, taking you deep into the experience of a number of superb psychiatrists as they talk about their work with patients. In this era of managed care and limited insurance coverage, the essence of psychiatric treatment seems too often lost in debates on cost-effectiveness, and I hope this volume may serve as a reminder of what must always remain the central issue: that all effective psychotherapy grows from the unique and healing bond between therapist and patient.

This book is about the nature of this healing bond, in all its uniqueness, complexity, and paradox. Much of what I have written inevitably applies to good psychotherapists in any profession, whether psychiatry, psychology, social work, or psychiatric nursing.[2] However, my focus is the psychiatrist, for he or she[3] is the only physician specially trained to treat mental disorders and the only psychotherapist generally allowed to prescribe medications.[4] I chose this focus because psychiatry is at the pivot of an explosion in pharmacology that has revolutionized the treatment of mental disorders in the last two decades. The new medications are as important as antibiotics, offering weapons against disorders that afflict up to one-third of all Americans in the course of their lifetimes;[5] and they have changed the ground rules for what constitutes good care—even for psychotherapists who are not allowed to prescribe medication. I have written this book for anyone in psychotherapy or counseling, for anyone considering getting treatment for themselves or someone they love, and for anyone who simply wants to understand what goes into the practice of really fine psychiatry.

✍

This book takes us behind the closed doors of the psychiatrist's office as we listen to a few of the best psychiatrists in the United States. As they speak, they bear no resemblance to psychiatrists portrayed in novels or movies or on TV. Indeed, they reveal a world that is unknown to anyone outside it.

As far as I know, these interviews are unique for three reasons: they include only psychiatrists who are extremely gifted at their work; they are limited to psychiatrists who are as comfortable with psychotherapy as they are with the uses of medication; and they take us into the psychiatrist's own experience working with patients.[6] Because the practice of good psychiatry demands the intimate interweaving of professional skills with the most private self, these psychiatrists also revealed a great deal about themselves as they described what they think and feel in the course of doing treatment.

✍

I have a Ph.D. in experimental psychology from the Johns Hopkins University and have spent most of my working life around psychiatrists. Because I married a medical student who became a psychiatrist, I was also around psychiatrists-in-training throughout my marriage, seeing their lives unfold as they moved from medical school through internship through three-year psychiatry residencies in hospital training programs.

As they grew from anxious students to seasoned psychiatrists, I marveled at the changes in them. And I couldn't understand the nature of the bond between them and their patients: intense but bounded, loving but dispassionate, protective but distanced, intellectual but emotive; and always complex, convoluted, and to my eye self-contradictory. I wanted to know how they could bear to listen to so much pain and shut it off at the end of the hour; how they could tolerate the responsibility for patients' lives or endure the inability to take control of them; how they could remember all the details patients told them. And what did they do about anger or lust or boredom during the treatment hour—or simple fatigue? Ultimately, I wrote this book to understand.

I prepared for these interviews by reading the books psychiatrists themselves read during their residency training and afterward. I went back to Freud's own writing in the multivolume *Standard Edition,* to a host of books by those who followed after him, to the last fifteen years of the profession's scientific voice, *The American Journal of Psychiatry,* and to the monthly newsletter of the American Psychiatric Association. Then I began to cull psychiatrists.

I couldn't use academic credentials or the number of papers someone had published because eminence does not predict actual performance as a doctor. On the other hand, all doctors know a few others for whom they have great regard; these are the doctors they send their own family and friends to see. So I asked a number of highly respected psychiatrists who they themselves called on when friends and members of their own family needed treatment.

They named psychiatrists whose patients get better even when they've failed with other therapists or been in and out of hospitals much of their lives.[7] They also said that when they ask these psychiatrists for advice about their own patients, they get suggestions that work. To my amazement, certain names were repeated over and over. These were the people I interviewed: a dozen psychiatrists in the New York metropolitan area, nine men and three women. (For the sake of clarity, I featured only seven of them in the writing: Laura, Steve, John, Gary, Emily, Michael, and Rosemary.)

Although they came from different hospital training programs, they'd all been taught how to be psychiatrists when psychoanalytic thought still dominated residency training, a domination which passed in the course of the 1980s; they were skilled in the use of medications as well. Licensed physicians and board certified[8] psychiatrists, all but two had also undertaken six years of additional specialized training at a psychoanalytic institute to graduate as psychoanalysts;[9] several had completed residency training in internal medicine or another medical specialty before beginning psychiatry training; most held academic positions; and a few were famous within psychiatry. They offered patients a range of treatment, from short-term psychotherapy, to classical psychoanalysis, to behavior modification, to fifteen-minute meetings once a month to monitor medications.

They talked to me for up to seven hours. Because I worked with an outline of the areas I was interested in, all were asked a similar set of questions, and we tape-recorded the entirety of each interview. At first many of them were suspicious, wondering what sort of exposé I planned, doubting my concern for patients, and sure that they couldn't convey their worldview to me. But as we gained confidence in each other, the interviews came to mirror the experience of a session, with each of us trying together to close in on the complex and mysterious processes we were examining, and they became extraordinarily frank. They insisted only that neither they nor their patients be identifiable, and so I have changed their names, their patients' names, and any physical characteristics of the psychiatrists that would allow identification.

Initially, I saw the interviews as adornments, to flesh out the skeleton I'd built from reading. I'd expected variability, even disagreements. But as the interviews progressed I made another unexpected discovery: They all said the same things about patients and the therapeutic relationship, and about the critical and ever expanding role of medications.

They made it clear that psychiatry is in an uproar at the moment, rediscovering its medical roots after forty years of Freudian domination, propelled by revolutions in drug therapy and brain research to integrate the very different and often inimical traditions of medicine and psychoanalysis. The psychiatrist must attempt a new synthesis that includes both the prescribing physician and empathic therapist; and the blend is extremely difficult because many of the underlying assumptions of the two approaches clash.

This book is not a cookbook, but it *is* a guide to the ingredients of good psychiatric treatment. Although I had no formal clinical training at the time I began the work, I became a resource for friends and friends of friends in the course of writing it, able to suggest what they should expect and look for in good treatment, and what sorts of things were signals that something was wrong with the care they were receiving. I believe that you will finish this book with a new understanding of the texture and quality of good psychotherapy and a new ability to make your own judgments of good and bad psychiatric care.

LAYER

1

ESSENTIALS

1

Background

This chapter covers background material about psychiatry that will help the reader in later sections. Largely historical, these pages give a short explication of the backdrop that psychiatrists take for granted, particularly in three areas: the differences between psychiatry and psychoanalysis; the interconnection of medicine, psychiatry, and psychoanalysis; and the enduring conflict within psychiatry between biological and psychological explanations of mental disorder. By putting this material in one place at the beginning, I hope to quickly orient the reader.

✍

When Freud graduated from medical school in 1881, the European world believed mental disorders to be the creation of a diseased or injured brain or—most often—degenerate heredity. These beliefs had become part of the general climate of thought that was created by advances in the sciences and by the scientific hypothesis that all the complexity of life—and mind—would ultimately be reduced to a few fundamental principles of chemistry and physics.

Freud himself was profoundly influenced by this grand scheme, and was extraordinarily well-trained to pursue it, having worked for years in the laboratories of Europe's greatest physiologist (Ernst Brücke) and finest brain anatomist (Theodore Meynert), and having studied with the brilliant French neurologist Jean-Martin Charcot.[1] Freud never abandoned the hope that mental function would ultimately be described in terms of physical processes in the brain, and he gave up his own attempts to reduce the mind to physical biology only as he became convinced that there sim-

3

ply weren't enough physiological data for what he called "The Project."[2]
Even so, his later psychoanalytic formulations were in large part metaphors
for the biology he couldn't get at, involving energy flow, balance of forces,
and other basic nineteenth-century concepts of physics. And he continued
to believe in the central role of heredity.[3]

When Freud began his work with "nervous" patients in the 1880s, psychiatry was a branch of neurology, and most psychiatric patients were seen
as people with obscure but nasty neuropathology that demonstrated
hereditary taint. His position was revolutionary not because he denied
hereditary influence but because he argued that in many patients mental
illness could be treated anyway, by psychological means. If Freud had been
armed with modern medications, he would have used them to attack the
constitutional vulnerabilities we now describe in the language of brain
biochemistry.[4] But the medicines didn't exist, and Freud turned to talk because he had nothing medical to offer. "Anyone who wants to make a living from the treatment of nervous patients must clearly be able to do
something to help them," he was to tartly observe years later in "An Autobiographical Study" (1925).[5]

In 1891 he published a remarkably accurate work on aphasia, and by
1893 two exhaustive studies of childhood paralyses, one of which is still
considered a classic.[6] During these same years he turned his genius to
mental disorders. Opening a world that had only been glimpsed before, he
was to create—in psychoanalysis—a new vision of the human mind and a
revolutionary treatment, the first attempt to cure mental illnesses by
purely psychological techniques.[7] In this context, Freud's emphasis on the
importance of childhood events and the critical role of sexuality are merely
details, a gloss on the overriding shift in viewpoint that came with psy-
chologizing what had been seen until then as purely physical, and, most
often, a matter of immutable hereditary weakness. And as Freudian
thought was adopted in America, it became ever more psychological, with
heredity, constitutional vulnerability, and questions of abnormal brain
function the Freudian equivalent of dirty words.

The first psychiatrists in the United States were superintendents of institutions for the insane.[8] Practicing "psychological medicine,"[9] they generally accepted the contemporary view that their patients had some sort of
brain malfunction. As Americans, however, they were shaped by dreams of

equality and by the fluid class structure of a nation shaped by immigration and an expanding frontier. The tone was set by Benjamin Rush, the titular father of American psychiatry (and signer of the Declaration of Independence). In the only textbook of psychiatry printed here until the end of the nineteenth century, he wrote, "Man is a single and indivisible being for so intimately united are his mind and body that one cannot be moved without the other."[10]

Retreating from European images of hereditary taint, American psychiatrists in the nineteenth century looked for the causes of brain disorder in the environment—in disease, diet, or injury—and stressed the importance of environmental influence on the course of mental disorders. The "moral therapy" movement that flourished during the nineteenth century emphasized humane care and simple manual labor to counteract mental disorders.[11] The most influential psychiatrist of the twentieth century, Adolph Meyer, stressed the interrelationships of multiple biological, social, and psychological factors in normal development as well as disease states.[12]

In fact, head wounds among soldiers during the American Civil War had provided important evidence that environmental factors—in the form of injury—induced certain psychiatric conditions. Then, in 1886, the Russian psychiatrist Sergei Korsakoff described a remarkable kind of amnesia brought on by chronic alcoholism, in which alcoholic patients confabulated—and believed—involved stories about themselves to cover loss of memory, frequently changing their stories from day to day as they'd forget what they'd already said. Korsakoff syndrome became a model of the potential effects of brain injury.[13]

Two decades later, when Freud was publishing his early papers on psychoanalysis, a test for syphilis (the Wassermann) and a cure (Salversan, "the magic bullet") were both discovered. The spread of syphilis to the brain accounted for up to one-third of all mental hospital admissions—apart from those cases that never reached the hospital, for untreated syphilis (that hadn't yet attacked the nervous system) was a common plague. Like AIDS, it spread to sexual partners and unborn children; once a cure had been found, neurosyphilis became the most exciting disease of the era for medicine.[14]

Meanwhile, vitamin deficiencies were found to be the cause of pellagra, another dementia-causing disorder that filled mental hospitals (causing the characteristic bronzing of the skin seen in many derelicts today). Almost always reversible with vitamin treatment, pellagra essentially disappeared in the United States once niacin and other B vitamins were added to flour.[15] Vitamin-B deficiencies also turned out to be responsible for Korsakoff syndrome.[16] Between 1910 and the late 1920s, then, psychiatrists uncovered the physical causes of three of the most common major mental illnesses—and found medical treatments.

Unfortunately, the origins of illness in the majority of patients remained stubbornly elusive as the following decades wore on. And psychiatry remained isolated from the rest of medicine. Psychiatrists had created the earliest American medical society in 1844 (the Association of Medical Superintendents of American Institutions for the Insane), and worked to have psychiatry taught in medical schools and psychiatric patients moved from the freestanding asylums to psychiatry wards in general hospitals. But as late as the 1930s most patients were still in mental hospitals that had no medical school affiliation for their staffs, only half of all medical schools had any study of psychiatric patients in the curriculum, and only a few general hospitals had added psychiatric wards.[17] Meanwhile, Freudian theory and practice offered an entirely different track, at first infiltrating and, after World War II, dominating, American psychiatry.[18]

Even in 1909, Freud was greeted by a surprisingly large and enthusiastic audience when he gave a series of lectures at Clark University, for his work resonated with American interest in psychological forces. In the following decades, his theories were widely disseminated by a variety of psychiatrists,[19] particularly William Alanson White and Adolph Meyer, the two most influential American psychiatrists of the twentieth century. Meyer, in particular, shaped every aspect of modern American psychiatry, from the psychiatric interview to hospital organization and residency training; and Meyer and White together gave psychiatry its present form as a hospital-based medical specialty rooted in psychoanalytic insights.[20]

From 1945 until the late 1970s, psychoanalysts controlled psychiatry, holding most of the academic positions, teaching classes, supervising residents-in-training as they worked with patients, and making a psychodynamic orientation central to almost every residency program.[21]

Psychiatrists who wanted the ultimate education capped their residency with additional training at a psychoanalytic institute, focusing solely on psychoanalytic theory and technique; graduates got diplomas certifying them as full-fledged psychoanalysts. It usually took candidates about seven years to finish classes and to carry through the analysis of two or three out-patients plus their own personal psychoanalysis with a "training" analyst appointed by the institute. (Some psychoanalytic institutes also accept psychologists, social workers, and, occasionally, professionals not in the mental health field. Nowadays there are, if anything, more psychologists graduating from psychoanalytic institutes than psychiatrists, in part because there are many more psychologists, and in part because fewer psychiatrists want psychoanalytic training.)

But few hospitalized patients were ever cured by psychoanalytic techniques alone, and Freud himself never tried to treat all psychiatric diseases psychoanalytically, initially developing psychoanalysis to treat hysteria, and then gradually extended his theories to other forms of neurosis. Along the way, he concluded that analysis was an inappropriate form of treatment for still other mental disorders, and he limited psychoanalytic treatment to people well enough to see him in private practice.[22]

On the one hand, he thought the most serious psychiatric abnormalities might well be signs of true brain disease. Apart from acknowledging the impossibility of affecting a truly damaged brain by talk, he also stated that analysis was out of the question for sicker patients because they hadn't the ability to tolerate the frustrations of the analyst's neutrality and often had too weak a grasp of reality to follow the rules of the psychoanalytic game.[23]

But a few pioneers began to build on Freud's work as early as the 1920s to extend the psychoanalytic domain to the kinds of patients Freud rejected. Modifying Freud's procedures over many years, these brilliant psychotherapists[24] worked with even the most psychotic patients in hospitals, reporting improvement and, sometimes, cures. They also began to hypothesize a continuum from normalcy through the most severe mental illnesses, and to contend that psychological issues were causal in even the most bizarre psychoses.[25]

Standing on Freud's shoulders, they vastly increased the range of psychoanalysis, extending both theory and practice to patients far sicker than Freud ever intended to treat. And as psychodynamic theory permeated psychiatry at large, so did the new belief that *all* kinds of mental disease could be traced to essentially psychological causes and treated by variations of the psychoanalytic method. As psychiatrists trained by Freud and his disciples began to teach and supervise the next generation of psychiatric residents, the American interpretation of Freud's work and this psychological view of mental illness came to dominate psychiatry.[26]

But before medications existed, only a handful of the most dedicated and talented therapists were actually able to treat sicker patients with variants of traditional psychoanalysis. Most patients were relegated to the crowded wards of state hospitals, where a few organic treatments (such as electroconvulsive shock) were available, and patients faced the prospect of a lifetime locked away if these efforts failed. Most psychiatrists limited their work to relatively healthy patients, and psychiatry after World War II split into two fields: the more or less psychoanalytic treatment of neurotics seen in private practice, and the locked ward for those with generally immutable illnesses. During this time, psychiatry's interest turned away from the medical and began to meld with a version of psychoanalysis in an approach most of us still associate with psychiatry, largely purged of Freud's emphasis on the interpenetration of biology and psychology.[27]

Then came the observation in 1952 that chlorpromazine (better known here by its brand name Thorazine), a sedative used by surgeons in France, also acted on patients suffering from schizophrenia. A few years later, in 1958, Thomas Kuhn found the first antidepressant, imipramine (Tofranil), Nathan Kline reported on the efficacy of another class of antidepressants called monoamine oxidase inhibitors,[28] and in the course of the sixties and early seventies, the Food and Drug Administration approved lithium to treat mania and to prevent recurrences of both mania and depression. Suddenly the psychiatrist had effective treatments for the three mental illnesses that were most likely to bring people into the hospital.[29] In the first wave of excitement, the state hospitals released one-quarter of their patients.[30]

During the next few years, a flood of other medicines, including the anti-anxiety agent Valium (and more recently, the antidepressant Prozac), extended psychopharmacology to more and more of us. Psychiatry was transformed as dozens of drugs for all kinds of mental problems followed Thorazine, drugs that worked not only against derangements that required hospitalization but also against less severe, but still disabling, disorders of mood and thought. In all, this revolution takes in mental illnesses affecting a minimum of 10 percent of Americans, almost thirty million people, in any given year.[31] Now we have medicines for depressions, phobias, compulsions, panic attacks, and a range of symptoms that only a blink ago were considered character defects requiring years of psychotherapy. And new classes of medication keep appearing monthly.

As a result, the definitions of both psychiatrist and patient have been forced to change, and the relationship between them has been profoundly altered. For the relative roles of biology and psychology must be reconsidered in all types of mental disorder, and the interplay of the two considered in all psychotherapy. Powerful medicines exist now that did not exist even a year or two ago, much less five, ten, or twenty years back, and they can do a great deal of good—if the right diagnosis is made.

2

Learning to Listen

All societies have shamans, magicmakers with the right to probe both the body and the mind, healers who have no doubt that the two are inextricably interwoven. These wizards have sanction to prescribe medicines and perform ritual ceremonies, license to touch the naked body, and liberty to ask questions allowed no one else. They are permitted to cause pain in the name of healing, using sharp knives to cut into the body and sharp words to excise the most shameful secrets from the mind. In Western tradition, the shaman's role is most closely approximated by the physician's.

In our society, however, mind and body are usually seen as independent—the body a fleshly machine, the mind mysteriously different. And most modern doctors prefer to stay firmly within the first sphere, concentrating on the patient's physical functions and staying clear of feelings and the inner life. In our society, only the psychiatrist routinely straddles the two domains of mind and body, balanced, however precariously, with one foot in each camp.

But all psychiatrists were doctors first, molded by medical school and immersion in medicine. Although their bond with patients is much like that of other psychotherapists, being a doctor becomes central to their identity in the course of their training, and, for better or worse, remains an indelible part of them and of how they relate to patients.

Like other physicians, psychiatrists begin with two years of science courses, comprehensive graduate-level classes in all the basic sciences of the human body, memorizing thick volumes of anatomy, physiology, biochemistry, neurobiology, genetics, and immunology. These two years are essentially academic years during which students are expected not only to learn raw facts but also to master at least the fundamental relationships among them. As textbook learning becomes a working understanding of the human body, so medical students can never again look at another person without an awareness of the machinery under the skin.

The second half of medical school is different, harking back to the apprenticeship the beginner served with the surgeon-barber in medieval times. In the clinical experience of the third and fourth years, students begin to face patients themselves, learning what to do by trailing after more experienced doctors on hospital rounds. Watching and imitating their teachers' every gesture, they learn how to take a medical history, do a physical exam, make a diagnosis, and set up a plan of treatment. These are the basic skills of the physician and, to a great extent, of the psychiatrist. In 1989 American psychiatrists rated interviewing and establishing the doctor-patient relationship, diagnosis, assessment, and treatment planning their five most important skills, even ahead of doing psychotherapy.[1]

But the aim of medical school is not just vocational training. It also calls for the very reshaping of character, transforming old ways of responding to the world and to the people in it. In the teaching hierarchy[2] that extends from medical students through interns, residents, and faculty members, students are constantly watched, taught, and judged. Although some teachers are supportive, others use shame and terror as a molding force. At many schools, students are publicly questioned all the time, and exposed and humiliated if they don't measure up. Students are told outright that their ignorance or stupidity will someday kill someone, and they are deliberately pushed to superhuman efforts to harden them for the responsibility of patient care.[3]

Laura Cameron is a California-born psychiatrist who's made New York her home. Childless, Laura married and divorced while still in medical school; a year ago she married again. An intense, hard-driving woman in her mid-forties, she is fashionably thin and attractive, with what are known as "good bones." Her seriousness is frequently punctuated by an uninhibited and joyous laugh.

"You learn to be a doctor by being forced beyond your natural limits," she said. "It begins with anatomy and two years of cramming more facts into your head than you thought possible. Except for anatomy, where you have a cadaver, the kind of work is familiar—it's all memorizing from books—but you gradually realize that from now on you'll never know enough, that you can't remember everything, that there's simply no way for your mind to absorb the sheer mass of material it's faced with. Then you start the clinical work in the third year, the clerkship, and you're expected to immediately pull all the book learning together and use it with real patients. No one cares that you've never taken out a suture before. 'It's easy,' the intern says. 'Take the tweezers and scissors to Room 630.'"

Steve Blake agreed with Laura. In his fifties, Steve is fair-haired, tall, and almost as handsome as Robert Redford but far less relaxed, with piercing blue eyes, an impatient manner, and an aura of barely suppressed energy. The youngest of four brothers by many years, Steve's childhood was a lonely one on a Kansas farm, and he is given to long silences. Like the other psychiatrists I interviewed, he is incisive and articulate.

"At rounds, you tag after the residents and interns and take notes on everything. You're wet behind the ears, and you know you don't know enough even though you've been up reading until three A.M. Because you also know that someone by the patient's bed will say, 'Dr. Blake, perhaps you can tell us why Mrs. Jones has turned purple with yellow polka-dots this morning?'" Although I smiled, he didn't. "The whole clerkship is like being a little kid in school when you don't know the answer and the teacher is looking around for someone to call on. Except that none of it is trivial. Once you graduate, you're going to be responsible for people's lives."

Students are taught that doctors must think clearly in any situation and take charge even if their best is only an educated guess. So students push themselves to the limit, taking a history from a man old enough to be their father, palpating a teenager's breasts, or explaining a diagnosis of childhood leukemia to distraught parents to whom a white coat means doctor. But coolness has its price. Denial of feelings becomes central to the professional identity, just as being a doctor becomes part of the core self. As Steve said wryly, "Everyone else can run in circles. Not you. Not from the first day."

Good doctors ultimately become able to be warm with patients once again—and psychiatrists *must* have access to such warmth if they are to be of any help at all—but rediscovery of feeling is not easy. On the first day of medical school, students sometimes vomit when they unwrap their cadaver from its plastic bag, but they begin the dissection anyway, for the first rule of medicine is that the doctor's feelings are irrelevant. "You're surrounded by pain and death," Steve said, "and patients are turning to you for help when you barely know how to find the nearest bathroom. Of course, you leave medical school less human than you were when you began. If you didn't put up barricades to hide behind, you'd never survive the experience."

The pages of medical journals frequently bemoan the dehumanization of the medical student, comparing the emphasis placed on technical expertise with how little attention is paid to the doctor-patient relationship. Although a number of schools have experimented with changes (such as assigning each medical student the care of the same family from the first day through graduation), dehumanization may be an inescapable by-product of advances in medical technology, for only so much can be crammed into a given training program. Indeed, some of the old-time doctor's warmth was offered in lieu of effective treatments. Given the potency of modern medicine, no school dares risk dropping one hard-edged fact to make time for the teaching of warmth.

"When I was in med school in the 1960s," Steve said, "our chief of medicine could diagnose patients just by walking into the room and sniffing the air. He was one of the half-dozen best diagnosticians in the United States, and he knew what certain sicknesses smelled like, he knew just what a particular tinge to the skin meant, and when he needed more information he'd smell the urine—or taste it. If he still wasn't sure, he sometimes climbed into bed with the patient. He said talking with someone while lying next to them in bed told him what he needed to know." The lines at the corners of Steve's mouth deepened as he smiled. "Obviously, he was the old-fashioned doctor carried to the ultimate level of sophistication. No patient ever felt himself an object in his presence, and you won't have the same experience when a technician sticks you for blood samples and the doctor reads the lab results. . . . But he was extraordinary—while you don't have to be extraordinary to read lab findings and order penicillin."

On the other hand, students' dehumanization may lie less with the technical demands of modern training than with the tradition by which they are thrown into medicine and told to swim. The demands only intensify after graduation.

The hospital year begins July 1. On that day, everyone in training moves to a new position—and the medical school graduate becomes an intern. Usually the first doctor to see the patient, take a history, diagnose, and treat, the intern may also be the only doctor present on the ward all night. Just under first-year residents in the training hierarchy, interns can always call the resident on duty for help. But in most programs residents are essentially supervisors, teachers, and backups, immersed in their own specialty training in a particular branch of medicine, and not the patient's prime caretaker.

"All medical training is apprenticeship," Steve said. "Internship is more of the same. But now you're the one the medical student follows around." He fell silent, his face pensive. After several seconds he said, "You never forget the first time you lose someone. Until then you believe in your gut that you can beat the odds, that you can save your patient if only you work hard enough. That first time, it doesn't matter if you've done everything right. You feel it's your fault—there must have been something you missed. But that's a turning point, when you know you can be truly helpless. The family is pleading for help, even for a miracle, and you have nothing left to offer. And the next morning, you have to show up for rounds and take care of your other patients, and you can't say, 'I'm scared.'"

The intern is expected to treat any disease that puts someone into a hospital bed, and in the emergency room interns decide who gets a bed and who goes home. Internship is the year of endless cups of coffee and ten-minute snatches of sleep, of frenzied on-the-job training, of taking charge no matter what.[4]

"Your medical school diploma doesn't make you a doctor," Laura said. "Your internship does. My first diabetic coma, I spent the night next to his bed, taking hourly blood chemistries and reading the book for what to do next. My resident was available when I needed him, but the man in the bed was *my* patient.

"My father [a surgeon] had mixed feelings about my becoming a doctor," she added. "Women in my family don't have careers. But he told me that when I became a doctor at least I'd never have an identity crisis. He was right: the internship fixes your identity forever."

Having gotten the experience required of a medical doctor, graduating interns are eligible to take the national licensing examination for physicians. Once they pass, they can legally set up in private practice, seeing patients for any medical problem in any area of medicine.[5] However, almost everyone continues on with specialty training at a hospital in what is called the "residency."

In most training programs, the resident builds on skills that already feel like second nature, solidifying an already firm professional identity. But psychiatry is different.

Psychiatry is medicine's poor relation, barely respectable or acknowledged;[6] in fact, medical students are often discouraged by their teachers from pursuing a career in psychiatry.[7] According to a 1990 survey, the average medical student has only seventy-seven hours of psychiatric instruction in four years of medical school, and six-and-a-half weeks on a psychiatry service during the third-year clerkship—and that assignment is frequently in an outpatient clinic, where even the sickest patients are still well enough to take care of themselves outside the hospital.[8] Having finally learned some medicine but little psychiatry, the new psychiatrist-in-training is once again a floundering beginner.

"The beginning of residency is a disaster," Laura said crisply. "You've spent years learning how to be a doctor, and you've finally begun to feel you know something. You've just stopped looking behind you when someone says, 'Dr. Cameron,' and suddenly most of what you've learned is irrelevant. The nurses are calling to tell you that Mrs. K. is crawling around on the floor like a snake and what should they do, and you have absolutely no idea."

In a well-known joke, the psychiatrist is a doctor who hates the sight of blood. Indeed, many doctors believe that psychiatrists view medical school as no more than an inconvenient necessity, a union card leading to a couch. However, many psychiatrists seem to make their career choice unusually late in training, entering psychiatry only after gaining experience in some other branch of medicine.[9] In any case, they now face a new kind of patient, a new pathology, and a new set of demands. Moreover, they generally begin to learn psychiatry with the sickest and most frightening patients: like other medical specialties, psychiatry begins training on inpatient units, with hospitalized patients.

Steve served his internship in Vietnam, completed a residency in internal medicine, and practiced as a general practitioner before switching to psychiatry early in the 1970s. "I'd begun to practice medicine near Boston," he said quietly, "but about half the people who came to my office had more emotional problems than physical.[10] I prescribed Valium and told them to relax, but I didn't have the time or the training to do anything really useful. After two years I decided that psychiatry would be more interesting, and I applied to a psychiatry residency in New York.

"The best places then had long-term inpatient units, where you were assigned patients for intensive psychotherapy for a year or more. My first patient was a twenty-year-old schizophrenic man who thought he was pregnant and wrote my department chief long letters about my telepathically raping him. My second was a beautiful fifteen-year-old girl who was completely mute. And my third patient, my 'good' patient because she liked me and talked to me, slashed her arms with a plastic fork when I was out with flu." He sat back in his chair, his voice dry. "These were not the kinds of problems I saw in medical practice.

"My schizophrenic patient frightened me," he said slowly. "At the same time, he was so strange that I could distance myself. But Carole, my adolescent patient, didn't seem crazy at all. She was beautiful, with long blonde hair and huge green eyes, and she sat as far away from me as possible—which wasn't far because the office was only six by nine. And she never spoke. And I—in a quite childish way—couldn't bring myself to believe that anyone that beautiful could be so ill. I kept thinking that she was really just an extraordinarily stubborn adolescent and that we were in a power struggle. And I told her that it was no victory keeping silent because I wasn't an enemy, I wanted to be of help." He stopped looking at me, as if he were gazing inward at the memory.

"And then I began hating her for subjecting me to three hours a week of a void. No matter what I said, it fell into the silence, and in that room I began to feel I didn't exist. I couldn't exist because nothing I said elicited a reaction. I was convinced she was doing this to me deliberately, and I felt so trapped I even had fantasies about killing her ... and I was too guilty to tell my supervisor...." His voice trailed off. When he began again, he spoke more quickly, as if he wanted to get the story over with. "And so I became even more attached to my third patient, an intelligent, lively woman I really liked. I knew she'd been hospitalized because she cut up her arms, but she always wore long-sleeved blouses, and I never asked to see the damage she'd done. My supervisor kept telling me that she was really ill, but I refused to think about it. She was my relief from the other two. I'd drop by just to chat with her. Then she slashed herself with a plastic fork when I was out with flu, and she needed over a hundred stitches."

Modern psychiatrists use medications freely, fill out standard insurance forms, and consider psychiatry a medical specialty. But the technology of the CAT scan and the MRI is still largely peripheral to daily office practice. With most of their time still spent doing psychotherapy, the realm of most psychiatrists remains the underworld of emotions and the unconscious.

Like Steve, John Hames maintains a private psychiatric practice in Manhattan and teaches part-time at a major psychiatric hospital. In his early sixties, he is grey-haired and balding, his suits unfashionable, baggy, and wrinkled. An academic behind thick glasses, he has round shoulders and a slight paunch, and he looks clumsy, although he likes to work with his hands. John grew up in a working-class Italian family and came to New York on a college scholarship.

In describing the transition from medicine to psychiatry, John focused on one patient who had seemed less ill: "In my second year of residency, one of my outpatients was a sweet, middle-aged housewife with four children," he said soberly. "She was so terrified of going outdoors that she couldn't even shop for food unless someone in her family came with her.

"Today she'd probably be given one of the newer medications. She might not even be offered psychotherapy—although that would be wrong. But in those days, the medicines weren't there. You looked instead for the unconscious meaning of the symptom, and my supervisor, who took a standard position about this kind of phobia, insisted that the meaning was sexual.

"I thought he was obsessed with sex," John mused, "but I was a dutiful second-year resident, and so I tried to ask her about sex. She'd blush and change the subject, and I was too embarrassed to press her. Not only was it like asking my own mother, but I was sure my supervisor was wrong—that he'd read too much Freud. So we chatted about her kids, and movies, and she brought me cookies. I was on the outpatient service for only ten weeks, and at the end of the ten sessions I still had no idea what was wrong with her." Removing his glasses, he leaned back, his hand clasped on his stomach, his voice deliberate. "A few months later, she wrote to me, saying that she was cured, and that I was such a nice doctor she felt guilty not confessing that she hadn't been able to go outdoors because she'd had [oral] sex with her dog. That she'd been afraid people could see it. But I'd been so nice to her, and talked with her as if she was like any other person, that she felt she could hold her head up in public again.

"I'd gone into psychiatry because medicine was too mechanical," he concluded. "There was never time to talk with patients; I was always too busy to know them more than superficially, to know their real concerns. I wanted to feel like the old-fashioned doctor on the Norman Rockwell cover, and I thought psychiatry would be the closest I could come." He smiled ruefully. "Well, it was different from medicine, but it sure wasn't Norman Rockwell."

Psychiatry training has changed considerably since Laura, Steve, and John left medical school. Then, medical students entered free-standing internships in medicine regardless of their future specialty. But in the 1960s, free-standing internships disappeared, transferred into residency programs in medicine. In order to continue the internship for future psychiatrists, psychiatry created its own internship-residency programs in 1977. (P)ost (G)raduate-(Y)ear I, is now the internship, currently offering six-and-a-half months (on average) of medicine (in conjunction with the departments of medicine, neurology, etc.) and five-and-a-half months (on average) of psychiatry (still generally on an inpatient unit). Although there is some fear that the PGY-1 is less medically demanding than the old internship, it is still considered the year which fixes the physicianly identity forever. And some psychiatrists still do internships in internal medicine residencies, coming into psychiatry residencies in the second, PGY-II year.[11]

Other changes in psychiatry training have more to do with the uses of medication and with shorter hospital stays, partly because people can be stabilized earlier but mainly because of insurance limitations. Now that most patients are in and out of the hospital in less than two weeks,[12] beginning residents don't even have the option to do psychotherapy; they must wait for the third year of training, which focuses on outpatients and includes both long- and short-term psychotherapy.

In today's programs, residents starting to learn psychiatry are asked primarily to learn how to take a psychiatric history; to distinguish different psychiatric disorders; and to get patients under control, ordering medication, managing drug side-effects, and making day-to-day decisions about life on the ward.

To some extent, residents are cushioned by the structure of the hospital ward. As part of a team that includes nurses, social workers, attendants, occupational therapists, and other support staff, they belong to a real community, with all the moral support that that implies, and even share some of the responsibility for patients with other members of the team. Supervised, moreover, by a senior resident and by the unit director, residents are constantly under observation and are protected from the worst of their own ignorance.

Even in premedication days, an inpatient floor provided the support of a known hospital structure. Now that most patients receive medication without psychotherapy, residents can more easily try to approach psychiatry as a medical subspecialty. In the familiar paternalistic role of physician-in-charge, they may focus on the medical aspects of patient care, checking for rare organic syndromes, reading up on the specifics of diagnoses, becoming expert in drug treatment, and spending time with other staff members discussing issues of "management" (meaning the rules of behavior patients must abide by while in the hospital). Residents may immerse themselves in psychiatric journals but spend as little time with patients as possible. As one senior psychiatrist said, "The new resident acts as if mental illness were contagious. Put him on the ward with patients and he'll catch it."

In fact, the experience many older psychiatrists had of working with very ill inpatients is unavailable nowadays. But psychiatrists-in-training must still learn how to find the person in the welter of unorganized and conflicting details of patient history. Despite their fears, beginners can learn to do this only if they sit down with patients and listen.

"There are two aspects to inpatient care," Steve said. "In the acute phase, the patient is usually psychotic: out of touch with reality, hallucinating, delusional, suicidal, or violent. Thinking is disorganized. . . ." He stopped and retraced his path. "Most people have no experience with someone who's acutely psychotic. The average person thinks we're just talking about a little eccentricity. In fact, patients are generally hospitalized because they can't follow even the simplest rules of society anymore.

They don't wash, they can't get out of bed, or they're assaultive, or talking to voices on streetcorners.

"Anyway," Steve continued briskly, "the first issue is control and containment—medicating the patient and protecting him and everyone around him from overwhelming and irrational impulses. Patients usually don't remember much of what happened during a psychotic episode, but they're glad you didn't let them do something they'd bitterly regret. And even in this phase, with acutely ill patients," he added, "I teach residents to sit for ten or fifteen minutes at a time to show they care and are trying to understand. You can't begin psychotherapy, but you can start to establish a relationship. . . . Because a patient has to know he can trust you and count on you if you're going to be of real help when he's better."

Laura said, "When I teach, my first goal is to get the resident to really listen. Not to have conversations, or rap about stuff. But to contain his own horror, his own fears and anxiety, and learn to grasp what the other person in the room is conveying. No one wants to, because then you lose track of the separation between the two of you. It's much easier to take a history and get the dates right, but I tell them they're not lawyers, they're not listening for facts. However much it scares them, however much they want to deny the patient's inner experience, that's where they have to start."

As beginning psychiatrists begin to face the reality of mental illness in patients they may have conflicting feelings. Often they find patients incomprehensible, even alien; at other moments, even the sickest patient seems to have just a few oddities of behavior. Some of this confusion is plain ignorance, and some of it denial. Some is also the reflection of the patchy quality of mental illness, for all but the sickest people are quite rational part of the time and able to hold a rational bit of conversation. Many patients can even manage to talk calmly about the very issues that led to hospitalization, whether it be an attempted suicide or their belief in messages sent them via the TV or their conviction that strangers are talking about them on the street. And beginning psychiatrists can't understand how the person across from them can remain absolutely untouched by reason, as much in the thrall of pathology at the end of the meeting as at the beginning.

"Every beginner thinks he can reason people out of craziness," Steve said. "He sits and talks with someone for an hour, and the patient admits that it doesn't make any sense that he's afraid to walk down the street or into a store. He admits that it doesn't make sense to be sure his wife is unfaithful because he saw her talking with the mailman. She admits that slashing her wrists isn't going to bring back her boyfriend. And the resident feels great—that he's just done wonders... and then nothing changes. Logic is irrelevant."

But the twist of the knife is that residents can no longer keep their distance while getting their bearings, for their new role requires dismantling the very barriers built up over the preceding years. Not only is so much knowledge that was once central seemingly irrelevant; beginning psychiatrists must now discard the very role so painfully fitted to the skin. The new domain is the world of feeling and emotion they have tried so hard to deny.

✍

The scene: a lecture for first-year residents on conducting the initial psychiatric interview, part of a course on outpatient therapy. The residents are in white coats, like other doctors at the hospital, and those on call carry beepers in their coat pockets. In the course of the class, several leave to answer emergencies. They look tired and tense, and exchange anecdotes about patients while waiting for the professor to arrive. The professor is in his forties and self-assured. He wears a slightly rumpled, expensive grey suit and a red silk tie, rejects the podium, and asks them to pull their chairs into a semicircle around him before he begins.

"In medicine," he says, "you introduce yourself to the patient and take a history. But in psychiatry the data about the patient come second to setting up the conditions for treatment. You have to offer him safety, you have to stimulate hope, and you have to protect him from injury—or he won't come back. You do this every day, and it's easy to become routinized and forget how crucial the first interview is to the patient. It's one of the most important experiences of his life—he's going to remember everything you say, every move you make. And you'll lose him if he doesn't feel he can work with you or if his self-esteem is damaged by the interview. However good your diagnosis, you can't treat the patient who doesn't return."

Pausing, he looks around the semicircle. "Now," he asks blandly, "have any of you had patients not come back?"

The room is silent, the residents stiff as the tension rises. Then a grim voice: "Many." The tension dissolves into relieved laughter, and the subject turns to the patient who cancels even before the first appointment.

When a resident suggests asking the reason for cancelation, the professor disagrees. "Too judgmental," he says. "We're not in a position to make any interpretations. All we can do for the patient is schedule another meeting." He smiles wickedly. "He cancels the day before the second appointment. But he asks for a third. What do you say now?"

The silence lengthens, broken at last by a low growl: "Three strikes and you're out!"

The class explodes with laughter, but the lecturer ignores it. "What about coming down on the other side of his ambivalence?" he asks. "Say to him, 'You seem to have mixed feelings about treatment. When you've decided, call for another appointment.'"

The group nods in agreement. Relaxing in their hard chairs, the residents look pleased and triumphant. After a moment the professor zaps them: "Do that and he never calls back!" As they wilt, he adds, "You're the expert, and you told him he's not ready."

✍

The lecturer's point about an unconscious communication from therapist to patient takes us to the core of psychiatry. It is not merely feelings that the psychiatrist confronts but the landscape of the unconscious, the entire range of perception, cognition, and emotional life that is normally out of awareness.

Although Freud's ideas captivated Americans as early as 1909, when he packed the lecture hall at Clark University, few of us really accept even his basic premises, much less the psychiatric edifice developed after Freud—and not because the terminology is incomprehensible or more difficult than any other field's, but because we don't want to. The everyday concepts of psychiatry are not only contrary to commonsense experience; they are repugnant. Ordinary life, however less repressed than in Freud's Vienna, still depends on channeling or covering up a wide range of primitive impulses. If we're healthy, we don't even know we do it. We are no more conscious of mental barriers than we are of the process of breathing in and out. Of course, we don't know what we've shoveled out of consciousness: not knowing is exactly the point. But psychiatry is a world in which those buried impulses are the working medium, a primitive and bizarre world more akin to nightmare than everyday experience. A great deal of psychiatric training, in fact, involves residents' unhappy confrontation with these unconscious realities in patients and in themselves.

✍

The scene (as described by Gary Rosenblatt, the psychiatrist interviewed in the next chapter): a conference presentation at a psychiatric hospital during the 1960s. The room is a small lecture hall, complete with raised stage, microphone, and about thirty rows of wooden classroom chairs. The patient whose case is to be presented is Maureen K., a psychotic woman of twenty who has been hospitalized for most of her life. She has been at some of the best psychiatric facilities in the United States, and none have helped. Gary Rosenblatt, her current resident, considers Maureen a torment to his life. When he asked for a conference in which he could present her case to senior psychiatrists on the hospital's teaching faculty, one consultant sourly remarked, "Dr. Rosenblatt doesn't want help. He just wants me to feel as hopeless as he does."

The room is packed with nurses, social workers, residents, and the psychiatrists on the teaching faculty. The meeting begins with Dr. Rosenblatt's diffident but embittered presentation of Maureen's difficulties, but he is soon stopped by the patient herself. Pulling at her hair, Maureen charges into the room in defiant interruption of the conference from whose beginning she has been barred, derailing the group entirely as she passionately screams, "I want to suck Dr. Rosenblatt's cock!"

The scene was even stranger than it seemed, for Maureen's plea had nothing to do with oral sex. As someone who spent days at a time huddled with her blanket in a corner of her room, Maureen rarely felt as grown up as a two-year-old. Too ill for anything but the most fragmentary stabs of lust, she really wanted to possess the strength she felt emanating from her doctor's being, drinking it in like mother's milk. By one single act she wanted to incorporate and make her own a nurturing and powerful mommy-daddy. Violating a host of social conventions at that conference, even for a mental hospital, she hadn't even meant what her words said. Nothing was what it seemed, nothing of her plea matched the world of normal human interaction.

✍

Initially, the stories psychiatrists told me about patients seemed too melo-
dramatic, and I thought that most readers were unlikely to identify with
them. But these were the kinds of stories I was told, and their very drama
holds meaning: psychiatrists are thrown into the lion's den without prep-
aration, and by the time a few years go by, little more can faze them. I also
came to realize that the psychiatrists who told me these stories were describing their own initial lack of understanding of patients who were in
pain, patients they had been too inexperienced to understand when they
were beginners. In one of the most famous lines in psychiatry, Harry Stack
Sullivan wrote, "We are all much more simply human than otherwise,"[13]
and this is what these psychiatrists ultimately understand. By following in
their footsteps through these chapters, I hope we too will understand.

3

Empathy

Maureen was pudgy and pasty-faced, her hair stringy and her eyes dull. She mumbled, answered voices no one else heard, smiled while crying, and cried without seeming to notice. Shuffling around the ward in army boots, her feet wide apart and heavy, she often saw the walls melting, and sometimes she screamed as doorways changed into mouths ready to swallow her. Her thoughts seemed disconnected, tumbling past with little apparent relationship to each other or to anything going on around her. Her behavior was unpredictable, and she exasperated nurses by constantly begging for permission to kill herself. Despite high doses of antipsychotic medication, she was thoroughly psychotic (unable to differentiate the real from the unreal), comprehensible to the staff only by an enormous effort of will, and not always then.

Even her voice was strange, rough and guttural, unmodulated like someone gone deaf and no longer able to hear herself. Yet she could read, and wrote poetry, and the Stanford-Binet intelligence test showed an IQ well above average. Her favorite book was a much thumbed copy of *I Never Promised You a Rose Garden*.[1]

Gary worked with Maureen throughout his residency and for several years afterward, in a bond so tight that he often dreamed of her. By now it's been a decade since they stopped working together, but Maureen still calls occasionally, and when she visits the emergency room she tells staff that he is her father. She will always be one of the most important people in Gary's past, affecting not only his professional life, but his awareness of what it means to be human. For Maureen reached him at the deepest levels of his selfhood, where they shared their common humanity:

"She was the sickest person I'd ever seen," he recalled. "The first time we met, she was in an isolation cell under twenty-four-hour observation. She'd smeared herself with feces, wrapped toilet paper around her hair, and was hunched in a ball in the far corner. When she began to trust me, much later, she wrote me letters on toilet paper—because she 'was shit,' she said. And I told her she couldn't be—because I didn't work with anyone who was shit. And that reassured her."

Gary is now in his mid-fifties, and long established in private practice, with an office along the psychiatric strip in Manhattan's East Eighties. He is a confident man, tall and rangy, with a quick, wide smile and dancing brown eyes that miss nothing. He also has a reputation for being able and willing to work with patients no one else will tolerate, and for having an extraordinary ability to relate to very sick people. He said that he drifted into such difficult work because he learned so much from Maureen. Eventually she was able to leave the hospital and live in her own apartment. But his initial reaction to her was frustration and despair—even paranoia.

"At first I took it very personally, as if she were a punishment, a kind of scourge to take me down a peg. I'd always been a first-rate student, and in medical school I'd made a specialty of rare and exotic diseases. And here was this person who completely baffled me. I couldn't begin to understand her—and I couldn't imagine any way to help her.

"I ordered every endocrine test I could, because I kept thinking that no one could be that ill and not show physical abnormalities." He shrugged, his voice quiet as he remembered. "By then, it wasn't so much that I expected a miracle cure. It was more that I thought I might not have to talk with her if I could find an organic condition. I'd done two years of a neurology residency before I switched to psychiatry, and I thought it would be like that. I'd be patted on the head for my diagnostic skills, and no one would expect me to do anything more. But the tests showed nothing."

Although he was unable to do conventional psychotherapy with someone so ill, Gary was still responsible for her care, and he was expected not to give up. Turning to several different teachers at the hospital for help, he experimented with a variety of alternatives, and even developed a behavioral reinforcement schedule in which Maureen was rewarded for designated behaviors. From their experiences together, he became interested in using reinforcement techniques to foster autonomy. He was enthusiastic about describing these early efforts.

"We started out with M&Ms if she combed her hair, and worked up to having her spend five minutes with her favorite nurse for each hour she didn't ask permission to kill herself—moving from primitive physical rewards to those involving other people. She and I would agree together on the goal—another was having fewer tantrums—and on the appropriate reward—say, a movie pass." He spoke slowly, trying to reconstruct the sequence he and Maureen followed. "She also had to learn new ways of behaving, because some of her peculiar actions came from never having learned socially acceptable alternatives. And we'd try them out. I'd be the bad guy, turning off the TV show she was watching, and she'd practice different kinds of responses, and then we'd switch, because I thought playing the other person's role was one way for her to learn more about why people acted as they did."

Even if Maureen's condition had a biological component—and Gary believes it did—it had a psychological component too. "Her mother was psychotic, convinced that she and Maureen were telepathically connected and were essentially the same person. So whatever she felt, Maureen had to feel.

"When Maureen was a baby, her mother fed her whenever she herself was hungry—whether or not Maureen wanted anything—and kept on forcing her to eat even after she threw up. If Maureen struggled or cried, her mother explained it as Maureen's way of expressing love—it *had* to be love, because she loved Maureen." He looked sad. "Her mother never treated her as a separate person, and so she was never sure she was one—as if she were still a baby.

"And she evoked the same reaction a baby gets. Everyone who met her, even absolute strangers, responded to her neediness by wanting to take care of her. One man she met in the hospital cafeteria visited her every week for years afterward." He rubbed his chin absently. "I couldn't stop thinking about her, and my wife said I never stopped talking about her. But she wasn't really like a baby because she was insatiable. Her neediness had no end." He hesitated. "She was the most pathetic person I'd ever met, but she could also be the most hateful. When my own mother died, she found out about it, and she stomped around my office screaming that she was glad my mother was dead. That she didn't have a real mother, so why should I." He suddenly looked strained. "I couldn't treat her after that. She went too far. I couldn't forgive her."

✍

By the time internship is over, the doctor's nerves are steely, her sensibilities, at least during working hours, nonexistent. Yet the average doctor finds the inner experience of the psychiatric patient incomprehensible and frightening. Moreover, the patient's state of mind is only part of what makes psychiatry so wrenchingly different from medicine. Even with someone as ill as Maureen, the most disturbing aspect of psychiatry is not the patient's inner experience but the psychiatrist's.

In working with patients, the psychiatrist encounters a new world, whose shape is formed less by the nature of the individual patient than by the psychiatrist-patient duo. The bond between them is the core of psychotherapy, and the bond depends on the psychiatrist's opening herself to the patient's experience, regardless of what that experience is. The issue is not that beginners are afraid that mental illness is contagious, but that they are told in effect to catch it.

"As a psychiatrist you have no option," John said quietly. "Although the whole trend in the field now is toward biology, toward explanations of mental disease that include a physical imbalance, you can't do the work from a distance. Even if the illness has an organic component, some malfunction of brain neurotransmitters, patients order their lives around their vulnerability—there is no disease apart from the person. You have to try to understand the patterns of their lives and see what might be changeable and what's too central, what they might like to change, and what they're perfectly comfortable with. It's not like other specialties. You have to get under your patient's skin."

In other words, the psychiatrist must develop the tool of empathy, "the process of entering fully, through imagination, into another's feelings or motives."[2] For empathy stands at the heart of the therapeutic relationship, the psychiatrist's most essential ability. In its absence, treatment fails. Most psychiatrists consider empathy to be a healing force all by itself, reducing the patient's loneliness and despair by providing the experience of being deeply understood. Empathically being with the patient moment by moment is the keystone of treatment, a partial substitute for the parental understanding children need if they are to grow up normally—parental understanding that many patients grew up without.

"In a sense, you love every patient you work closely with," Laura said softly. "The empathic relationship is so tight that there's no room for anything but caring. During our meetings, with the boundaries between us as fluid as they become, I know their pain, how crippled they are, and how they struggle against themselves. Not merely from their side, but better, because I understand far more about them than they do. Because they've walled in their pain, and blocked off the connections I make—or never made the connections in the first place. Or they hate themselves too much to see themselves clearly."

Half-smiling, Laura told me a story. "During my own analysis, I remember excusing one of our housekeepers for some bit of cruelty to me as a child, telling my analyst that I could in retrospect see how lonely and depressed she'd been. I went on and on until at last he said, 'Do you excuse Hitler because he flunked out of art school?' And he was right; you don't excuse someone's behavior on the grounds that you understand why they act as they do. You have to hold people accountable for their actions.

"But in the office," she continued, "you don't think in these terms. You're so tightly bonded to your patient that all that's left is a kind of love: absolute acceptance. No judgments. I sometimes think that nothing I say is as important as this experience, as if we went back in time and made up for the wounds they received in childhood. And my caring also becomes part of them, so that they begin to feel toward themselves what I feel."

One prominent psychoanalyst, Ralph R. Greenson, defines empathy as "an emotional knowing" of the other person;[3] another, Hans Kohut, labels it "vicarious introspection,"[4] without which we cannot conceive another's inner life; while Freud wrote that without empathy we have no way to comprehend anyone outside ourselves.[5] To each of them, empathy connotes an awareness and deep understanding of the other person that goes far beyond words, and that at its best looks telepathic.

Empathy requires a blurring of the boundaries between the psychiatrist and patient, in a kind of controlled identification, a temporary and limited, but very real, trying on of the patient's inner experience. Empathic ability seems in part a talent, perhaps an unteachable one, that the best psychiatrists have to an extraordinary degree. Indeed, some psychiatrists offer their classes demonstrations of interviewing techniques that are legendary for their leaps of empathic intuition, such that residents despair of ever imitating them.

"When I was a first-year resident," Steve said, "I presented Deborah [the woman who cut her arms] at a hospital conference, where she was interviewed by one of the big guns in psychiatry. This was right after she'd stabbed herself when I was out sick, and I was feeling hopeless about her, and fed up, and betrayed. I couldn't understand how she could do something so self-destructive when we'd been getting on so well and talking so rationally about her problems."

Steve spoke contemplatively. "At the conference, the consultant sat down facing her, ignoring the audience, and said without any preamble, 'Let's see if we can find some other way of proving to yourself that you're alive.' . . . And she began to cry. I'd been thinking that she was furious with me for being away, and that she'd turned her fury inward in an attempt at suicide . . . and I was entirely wide of the mark."

Steve sat very still, only his hands moving, making designs with some paper clips. "The issue wasn't fury but despair. . . . I was right in feeling we'd established a close bond. What I hadn't comprehended was how primitive it was. To Deborah it was like the symbiotic tie between mother and infant, in which her very sense of existence depended on my being with her and, by my responses, telling her who she was. She was like the babies Spitz[6] studied, who died in the absence of mothering: she couldn't live without me. The consultant said that he felt himself turning transparent as soon as he saw her, as if he were fading away to nothing, and he felt frantic to act before he disappeared. And that's how Deborah felt . . . but if she made herself bleed, it meant she was still alive. And so she slashed herself."

Steve slowly continued. "Although I've read that interpretation of self-mutilation since, it would have been irrelevant if the consultant hadn't felt her despair. If he'd felt rage instead of despair, then my assumption would probably have been right—that she was turning her fury at me against her own body. Fury and revenge would have been the issues, not Deborah's feelings of deadness."

The capacity for empathy is thought to develop spontaneously from the intimate and nonverbal communications of infant and mother as they

act and react to one another, although some people clearly have more talent for empathy than others. Calling on skills we only partly understand,
empathy often operates outside of consciousness, tapping the deepest re-
cesses of the psychiatrist's mind, as mysterious to her as it is to the patient.
At the same time, empathic skills and processes can be honed with experience and hard work. While the naïve therapist, for example, may have no
idea at all of what the patient is feeling, the experienced therapist has a
gamut of known possibilities to pick from. The consultant, unlike Steve,
knew all the theories about self-mutilating behavior, so that he was on the
alert for specific feelings in himself. Moreover, he could also understand
Deborah more easily because he'd seen other patients like her.

"You can't learn diagnosis from a book," Steve explained carefully. "You
have to see for yourself again and again in order to absorb the way in
which a syndrome really presents itself. Without the hands-on experience,
you don't have a real sense of the cues. The clearest examples are in derma-
tology, where you learn *only* by comparing the skin lesions in front of you
with the plates in the book, until eventually you begin to know what the
range of possibilities is for a given diagnosis. . . . But it's the same in all specialties. When you're a beginner, most of your supervisors look like ge-
niuses just because they've seen so much of it before."

He grimaced. "When I was a resident, I presented a case,[7] a woman in
the hospital with the compulsion to pull out her hair. But her hair looked
fine to me." He looked at me questioningly, and when I told him I didn't
know what he was getting at, he smiled slightly. "I knew that wasn't her real
complaint, and I made a number of dumb statements during our interview.
Finally one of the senior faculty raised his hand and asked her how long
she'd worn a wig." We both laughed. "What I hadn't known," Steve continued, "and he'd seen before, was that this woman was in the hospital because
she'd pulled out *all* her hair. . . . Even her pubic hair. She wasn't going to tell
me, because she was embarrassed, and when she said she pulled her hair, I
missed the point." He smiled and raised an eyebrow. "Given my total, absolute ignorance, I couldn't begin to empathize with her."

But while knowledge and experience help, the development of empathy
also requires certain attitudes of mind. To begin with, the psychiatrist has
to give up her preconceptions of the patient. Even if she and the patient
come from the same background, which gives an extra edge of under-

standing, she can make false assumptions and be plagued by blind spots. To really listen, to really understand the other soul in the room, the psychiatrist has for the moment to put aside her own self, how she feels, how she would react in the other's situation, for the moment deliberately losing her own egocentric view.

In talking about his early experiences in psychiatry, John Hames returned to his first outpatient, the woman who later wrote him that she'd had her dog perform cunnilingus on her. If anything, his inability to see the world through her eyes stood at the opposite from Gary's inability to see the world through Maureen's eyes: Instead of finding his patient too ill to comprehend, John failed by misperceiving her as essentially well.

"If I'd been more experienced," John said thoughtfully, "I would have heard how frightened she was about sex, and I would have been able to talk with her about the meaning of her inability to go outdoors alone. Ultimately, we might have explored what led her to turn to an animal, a pet, rather than to her husband. What was she afraid to admit about herself, or about her sexuality, to another human being? But I was both naïve and stubborn, rejecting my supervisor's advice and unable to really hear my patient. Instead of letting go of my own presuppositions, I persisted in seeing her as sexless, the way I saw my own mother." He turned his head slightly to look me full in the face. "But it's difficult to really listen, and it can be very frightening."

The psychiatrist's impulse is always to reach a conclusion, to decide that she understands and to force everything else the patient offers into its proper pigeonhole. It takes effort for her to maintain an open mind, refusing to allow herself to prematurely categorize what she sees and hears. For the patient is a blurred and shifting figure in the absence of such categories, his essence too complex to take in intellectually. But to really understand the whole person in all his moment-by-moment buzzing presence, the psychiatrist has to let the reality of the patient build up inside her, moving beyond categories to feel her way emotionally into the other's world. She must act for the moment as if mental disorders really were contagious, inoculating herself with the patient's illness and experiencing at least a portion of his pain.

Maureen didn't want sex with Gary, but to take him into herself, making him part of her being, protecting her from annihilation. Her inner experience was of shifting bits and pieces, her consciousness fragmented like shards of broken glass, while the boundaries separating her from the rest of the world were so fluid that her sense of identity was often blurred, confused not only with other people but even with things. In working with her, Gary had to open himself to the specific quality of her desperation and feel within himself some of her terror of losing what little selfhood she had and dissolving into nothingness. He had to feel at least a shadow of her terror to understand the least part of what she said to him, and to be able to say anything helpful to her in return, not only surrendering his own preconceptions when he was with her, but exchanging them for her experience.

"She felt her existence to be at stake every moment of her life, but I sometimes felt mine was at stake when I walked into a session with her." Gary smiled painfully, distancing himself from the memory, but his voice was earnest. "It was like bringing a candy bar to a starving child, except that I was the candy bar. I'd sit there in her room, and she'd be rocking back and forth, hugging herself and mumbling, and I'd be afraid to turn my back on her because I had such a vivid image of her eating me until nothing was left. I felt so threatened I had the persistent fantasy that only one of us would survive the session."

He gazed at me shrewdly, aware of how open he had decided to be with me, and aware of my total absorption in what he was saying. Then he continued thoughtfully, choosing his words. "In fact, I was taking her feelings and fantasies into myself. I remember after one session... I couldn't use the elevator. I knew it was crazy, but I kept thinking it would swallow me once the door closed." He shook his head ruefully. "It was as if I'd caught her sickness. I had to walk all twelve flights to get out of the hospital that night."

In learning to empathize, the psychiatrist creates a split in her own consciousness. Sometimes she makes deliberate use of her imaginative powers to actively construct an image of her patient that goes beyond her own experience; sometimes she is more passive, allowing the patient's selfhood to wash over her and imprint itself on her waiting and receptive psyche. In reality, of course, the lines between these differing empathic processes are nonexistent, the psychiatrist dependent on shifting modes of experience in any given session.

"Maureen was twenty when I began to see her, but she looked more like a very sick—and young—fifteen," Gary said. "And she often seemed even younger. She had a doll she dragged everywhere, a beat-up little thing she'd knocked the eyes out of. One of the other patients once got furious at her and hid the doll under his bed until Maureen freaked out in a panic that made my skin crawl.

"The more I worked with her, the younger she felt to me, even though her behavior improved with the reinforcement schedule she and I worked out. Meanwhile I read everything I could find on treating people as regressed as she, and I finally came upon the very respected French analyst Marguerite Sechehaye. Sechehaye suggested that some very regressed schizophrenic patients needed to have their infantile needs satisfied—in real life—in order for them to move on to later stages of ego development. And she described bottle-feeding a patient much like Maureen."[8]

Sechehaye's work was part of a legitimate tradition among psychoanalysts, dating to premedication days, of doing long-term intensive psychotherapy with schizophrenic patients. Few psychoanalysts ever chose to do intensive psychotherapy with these patients because it was just too technically difficult and emotionally demanding. But some of the most extraordinary members of the profession dedicated their working lives to exploring the possibilities such treatment opened, and some of them reported profound interactions with their patients very reminiscent of Gary's.[9] However, these were eminent analysts with years of psychoanalytic training and experience behind them, not psychiatry residents; and Sechehaye's recommendation was seldom, if ever, followed even by them.

And in today's climate, the likelihood of bottle-feeding a schizophrenic patient would be still lower than when Gary did it. Schizophrenia is once again viewed as a disorder of brain function, to be treated by medication. Exploring the psychology of schizophrenic patients is out of fashion, and almost none receive long-term intensive psychotherapy with their medicine. (Even if they were in intensive treatment, no psychiatrist, including Gary, would be likely to recommend bottle-feeding—not for any patient whatever to any psychiatrist today. The risks of violating therapeutic boundaries are much too great. In any case, the risk of a malpractice suit is not worth taking.)

Gary went on with a tinge of defiance in his smile. "It was totally unorthodox, at least in this country, and I was afraid to tell my supervisor, even though he was famous for the intensity of his work with schizophrenics. I sneaked in one morning with a baby bottle, locked the door to my office, and took Maureen on my lap. And she loved it. She melted into my arms the way a baby does. I felt incredibly peaceful holding her, and after a long time she giggled and said she had to pee and probably shouldn't pee on me.

"When I was feeding her, I felt her desire to go back and be the baby again. Not to have to struggle with becoming a person. And when she giggled, I felt her get less boneless, more defined. When she spoke to me it was a shock, an older person I didn't expect."

Gary's voice had been so gentle that I, too, wanted to crawl onto his lap. Then his tone sharpened. "In many ways, doing treatment isn't so different from other highly focused work. You become so absorbed in the process that you have no other existence for that time."

To understand what she hears, the psychiatrist must surrender some of her own identity with each person she sees. Empathy is difficult, painful, and unnerving, even with patients far less ill than Maureen, and particularly when the psychiatrist must, like a chameleon, change guise at the end of each hour. But her job is even more paradoxical, for her capacity to comprehend her patient's world depends on how fully she can plunge into her own.

However unique each person's experience, we make a start toward empathy by working from ourselves outward, and so the psychiatrist must learn to mine herself and explore the limits and boundaries of her own selfhood. The simplest component of empathy is the rapport of shared experiences, as when Gary says, "I have doubts about a childless psychiatrist treating someone who has children. If you've never been a parent, I wonder if you tend to be too hard on patients when they describe problems with their kids. Because you have no idea of the amount of work and frustration that parenting necessitates, and you side with the child in yourself. I even wonder about psychiatrists who've never married or lived with anyone: I don't feel they can really understand the daily experience of sharing where you live, of adjusting to another person's habits."

Psychiatrists themselves are data sources. Nothing in their lives is irrelevant—no memories, feelings, or ideas. "My first wife and I were good friends," Steve said carefully, "but we weren't terribly passionate about each other. After my divorce, I met Barbara [his second wife], and for the first time in my life, I could understand someone risking everything they had for passion. I pay more attention now to a patient's sexuality, and I've been surprised at how much more tuned in I am to sensuality in general, not only around sex, but around food, or clothing, or even vacations.

"I grew up on a farm, where working hard was part of the life, and your body was something you took care of the same way you took care of any other machine. But a whole universe of physical existence became real to me through Barbara, and I suddenly found myself wanting to wear a good-looking shirt or sweater, or paying attention to cologne, or appreciating the texture of a chair's upholstery." He moved restlessly and was silent for a few moments. "In the past, most of my patients were obsessional in character, rather insensitive to physical experience, their defenses organized around thought. I do much better with them now, because I'm much more aware of what's absent."

Rapport based on real-life similarities of experience is ultimately a far less important component of empathy than is the therapist's self-awareness. The psychiatrist can comprehend her patients only if she becomes open to her own needs and desires, her own motives and defenses, only if she is at home with the feelings and emotions that lie below the surface details of our lives, and that we all share to a surprising degree.

Gary had so immersed himself in Maureen's world that his own identity took on characteristics of hers. The night he couldn't take the elevator (or when he held her in his lap), her perceptions became his, and her fear and desires his own. To become so mixed up with someone else can be terrifying, an experience few adults have and which they ordinarily defend themselves from as if it were a death threat. But Gary didn't literally take on Maureen's feelings and perceptions, or lose himself to become her. Instead, he used himself, mining his own being for psychic treasure, quarrying himself for experiences related to hers, finding aspects of his most hidden self that resonated with her.

To use yourself this way is to add your own buried memories to whatever empathic experience you already have of the patient. For the aspects of self that are most useful in treatment are walled-off in the unconscious, involving material that is threatening, painful, and barely tolerable. What we know best in ourselves is the tip of the iceberg: the ever shifting stream of consciousness, and the thoughts and feelings we can easily call into awareness. Freud's monumental contribution to our understanding of ourselves was his exploration of the base on which consciousness sits, his discovery of the overweening importance of deliberately hidden unconscious processes. Many of our most important experiences, and the motives that most determine our behavior, lie below the surface in us all, unknown to our conscious self, buried and denied. These are what the psychiatrist must tap if she is to understand her patients.

Some of our experience never takes place in consciousness: the brain controls breathing or heartbeat, for example, without our awareness. And very early experiences may never have been stored in ways we can get at verbally, in part because much of the brain isn't working yet, the neurons not even formed, and the connections between them not activated until many months after birth—and in part because we haven't yet learned to make sense of so much that happens. The earliest memories seem to be chaotic and fragmentary, bits of sound or smell, or isolated images that reflect the baby's limited understanding and ability to process information. Even after the first year, much of our experience seems stored mainly as direct physical memory, locked into posture, muscle spasms, and a whole range of bodily responses known as character armor. Only with the continuing development of speech is there a change—memories becoming less physical, more cerebral, and far more complex and coherent. But the bulk of unconscious material relevant to psychotherapy has been locked away purposefully. Some of this material comes from adult life, but most goes back to childhood, and much of psychotherapy involves uncovering unconscious forces that have little to do with current reality, forces rooted in the past that keep us tied to ghosts, refighting ancient battles irrelevant to our present lives.

We were all infants once, and children, and we all have some experience of being cold or hungry or wet, of being alone and helpless, terrified or enraged. We all coped with baby bodies that we couldn't control, with wishes we couldn't express because we had no words. We've all been frenzied infants, furious toddlers, jealous children. All of us have had powerful experiences that we've shut away as too painful or frightening; we've shut out not only real experiences but secret wishes and impulses, skeletons in the unconscious closet that we labeled bad or forbidden, unacceptable in a child who wanted to be loved; we've driven those wishes and impulses underground as fully as if they had been memories of real acts.

The infant is totally at the mercy of those around him, the child only a little less so, and experiences or impulses we might cope with as an adult are too threatening to a child with meager resources of self-protection or strength. Much goes into the unconscious that is part of normal growing up, overwhelming not to the adult but to the child in us. And we bury not only the impulse and memory but knowledge of the burial act itself: even our defensive maneuver is part of an unconscious process.

The patient is not so much a child caught in the body of a grown-up as a grown-up deranged by uncontrollable intrusions of childish thoughts and feelings. The product of all his successes and failures, joys and disappointments, he is a mix of different stages of development, responding sometimes at one level and sometimes at another; and he usually carries adult desires along with the child's, and in all but the most regressed moments, the adult's additional experience and sophistication. But much of the therapeutic work is going to take both patient and psychiatrist back to the time when development began to go wrong, and for many patients seen in psychotherapy, that time is prior to the age of five or six. Most of the concerns of doctor and patient center on issues of the first years of life, developmental tasks such as differentiating self from other people, getting a sense of the stability of the physical world, gaining control of one's own body, separating from mother, making the first moves toward an independent identity, making one's will clear without bringing down the world— the issues one sees in growing children in the early years of life.

✍

In his fascinating book, *Becoming Psychiatrists: The Professional Transformation of Self,* Donald Light drily remarks that having to unearth their own unconscious desires and terrors may well produce [serious] emotional disturbances in psychiatrists.[10] Certainly, there is no doubt that the beginning psychiatrist finds empathically being with patients, particularly sicker patients, terrifying. Even when they suffer from illnesses now thought to originate in abnormalities of brain biochemistry, with medication the first-line treatment, patients may describe feelings and perceptions that seem to resonate to early experiences and stages of childhood development in us all—or the psychiatrist may simply feel directly what the patient is feeling.

"The first year of residency," Steve said, "sitting with Carole [his mute adolescent patient], praying that she'd speak, I'd start to feel myself go numb. I began to have dreams that I was dead, or that I was in a coffin, buried under the earth, and no one knew I was still alive. And finally I dreamed that my supervisor was staring at me, only I was a piece of furniture, a table. And then he put his feet on my back, and he said, 'At least he's good for something.'"

His expression was grim. "Some of the major psychoanalysts talk about the fear of becoming an inanimate thing, not only inhuman, or dead, but without even the semblance or possibility of life. Harold Searles[11] writes that everyone has that fear buried deeply within themselves, that it is the experience the infant has when he cries and cries and is ignored. Sitting with Carole, I went back to that fear in myself and began to feel as if I were just a thing myself, no more than a piece of furniture. It was one of the most frightening experiences of my life, worse in a way than anything that happened to me in Vietnam. I've never forgotten the total hopelessness of it."

Freud compared the analyst to a surgeon: aloof, clearthinking, ruthless in the pursuit of truth, excising the tumors of the unconscious with the scalpel of reason.[12] This description has a great deal of reality in it, but the beginning psychiatrist is more likely to feel like one of the blind leading the blind. Even the way in which the psyche reveals itself is unsettling to her, for this aspect of our mind uses imagery and metaphor instead of logic. Like a small child, unconscious processes forever mix up literal and symbolic meanings, converting a feeling of confusion into an image of the world turned upside down, or an angry impulse into a dream of a roaring lion.

"Carole was treating me like a thing," Steve said, "but I dreamed I *was* a thing. Part of the dream's power was in its literalness. I wouldn't have been as frightened by it if it had been symbolic."

The medical doctor prides herself on her logical abilities, on the ease with which she can reason from point A to point B, but connections made outside of consciousness follow the rules of magic instead, and they never run in a straight line. No longer able to count on her reasoning skills, the new psychiatrist has to cultivate a new mind-set as well, one that is far less focused than the medical. She must learn to tolerate a kind of free-floating awareness, in which, however sharply part of her is following the patient, however clearly part of her is making hypotheses as to what the patient means, the rest of her must remain much less focused, letting float to the surface whatever appears, and attending to all her associations impartially. One of the many disturbing experiences of the novice is getting used to the fact that the most significant empathic connections are often on the margins of her awareness and appear less as connections than as bizarre wanderings of the mind.

Gary said, "You sit with a patient, and you listen to the best of your ability, trying to make sense of what he's saying, and suddenly you realize you've been thinking about your Aunt Suzie, whom you haven't seen for the last five years. Now in medicine you'd likely feel you had a lapse of attention, and you'd just work harder at keeping your mind on track. But in psychiatry, you're taught that thinking about Aunt Suzie is an empathic cue: Something about this patient will be clarified when you comprehend why you thought of Aunt Suzie. But this isn't a connection you've consciously worked toward or can control. If anything, it appears out of the blue; it doesn't even seem to be a connection as much as a random thought dependent on brain fatigue or inefficiency. And thinking about Aunt Suzie isn't in itself threatening." He gave me that sudden wide smile. "She's the nice aunt who always baked your birthday cake. What about sitting with a patient and finding yourself thinking about Uncle Joe, who tried to pull down your pants when you were ten?"

4

Identification

The person in treatment addresses universal human themes and arouses in the psychiatrist memories and emotions that might otherwise have remained outside of consciousness. The psychiatrist is especially vulnerable because he is told to deliberately mine himself, unearthing whatever in his own life resonates to his patient's experience. Furthermore, he may go too far, confusing his own problems with the patient's as he strives for empathy. Opening the Pandora's box of his own unconscious, he may cross from empathy to identification and lose track of the genuine differences between himself and the patient. Psychiatrists can fall into this trap at any stage of their career, but it happens most often in the early years.

"You and the patient are stumbling around in the dark," Gary said. "And you recognize your own conflicts coming back at you in what you hear. You lose sight of who's who in the room, so that much of your initial experience revolves around uncontrolled identification."

Gary sprawled in his oversized leather chair, his thoughts organized into incisive paragraphs. "In part, you identify because so many of your patients are young, in their teens and twenties, and however sick they are, they're struggling with issues that are still alive for you. You're not that much older yourself, and in some ways you feel younger than your age because you're still in training. You're still establishing your own adult identity, you're still separating from your parents, you still haven't left school and gone out into the real world on your own.

"Near graduation, everyone talks about how terrified they are of leaving the nest to set up practice. Everyone's afraid they're going to starve to death. And it looks so lonely out there," he confessed, "because you've never been on your own before. So when a patient tells you they're scared to leave the hospital or look for a job, you identify with them, and you have trouble seeing why they're in and you're out."

In fact, identification can occur with any patient, regardless of age. "In the long run, it doesn't matter how old your patient is," John mused. "We carry our childhood with us until we die, and the man of seventy may feel as hurt about something that happened when he was a child as [does] the boy of twenty. But when I started out, I was so naïve I thought it would be really different listening to older people.

"Of course the realities are different—they may be widowed, friends are dying, and their own death is much more real to them. But people still go right back to how they felt when they were eight and their best friend moved away or their dog died. One of my first patients was a man of more than seventy, a depressed, isolated lawyer, divorced, who'd alienated all his children and whose only social contact was a weekly game of poker. The second time I saw him he talked about having come here as an immigrant when he was six, how scared he was of the big city, how he'd never seen his father before, how he never felt able to reach out to people the same way again. And I felt I understood a lot of what he said from the inside, because it connected with some of my own experiences. And I had trouble setting limits with him because of my identification."

John shook his head wonderingly. "I was incredibly self-centered, and at first I marveled that his childhood was still as alive for him as mine was for me. And that I found his so poignant. But memory is never in clock time. Issues remain alive as long as they remain unresolved, and some very similar issues were alive for both of us." He took off his glasses and pressed his fingers against his forehead. "It's like the paintings by Rembrandt of the same woman at different ages. When you see the last one, she's an old woman, but she looks out at you from the canvas wondering how it ever happened that half a century has passed."

Empathy involves putting oneself in the other person's place, whether by an act of pure imagination or by searching out similar memories and feelings. But identification goes far beyond empathy to something more global and uncontrolled: a loss of boundaries and confusion of oneself with the other person—at least in certain ways. Whereas empathy allows the psychiatrist to see the patient more clearly, identification involves a loss of perspective and judgment.

"When I held Maureen in my lap," Gary said softly, "it was impossible to tell who was who. I had no sense of time. In retrospect, it had a quality of ecstasy that was almost frightening. You can lose yourself so completely with a patient... and it's just not acceptable. Someone in the room has to keep his head."

Freud wrote about "oceanic feelings," the sense of ecstatically merging with the other, and even with the inanimate universe, which he felt stemmed from our earliest experiences of nursing, before we develop a sense of self separate from the mother.[1] Most of the time, however, identification does not take the form of an ecstatic union. Usually it involves feeling the patient's pain instead, with the effort to get inside the other person's skin transformed into an assault on the psychiatrist's own psyche, during which he becomes unable to maintain any distance at all. No longer functioning as a medical technologist, using the tools of his trade to the best of his ability, he ends up merging with the patient, suffering with his suffering, and losing the very skills and judgment he most needs. Sharing his patient's turmoil, he's wrong when he worries about going crazy; the real problem is that his judgment is shot, and he doesn't even know it.

"To me, the overriding issue is not getting caught up in the patient's craziness," Laura said. "Everything else is secondary—safety, empathy, their trust in you. None of that is as important as you keeping your head." She smiled fleetingly. "Someone in that room has to be clear on what's happening. That's what you're getting paid for.

"The classic example is the patient in the emergency room at two A.M., absolutely desperate—she's going to kill herself, she can't go home, there's nowhere to go. Finally you get the story: She and her boyfriend had a fight, she took some pills, her girlfriend brought her in. And then you find out from the records that she was in last month the same way, and a year ago, and she always shows up the same way: frantic, at the end of her rope, and convincing everyone around her that they have to do something *now*, this minute, at two o'clock in the morning."

Laura's voice gathered momentum and finality. "I want to be clear: This woman is troubled. She has a considerable chance of ending up dead one of these nights, because pill-swallowing is dangerous. And she's not playing games. . . . The whole point is that she does feel desperate at these times. She feels she has nowhere to go. She's used up her usual ways of coping. But you have to keep perspective. You can't be stampeded because she's panicked. You have to understand how she feels, but you absolutely cannot share it.

"This is the classic example, and if you can, you get in her boyfriend, and the girlfriend who brought her in, and everyone else who's involved. And you find out exactly what happened *this* time: What precipitated her panic, what she thought she was doing, what it means to the people around her, and what should be done differently in the future. And you get them all engaged right there and then, and you get her involved. And then when they leave, you've actually made a change in her life, and she'll actually show up for the outpatient appointment you arranged for her." Her voice had an edge. "I'm in no way saying you're supposed to stand by passively. I *am* saying that you are effective only to the extent that you don't get sucked in and lose the ability to make your own assessment of what's needed."

Sometimes the issue in identification is the therapist's feelings of urgency, his own reverberation to the patient's panic. Other times identification takes the form of an acceptance of the patient's worldview, of how she characterizes the world around her.

"Sometimes a therapist takes sides against a patient's parents, as if they really were the malevolent devils the patient portrays," John said. "When I was in training, you saw a lot of this, where we discounted biological influences and talked about family dynamics and the patient being scapegoated,[2] or described someone's mother as 'schizophrenogenic.'[3] And we acted as if the parents were deliberately destroying their kid's life—when the child would have to rejoin the family whenever he came out of the hospital.

"You rarely hear this kind of talk anymore. Whatever their faults, most parents do the best they can—and they're already guilty as hell about what they've done wrong." He shrugged. "Family dynamics are a fascinating area of research. And you can't treat adolescents, or kids, or anyone who's so disabled that they can't live independently, without working with the whole family. You can't work with the individual in isolation.

"But I've wondered about some of the abuse parents came in for from [hospital] staff, how much of it came from our feelings about our own parents. Particularly because so many residents were at the start of their own psychoanalyses[4] and all stirred up about their own experiences. You'd tell your analyst how excited and guilty you felt when your mother slept in your room after an argument with your father, and an hour later you'd have an adolescent patient talk about his mother giving him baths when he was twelve, and you'd freak at his mother at the next meeting with her." He leaned forward and held my eyes. "Because you and your patient were both struggling with the same incestuous feelings, and the same need to separate and develop as an independent adult."

Laura said something similar. "When I was starting out, all my patients would say things that I felt could as easily come from my side of the room. But even when you've been in practice a long time, you still have some patients whose problems reverberate to live issues in yourself—and they're the hardest to do well by.

"I can never be thin enough," she added. "Before I was in analysis, I tried every crazy diet that came along. Between diets I often ate only one meal a day. I was never anorexic, but I certainly have some sense of the anorectic impulse from within myself. And that means I have to be particularly careful treating people with eating disorders. I may know just where they're coming from, but because I haven't fully worked out my own conflicts about food, I more easily make mistakes." The corners of her mouth turned up. "I'm not always alert enough to an eating disorder because I share my patient's bias: we both think we have fat thighs.

"Some psychiatrists will say their most difficult patients are those who are mute, or potentially suicidal, or acting out. I don't find that," she said pensively. "At this point, it's basically only the patient with whom I share some piece of craziness who I find difficult. I can't keep therapeutic neutrality then. They and I are all mixed up together."

Sometimes identification is sparked by an issue that revolves around unresolved conflicts in the therapist's own psyche. Other times it is sparked by real-life events. Steve talked about how psychiatrists in the throes of divorce, for example, often identify with patients whose marriages are troubled.

"You have such powerful feelings around your divorce," Steve said thoughtfully, "primitive feelings around failure, and blame, and loss. It's difficult in even the most civilized of divorces...and very few are...and meanwhile you're in the process of treating large numbers of married patients, with their marriage and marital relationship an inevitable part of their treatment."

"You're never a neutral mediator," he continued, "because your obligation as a therapist is to the person in treatment with you. And you know them intimately and empathize with them.... You're trying to see through their eyes. Of course, you try to be dispassionate, and it's not that you see your patient as a saint, but...there's a bias. In addition to your contractual obligation to them..." His voice trailed away. Then he spoke almost sharply: "And if your own marriage is in dissolution, with all the bitterness that entails, you can all too easily fall into a pathological merger with a patient, accepting without question their version of their spouse." He grimaced. "A few years ago, I sent a couple for marital counseling to a very respected colleague—not knowing she was in the process of divorce herself. And during their first hour, the therapist looked across the table at the husband, and said, 'You son of a bitch, you're doing the same thing to your wife my husband's doing to me!'"

In talking about psychiatrists' impulse to identify with patients like themselves, Laura said: "As a doctor's daughter, I know that doctors' families get the worst care precisely because doctors identify with them and lose their professional perspective. Special treatment almost inevitably leads to overlooking the obvious." She leaned back and pushed her hair away from her eyes. "But I've done it myself. About five years ago, I treated a very depressed medical student. He posed a distinct suicide risk but insisted that hospitalization would destroy his career. In my identification with him, I backed down." She shook her head. "I held his hand through a very long summer and gave him my home phone number, and I called him every day during my vacation. He recovered, but I realized afterward that I should have hospitalized him despite his objections. If he was truly at risk of suicide, then I owed him better protection."

In the 1971 movie *Who Is Harry Kellerman and Why Is He Saying Those Terrible Things About Me?* Dustin Hoffman portrays the hero who suffers a breakdown and eventually commits suicide. Much of the movie takes place in the office of his psychiatrist-analyst, who sits unblinking as Hoffman frantically describes his progressive disintegration. In one unforgettable moment, he turns to look at his analyst and sees him as a taxi driver, watching the meter tick off the minutes of his session. The analyst is totally uninvolved, completely walled off from his patient's desperation, so much so that he seems unaware that Hoffman is spiraling down into the suicide that ends the movie. Taken as one chooses, the movie offers either an accurate description of abysmal psychiatric treatment, or a more subjective view of the way the patient sometimes feels in the course of even good psychotherapy. As the patient suffers through the session, racked by crying, miserable, enraged, or trembling, the therapist watches in calm silence, his compassion apparently limited to providing the box of tissues placed carefully within the patient's reach. To the patient, the therapist may seem essentially untouched, reacting to the unfortunate soul sitting in his office as a technician to a piece of faulty machinery.

To the good therapist, however, they are a mutually interacting pair, intensely intertwined during their time together. Behind the controlled calm, he is dogging the patient with his own associations, trying as best he can to find glimmers in himself of the other. In this context, empathy can be seen as partial identification, in which the therapist can feel with the patient, yet keep his own perspective as well; whereas full identification is empathy gone wild, the therapist trapped within the patient's psyche.

Paradoxically, over-identification can sometimes lead to the psychiatrist's emotional disconnection from the patient, as he tries to defend his own boundaries. The psychiatrist's withdrawal is devastating, for the patient experiences the emotional distance as one more rejection, and a rejection from someone immensely important. The patient gets worse, but the psychiatrist is too out of touch to respond appropriately. The patient feels even more rejected and ignored, and the cycle goes on. At such times, even the experienced psychiatrist may miss an impending breakdown, a suicide, a homicide.

"You're more likely to see the despair of the chronic schizophrenic," Laura said with a frown, "than the desperation of the therapist-in-training who tells you he can't go on. None of us want to hear serious illness in a colleague—that's why medical doctors often get the shittiest treatment from other physicians. Half your efforts in medicine are spent walling out your awareness of your own mortality, and another doctor's illness is a

frontal assault on your denial. Doctors get laughed at for being hypochon-
driacal when they've correctly diagnosed their own malignancies, or else
they're given their own death notices as if it were a weather report." She
spoke bitterly. "A professor of mine in medical school called the entire
class over to look when he diagnosed a retinal tumor in a med student he
was using as a demonstration subject."

Nowadays, the psychiatrist's withdrawal often takes the form of prescribing medications without talking with patients, whereas in the past it
frequently took the form of "pseudoanalysis." As one older psychiatrist described it, "When I was in training, the model was psychoanalysis. And I
knew psychiatrists who'd watch a patient go down the tubes without doing
anything, calling their withdrawal 'analytic neutrality.'" And sometimes
the psychiatrist in the throes of identification oscillates between the poles
of merger and withdrawal. A great deal of the resident's supervision is
aimed at teaching appropriate modulation.

"One of my first inpatients was a history professor," Gary said sadly, "a
brilliant man who'd published several books I'd actually read in college,
but an awkward man who was physically unappealing, had never married,
had no friends. He was acutely suicidal, and I was desperate to keep him
alive. When he started to look better, I took him off suicide watch. And
the next night he threw himself down the stairs and broke his hip. And at
that point, I went the other way: I lost all feeling for him. And he got
worse and worse."

I asked what ultimately happened, and Gary spread his hands. "I have
no idea. He was transferred to a state hospital. To my knowledge he never
recovered.

"But the next year I treated a computer programmer who was also un-
married, isolated, socially awkward, and depressed—and at special risk because his own father had killed himself. After months of outpatient
treatment, he went on a blind date. And afterward he called to tell me it
had been a total bust, and he wanted to say good-bye before he turned on
the gas.

"But this time I had a much clearer sense of who was who in the treatment, and without even thinking I said, 'If you kill yourself, I'll piss on
your grave!' As I said it, I thought I'd gone crazy myself. I thought, What is
he going to make of this? Afterward, I realized how condensed my response

was, that in one sentence I was telling him that I had no respect for his throwing away his life; that no matter how angry he was, he couldn't destroy me by his suicide as he felt his father had destroyed him; that I cared enough about our work together to actually go out to the cemetery; and that regardless of his yearning to merge with me, we were separate people: I'd be alive whether or not he was."

Gary shrugged. "I couldn't have said all those things more forcefully if I'd stayed up all night thinking about it. And it wouldn't have been right for many patients. But for the moment, I heard myself on the phone with him, and I thought how hard it was going to be telling my supervisor what an ass I'd made of myself. And there was a long silence from my patient's side, while I tried to figure how I could unsay my words, and then he said, 'Thank you. I'll see you at tomorrow's session.'"

LAYER

2

NAVIGATING THE UNCONSCIOUS

5

Hearing the Unsaid Meaning

The ideal physician is beneficent, rational, and decisive. She is expected, if not to cure, then at least by her efforts to alleviate suffering. Having finally learned to defend herself from her own fears of death and illness, she is coolly knowledgeable, her medical decisions calling on all the scientific resources of late twentieth-century medicine. But the best psychiatrists are as much at home with the primitive unconscious as with the rationality of medicine, familiar not only with ordinary feelings and emotions but with the powerful forces of Freud's underworld. And they can never return to their earlier state of innocence: Once the threshold is crossed, their relationship with patients is inexorably changed and even their inner experience of reality altered.

In the annals of Western thought, Copernicus, Darwin, and Freud stand apart, having one by one reduced us from a position next to the angels to a place far closer to primeval muck. Copernicus moved us from the center of the universe to one side; Darwin took us out of Eden to be cousin to the apes; and Freud announced that we are not even masters of our personal fate, but puppets buffeted by unconscious forces that shape our lives without our knowing it. While Darwin deprived us of divinity, Freud humbled us before the hidden forces within ourselves. He wrote that the real resistance to his work arose from our wish to deny the reality of our helplessness and the limits of our own self-mastery.[1] Looking at ourselves as reflected through Freud, we see not captains of destiny but children chained to the past, doomed forever to repeat the same mistakes, driven by forces beyond reason, with the line between madness and sanity blurred.

Although Freud believed the unconscious to be the source of creativity, his emphasis was less on its creative potential than on hidden conflict, rigidity, and weakness. Freud thought us blind to our deepest motives; worse, he postulated motives that no one would want to acknowledge: a catalogue of sexual and sadistic perversions, and feelings ranging from the outright murderous to the embarrassingly small-minded. At first he believed in the truth of his patients' reports of early sexual trauma—of being witness to the primal scene, or of being sexually abused—but later he argued that their apparent memories were unreal, signs of unconscious sexual impulses (and the anxiety these impulses aroused).[2] Soon he suggested that the experience of lust goes back to the earliest days of life, and to states of arousal centered on the mouth, the anus, the urethra, and the genitals. But in the confusion of babyhood nothing is clearly differentiated, so that lust becomes intermingled with other drives, such as hunger or fear, and with our very sense of developing identity. Woven in this way into the very texture of our lives, underlying sexual impulses tinge almost every aspect of experience.[3] These yearnings are not leftover curiosities, he insisted, but needs that drive us now, however out of awareness they may be. They are the source of unacknowledged impulses that creep out in multitudinous disguises to determine our love and work and play, our every relationship and circumstance of life.

Freud wrote that these primitive impulses are usually well masked, kept out of consciousness by strong defenses and by compromises that allow us to secretly satisfy at least some part of the forbidden desires without acknowledging them. Normally the unconscious remains walled out, perceptible only in slips of the tongue and in dreams.[4]

Symptoms, on the other hand, indicate faltering defenses and inadequate compromises that reveal what they should hide. The symptom expresses the forbidden wish, Freud wrote, while simultaneously denying it: it is a kind of unconscious attempt to both have the cake and eat it.[5] And further, he said, we are compelled (if neurotic) to repeat ourselves again and again, helplessly reliving the conflicted experiences we couldn't master at the age of two or three or five.[6]

Almost all of Freud's points have since been challenged by psychotherapists (and others) within and outside of psychoanalysis, psychology, and psychiatry, and few of his theories have been left unchanged. It is now agreed that some symptoms represent a compromise between unconscious, conflicting impulses, while others seem more like habits, problems of faulty conditioning with little current psychological meaning. Some people who report sexual abuse are reporting fantasies, and others are remembering real events. The Oedipal complex may be seen, but it is rarely the focus of treatment Freud felt it to be. In fact, neither the Oedipal complex nor sexual impulses per se seem as important today as they did in the sexually repressed and conformist culture of Freud's Vienna. In our society, development is more often snagged on conflicts that revolve around individuality, independence, and assertiveness; and psychiatrists see far more patients who act out their impulses instead of repressing them—far more people who are promiscuous, aggressive, alcoholic, or drug abusers.[7]

Still, Freud's basic psychodynamic ideas remain the bedrock of residency training and psychiatric practice: Many mental processes are unconscious; unconscious motives often determine our behavior; we actively repress (push out of awareness) many anxiety-producing memories, feelings, thoughts, and impulses; we protect ourselves from anxiety by specific defense mechanisms (repression, isolation, displacement, rationalization, denial, projection, and so on); childhood experiences, particularly early ones, shape our adult personalities; and we pass through a predictable series of psychological stages in the course of growing up.

In Freud's schema, people get stuck at given stages of development because of constitutional vulnerabilities and environmental events, and the stage at which someone is "fixated" (oral, anal, and so on) determines a whole constellation of personality characteristics.[8] Psychoanalytic writers after Freud offered different developmental schemas with different names (for example, narcissistic personality, borderline personality), and they often focused on different patterns of traits, but they too looked for fixation at specific developmental stages. Only the labels are different.

There have been changes both in labeling and in emphasis. Freud stressed the centrality of sexuality in human development, and the ways the sexual drives are shaped by early parent-child interactions to create adult personality. Modern theory stresses at least equally the centrality of the emotional bond between parent and child, and the damage done by failures of parental empathy, although there is still considerable overlap of terminology in the two approaches, particularly in descriptive case material.

The most important single figure in the new approach is Heinz Kohut.

Kohut's theories, like Freud's, evolved from working with patients, but were shaped by the fact that he worked with extremely difficult and demanding patients who were far sicker than those seen by most conventional analysts, people who weren't helped by his interpretations of their ongoing experience in terms of their past history. In Kohut's work, the therapist's empathy is stressed rather than his interpretations, and his being with the patient moment by moment in the course of the session is more important than his analyzing the historical roots of the patient's symptoms. Kohut also argues that Freud was wrong in believing that what really happened in childhood is less important than the patient's fantasies and beliefs about what happened. Kohut insists that people develop the kinds of disorders he treats only if parental figures really failed them. Whereas Freud (who talked initially of the role of traumatic sexual experiences in creating neurosis) stressed unconscious fantasies that were rooted in the child's own sexual drive (which might lead to unconscious fantasies that appeared to be real memories), Kohut's formative experiences refer to failures of empathy on the parent's part, parents truly not paying attention to the actual child and his needs. It is the therapist's continued empathy, therefore, as he follows the patient's feelings through the hour without necessarily interpreting them, that Kohut sees as curative.

Relatively few therapists have read all of Kohut's work, for his writing is difficult and dense; and psychiatry continues to follow Freud on the importance of interpreting present experience in terms of the patient's past, particularly in analytically oriented psychotherapy and psychoanalysis. On the other hand, recent writers also emphasize the centrality of empathy and believe that treatment is doomed without it. So Kohut has infiltrated psychiatry.[9]

In any case, it is one matter to read about psychodynamic concepts in a book or to learn about them in an introductory college class where they may be blurred or trivialized by a teacher whose own clinical experience is limited. It is another to study the concepts while working with patients, to become aware of unconscious processes in them and in oneself, and to observe the pervasiveness of unconscious processes in daily experience: in slips of the tongue and in dreams, in someone's forgetting an appointment or coming late, in our very personalities and ways of being in the world. This kind of awareness extends to every part of life and to all our relationships. To the psychiatry resident, it has the force of a religious conversion.

"Now everyone around me had unconscious wishes," Gary said wryly. "No one could do anything without my seeing underlying motives and needs. People became types: My father was a 'narcissistic personality with anal-sadistic traits,' my mother a 'passive-dependent hysteric with major depressive episodes.'" He flashed his quick smile. "My kid's nursery school teacher said my daughter hid under the table whenever it was time to play outside, and I was haunted by the possibility that she was a 'schizoid personality with possible early autism.' I already had a bed waiting at a state hospital."

He stretched his long legs and rubbed his chin reflectively. "I had a key to a puzzle, mental file cards that helped make sense of people around me. My father's sarcasm and tight-fistedness were part of a larger constellation of personality traits described by Freud, and Freud's description of unconscious dynamics predicted other traits, like my father's collecting stamps and watches. . . . He walked out on Thanksgiving dinner when my wife and I disagreed with him about Vietnam, and I explained his behavior as a manifestation of narcissistic personality disorder.

"It was like putting on imaginary glasses that allowed me to see through people. When my wife complained about my working late, I told her the real issue was her penis envy, and when she didn't speak to me after that, I interpreted it to her as a passive-aggressive manipulation."

I winced, and Gary grinned at me. "Really," he said. "I was a royal pain in the ass, spouting pedantic jargon. You understand, even if 'penis envy' had been salient, I was leaving a very bright, college-educated woman home alone with two kids under five for twelve hours a day, and when I came home I'd had it with listening to other people's feelings. I was as empathic as a stone. If we hadn't had the kids, we would have divorced."

"You're like a child with a new toy," Steve said earnestly. "You bring it with you everywhere. It's all you can think about, and you drive everyone around you crazy. It's a new way of organizing experience, and of perceiving reality, and you can't turn it off."

"So much that you never understood about yourself suddenly falls into a pattern. It's like walking into sunlight from a dark room. I was driving home from the hospital one day—I'd been reading Freud—and I remembered a calf I'd raised when I was no more than seven, that my father had sent to slaughter. I'd pleaded with him, I'd cried, I'd offered to clean the barn every morning, and he said only that a farm wasn't the place for sentimentality. I hadn't thought about the experience in twenty years, but now I felt the connection between my helplessness then and a quality of cold hardness in myself, a door shut against emotion to protect myself from ever feeling so grief-stricken and enraged again. And with that image, I had a flood of associations to my father's harshness, and memories of my older brothers calling me a sissy, and of my mother circling my wrist with her thumb and forefinger and calling me the runt of the litter. And I thought, Childhood experience shapes the kind of person you become, and it had the quality of revelation, of a blinding flash of profound understanding. . . . It's like having a new sense added to your repertoire. You perceive a world previously unknown."

When I asked Laura how the developing awareness of unconscious processes had affected her, she said, "Most of us narrow our circle down to friends for whom psychological reality is predominant. They don't have to be therapists, but if they're not, they've had enough therapy to find the psychological view natural, or they're in some creative work that necessitates keeping the line to the unconscious open. Otherwise the gulf is too wide." Her speech was formal, as it often was when I asked a direct question. "You can share interests and enthusiasms, but you can't be close to people who are truly naïve psychologically." She frowned slightly. "I believe that's a major reason so many spouses of psychiatrists get analyzed, so they can think in the same language."

Nowadays, psychiatry's approach to labeling has changed. While the older typology was based on Freud's developmental stages, the modern approach (abbreviated as DSM-IV, a newly revised version of DSM-III-R) aims to be atheoretical, describing different psychiatric disorders only by the symptoms patients present without regard to their underlying meaning (so that some of Freud's terms remain only for their purely descriptive value). The idea is to avoid theoretical debate and focus on readily observable facts, and it is a particularly effective approach when the appropriate diagnosis calls for a specific kind of treatment. The psychiatrist had better, for example, differentiate depression from anxiety, anxiety from panic disorder, and post-traumatic stress syndrome from both because what she prescribes (and some of the psychotherapy) vary with the diagnosis. But the DSM-approach doesn't tell you anything about the etiology of different disorders. For all its faults, the older strategy, pioneered by Freud, did. Although insurance forms require DSM-IV for diagnosis, the new system and the most useful parts of the old coexist in the psychiatrist's thinking.

"When I go home to Rhode Island," John said sadly, "I feel I've gone back in time. Even now nothing has changed, and I have to bite my tongue and pretend to be blind. My grandmother is in a nursing home, and my mother gets a headache every time she sees her. My mother gives it no meaning. She even forgets that it always happens, and if I remind her, she blames the headache on the long drive." He leaned forward intensely. "She's fought with her mother all her life. She feels that she was the least favored child, that her mother never really cared about her welfare, and she's still angry that she was forced to leave school to work in a factory when she was fifteen. Whatever her affection or concern, each visit triggers resentment and anger—and guilt—with the whole complex of negative feelings pushed out of awareness. And I'm certain that her headache grows out of the tensions generated by her repressed conflict over making the visit."

He sat back. "On the other hand, she adored her father. She never felt her husband measured up, and she criticized everything my father did until the day he died. I still remember seeing her in my grandfather's lap when I was nine or ten, with her arms around his neck. Altogether my mother is still playing out the Oedipal drama: she is still unconsciously fixed in early childhood, struggling to take Daddy away from Mommy. But she'd be shocked and disgusted if I said it. She'd want to wash my mouth out with soap."

John removed his glasses and began polishing them. When he spoke again his voice was cooler and more impersonal. "That wish destroyed any chance of accommodation with her mother, ruined her marriage, and led her to be so competitive with her own daughters that she's alienated them. And my older sister's doing something not dissimilar with her own life." He looked fully at me. "You narrow your circle to psychologically sophisticated people because you have more rapport with them—and also because you're less likely to see gross psychopathology in people who've had intensive treatment. When I visit my family, I feel I'm watching a tragedy in the making—that the next generation will be no better off than mine was, or all the centuries of peasants before us. It's heartbreaking to see my nephews cling to my sister, and failing in school because they're too anxious to concentrate, with neither my sister nor brother-in-law willing to admit to a need for family treatment."

When people meet a psychiatrist socially, they often fear their minds will be read, or their emotions dissected. In fact, young psychiatrists (and people in other fields of psychotherapy) often go through a phase in which they try their new knowledge on everyone they meet. But established practitioners prefer to lock their office door when they leave at the end of a day. One psychiatrist I know sometimes tells people (with an utterly bland expression) that he's a plumber; another says he's a physician and immediately changes the subject. And the psychiatrists I interviewed talked about their unwillingness to use their professional skills in their social lives. I even wonder if some of the reputation psychiatrists have of being boorish, insensitive, and odd, comes from their frequent unwillingness to pick up on even the ordinary psychological cues other people use.

When I asked Gary about it, he smiled cheerfully. "My wife says she sometimes wonders if I'd notice if she began talking to herself, and that, if I did, if I'd think it was peculiar. Because it's not just that you don't want to wear your shrink hat at home; it's that you develop two disparate modes of being. When you're 'on,' you see unconscious material in neon lights, and when you're 'off,' you can act the role of psychological moron. My wife leaves a party knowing that one couple is on the outs, that someone else is having an affair, that so-and-so is fighting with his business partner, and I've noticed nothing."

"You tune out and turn your back," Laura agreed. "But it's automatic, out of awareness. Last week, a friend mentioned another woman I'd spoken to very briefly at a party as someone who'd had a difficult life, and I said, 'Yes, she's manic-depressive.' And when my friend wanted to know how I knew, I couldn't say. I'd thought only that although she seemed nice enough, I didn't want to spend more time with her. Yet clearly I'd registered enough to make a diagnosis, without even knowing it.

"To some extent you become callous," Laura said suddenly. "Once I become aware of someone's disturbance, I also know that I'm seeing just the surface, that the troubles are pervasive. And I don't want trouble—I have enough pain in my own life. I was at a meeting last week, and there was someone there who was obviously psychotic, and I thought, I don't care that this is a public place. He shouldn't be here. He shouldn't be allowed."

Although some therapists inappropriately flaunt their awareness of unconscious processes in off-the-cuff interpretations at parties or across the dinner table, almost everyone I interviewed thought of this as beginner's behavior, or else as something they saw in others and loathed.

"It's my job to listen in the office. It's not my job after hours," Laura continued. "My friends are friends, people who I enjoy being with—I'm not there to analyze them. If a friend has a serious problem and turns to me for advice, then I may, for the moment, try to listen as if it were a patient. But I find it extremely difficult because it's an entirely different mode of relating. Friends haven't given me permission to ask the kinds of questions I ask patients or to make the kinds of interpretations, and it's arrogant of me to feel that as a friend I even know them well enough to be right. And I try never to do it unless I'm specifically asked and agree that I will. Psychiatry is a role: When I'm being a psychiatrist, I'm not the person, Laura—I'm the person embedded in the role of shrink. I have to become absolutely accepting, absolutely nonjudgmental. I have to think about everything I say and formulate it carefully. I have to be professional. And I have to maintain a new kind of distance. I have to keep myself apart in order to be able to see so clearly. It's no longer a relationship between friends." She frowned. "And, of course, no matter how careful you are, you now know things your friend may be very uncomfortable with your knowing, or say something they really didn't want to hear. . . . It's too easy to risk a friendship."

Gary said, "When I start listening the same way, the way I do in my office, I know the other person is in serious trouble. Once I stop listening to the content of the conversation and begin hearing the underlying affect, once my own thoughts begin to drift into associations, I'm on duty. I don't want to be burdened with knowing that much about people I meet socially, and I don't want other psychiatrists listening to me that way. By the time you're in practice ten years, you want to leave your office behind at the end of the day."

6

The Therapist as Patient

Psychological-mindedness is a way of thinking, an orientation toward psychological explanations of behavior. But it is also grounded in simple observations, paying attention to the specifics of someone's posture, movements, tone of voice, or expression as much as to the words used. We all do some of this spontaneously; the psychiatrist must learn how to use these sources of information constantly and with control.

Gary said, "A great deal of my work involves paying attention to detail and looking for discrepancies, for what doesn't fit. This morning a patient talked about his son's illness—a terrible story, the child has leukemia—and by the time he finished, I had tears in my eyes. But he didn't, so I pointed it out to him: 'How come I'm crying and you're not?'"

"Sometimes I notice a piece of behavior, an odd posture, a movement," he added. After a moment's reflection, he offered another example. "A woman I've begun to treat, a writer, always offers me a cigarette at the beginning of our session, although I inevitably answer that I don't smoke. Yesterday I asked her why she insisted on asking the same question again each time. And she confessed that she was never entirely sure I was the same person from meeting to meeting, that this was one way she could test who I was." Gary searched my face. "I'd had some idea how frightened this woman is, but no notion she was having so much difficulty with reality testing. I'd only known that the oddity of her behavior had to have significance."

Facing a patient is much like viewing a work of art, seeing the unique and specific way in which particular needs and experiences have been organized into a personal gestalt. No person is reducible to another, so the psychiatrist must learn to take each patient's discrete symptoms and complaints and oddities and assets and construct from them a unique and coherent picture. To do this work, he has to learn the nitty-gritty details of the patient's life, and he has to have a substantial backlog of old-fashioned common sense. But he must also learn to do what Theodore Reik called "listening with the third ear,"[1] and developing this capacity depends essentially on direct experience.

There are only two avenues to this experience: by treating patients or by being a patient. Of the two, only the first is still an absolute requirement in training programs, particularly in the expectation that the resident learn to do psychotherapy with outpatients in the second and third years of training (although residents receive less psychotherapy training, see fewer psychotherapy patients, and see them for less time in recent years, mainly because of changes in insurance coverage, and partly because of the increased role of medications. It is said that in many modern programs residents come out with far too little psychotherapy experience. The issue of psychotherapy training is at the center of the debate between mind and body in modern psychiatry.[2]) But when I asked the psychiatrists I interviewed, who had considerable psychotherapy training in their residency, how long it took to feel that they *really* knew what they were doing, almost all of them said that they'd needed about ten years. As one said, "It takes that long just to see enough patients so that you can say, 'I've had experience with that kind of problem. I've treated that successfully. Or I learned to do this and not that.'"

As to the requirement that the therapist learn to "listen with the third ear," by being a patient, Freud wrote: "But where and how is the poor wretch to acquire the ideal qualifications which he will need in his profession? The answer is in an analysis of himself."[3] Freud saw analysis as a lifelong experience, involving continued self-examination and/or periodic returns to a formal analysis;[4] but he saw the initial analysis as a necessary introduction to the unconscious processes.[5] And one of the most wonderfully empathic of all psychoanalysts, Frieda Fromm-Reichmann, added wryly that personal analysis is a necessity because it is also the only way to convince the overwhelmed beginner that psychological change is really possible (1959). By seeing what happens to himself in the course of treatment the psychiatrist-in-training can "learn from his own experience to believe in the possibility of psychological change in himself and in others."[6]

The issue is not that would-be psychiatrists are sicker than the rest of us. Rather they need to be healthier, and analysis offers a profound self-exploration unmatched by any other technique. At best, analysis ends with the resolution of most of the therapist's own conflicts, leaving him not only healthier but better able to withstand his patients' turmoil. At the least, analysis ought to leave the therapist aware of his own weak spots; of what sorts of patients he shouldn't treat; of what areas of conflict and impulses in a patient should act as danger flags to him; of the areas in which his own judgment is weak and where he must be on special guard. Moreover, the person he goes to for treatment becomes a very important role model for his own work with patients.

Laura said, "For me, a direct experience is much stronger than something I read, and analysis was a very powerful experience in terms of learning how to do therapy. You see your supervisors once a week, but analysis was four times a week, and it was an immediate experience. Rather than being told what to do, it was being done to me—I know what it felt like. I developed my own style and my own way of doing treatment, but much of the time I found myself saying things my analyst said to me. Sometimes they didn't work, and I realized they were inappropriate, and sometimes I realized they'd been mistakes on his part—they hadn't worked with me, but I'd thought maybe they'd work with someone else. Real things, sentences, phrases."

Originally, the psychiatrist simply went to a disciple of Freud's and became a psychoanalytic patient. But requirements soon rigidified. Even before World War II the "training" psychoanalysis became attached to formal study at a special psychoanalytic training institute, where only psychoanalysts from the institutes' list were allowed to perform psychoanalyses on candidates.[7] In fact, few psychiatrists went on to psychoanalytic institutes even at the peak of psychoanalytic influence, when becoming a certified psychoanalyst was the capstone of training (and a requirement for academic rank and leadership). And the number of psychiatrists who have gone on to psychoanalytic training institutes has dropped precipitously since the 1970s. In the majority of training programs today, almost no residents go on to psychoanalytic institutes. Although it is not known how many psychiatrists receive treatment themselves, it appears that many psychiatrists are content with a personal psychoanalysis, as in Freud's day, or even some other form of psychotherapy. However the treatment is arranged, every psychiatrist I interviewed felt a personal analysis—or intensive psychotherapy—to be essential.

Although Freud's theories are the basis for almost all later psychotherapy, there are different theoretical schools that are based on emendation to Freud's work.[8] But Freudian analyses and some kind of Freudian-based psychotherapy are by far the most common in the United States,[9] and share a variety of parameters. In Freudian analysis, the analysand (whether psychiatrist or not) comes three, four, or five times a week, lies on the couch, reports dreams, and free-associates to an invisible analyst behind her. She is told to say whatever comes to mind, revealing herself as fully as she ever will to anyone, trying not to censor her speech for any reason whatever. Reporting all her thoughts, she not only explores material that wells from the deepest levels of the unconscious but is specifically asked not to set an agenda or prejudge what is relevant or makes sense. All the important problems of her life will appear in their own time if only she lets it happen, and any attempt on her part to decide what is most important can only interfere with the process.

In this collaboration, whose aim is a dissection of personality unmatched in any other kind of psychotherapy, the analyst serves as empathic listener and expert guide, commenting, clarifying, and interpreting; laying bare unconscious conflicts and peeling away defensive layers to expose the analysand's deepest fears and wishes.

The dismantling of psychological defenses sends every analysand backward in time, to the experiences that led to the raising of defenses in the first place. The experience is intense and often painful, and in the process the analyst becomes a central figure in the analysand's inner life. Indeed, the analyst becomes a stand-in for the significant figures of his past as the patient re-creates the sense of her childhood, not just in words but in feeling. (Because it is important in all psychotherapy, this "transference" of feeling to the therapist will be discussed at length later.)

"Sometimes I felt I lived mainly for my sessions," Laura said, "particularly when I wasn't going out with anyone significant. It was frightening that the rest of my life felt less real, less important than how my analyst felt about me that day."

The intensity of analysis—and the relative silence of the analyst behind the couch—makes it essential that the analyst be compassionate and empathic. But not all are, by any means. Several psychiatrists complained, with remarkable bitterness, of their analyst's silence and lack of responsiveness; this was particularly so when their analysis had been part of their training at a psychoanalytic institute.

Laura said, "When I work with someone, I tell them they have to tell me everything they're thinking, everything they feel in the hour—what seems weird, what seems crazy, what they don't understand, what they're ashamed of, what they're pleased by. That their job is to put all this muck down on the table between us so that we can look at it together. We'll both sit there with our hands in the muck trying to make sense of it, and I will help them understand what it's all about. That's my job." She sighed. "It hardly ever felt as if we were sitting together that way in my own analysis. I felt that I was in the muck, and he was over there observing this. It was a very lonely experience. And when I tried to talk with him about it, it was as if I were talking Chinese. He either didn't understand, or he didn't let on that he understood." She thought a moment, and corrected herself. "Except sometimes. Every so often I'd feel him really in there, working with me. And those moments were wonderful. But there weren't enough of them—so few I felt that I could count them."

Yet analysis is only one kind of psychotherapy; in fact, less than 3 percent of psychiatric outpatients are in psychoanalysis.[10] "Psychoanalytically oriented intensive psychotherapy" is closest in aim to psychoanalysis, and it is the likeliest approach to be taken in long-term psychotherapy. Like analysis, it is a stripping-down process, removing defenses and confronting the painful emotions they protect us from. In this work the patient sits up and faces the therapist, but is still expected to say whatever comes to mind without holding back. Because she comes to sessions only once or maybe twice a week, she is likely to talk more about events in her current life and less about dreams or childhood. But the therapist is still primarily empathic listener and guide, interpreting current issues in terms of unconscious conflicts, and collaborating with the patient to understand the connections between past events and current feelings so that those old bonds can be broken.

The goals of psychoanalytically oriented intensive psychotherapy are more restricted than those of analysis, more a partial renovation than a total overhaul. In intensive psychotherapy, the therapist (and patient) may have limits in mind, aspects of the personality that will not be touched, defenses that will be left alone. But the divergence from analysis is not absolute, and the more complete the attempt to change the personality, the more alike analysis and analytically-oriented intensive psychotherapy become.[11] At their best, these treatments bring about a kind of rebirth as they unlock us from the past and leave us free to become more truly ourselves, to approach the dimly sensed "what I might have been if the past had only happened differently."

And most psychiatric practice is still further away from psychoanalysis, toward what is called supportive treatment. Here the aim is less to change underlying characteristics of personality than to strengthen what is already there. In supportive therapy, the psychiatrist is more likely to give information, advice, suggestions, and even orders. In this kind of treatment, the therapist goes beyond empathic listening to act as coach and cheerleader, helping with problem-solving strategies and methods of coping, and offering a shoulder to lean on and emotional support that provides a "corrective emotional experience."[12]

Supportive therapy is the choice for people in the midst of a major real-life crisis (for example, divorce, life-threatening illness, and so on), or for patients who may be overwhelmed by terror, and even fall into psychosis, if the barriers against unconscious material suddenly drop; it is generally the choice for people recovering from psychotic episodes. Supportive therapy is also the primary treatment for patients who can't think psychologically, don't want major personality changes, have very specific problems they want to work out, or can come for only a few sessions or to sessions spaced far apart.

But supportive psychotherapy and analytically oriented treatment are most often used in tandem, the therapist using interpretation to increase insight in certain areas and for some of the time, and at others simply helping the person to function better without regard to increasing insight. When to do which is an ever present treatment decision.

Finally, there are still other kinds of treatment that are quite different. Outside of traditional psychotherapies, the two best known are behavior therapy, which makes use of conditioning techniques, particularly to reduce anxiety and avoidance behavior, and cognitive therapy, created by Aaron Beck,[13] which focuses not on the Freudian unconscious but on a semiconscious, free-running and self-critical internal monologue. Behavior therapy may be used without regard to psychoanalytic theory—although more sophisticated behaviorists are unlikely to ignore unconscious processes when they tailor behavioral programs to an individual patient. Cognitive therapy too, usually presupposes a familiarity with the psychoanalytic model. And either technique may be used along with yet other specific modalities—such as hypnosis—as adjuncts to psychoanalytically oriented or supportive psychotherapy.

✍

I close this chapter with a segment from an interview I had with an eminent elderly psychoanalyst, Emily Mandelson. Trained by one of Freud's disciples, she is white-haired and frail, and her hands tremble slightly. But her voice is firm, younger than her years, and she sits erect in her chair, her back straight like a dancer's, her ankles carefully crossed.

She told me that she pictured analysis as a journey: "setting off on a long voyage with a stranger in the course of which the two of you become terribly intimate. The reality is that both you and the patient are working together on understanding and helping him," she said. "Nobody gets that kind of attention outside."

She then continued, talking about the experience in particular of psychoanalysis, but what she said applied, I feel, to all psychotherapy of whatever kind, and to all psychotherapists. "There's a tremendous intimacy in this specialness, so that even though the patient says, 'I love you, I want to marry you, and you're the handsomest man, and why won't you make love to me,' and gets terribly upset, and angry, and so on, the doctor can truly point out—and I've taught this to many residents—that, Yes, [the patient] will have other lovers in her life, and other friends, and other people who will go to dinner, and so on, but there is only one person to whom she can really go and examine everything in absolute safety, that this is the purest kind of relationship, and it's unique. The care is both ways," Emily concluded, "and you can say to the patient, 'Of course I care for you,' because it's safe—the analyst won't go past the boundaries." She added suddenly, "That's why everyone doing therapy should be very well analyzed. We need all the help we can get to keep that relationship safe."

7

The Healing Bond and the Psychiatrist's Own Baggage

In psychiatry, the private and professional selves become completely interwoven, and the line between role and self is not simply blurred but in a fundamental way erased. Working intimately with patients, the psychiatrist has no choice but to bring her whole self into the room. Everything about her, including her own past and the reasons that brought her into psychiatry in the first place, is relevant to the bond that is created, helping to determine its shape and texture. So it makes sense to ask what kind of people psychiatrists are.[1]

Certain observations have been made repeatedly. Many psychiatrists, for example, are more intellectual than most doctors, more often drawn to abstract questions, and intolerant of intellectual boredom. Certainly the psychiatrists I interviewed said they couldn't stand the idea of being in a medical specialty that would become routinized, in which they would face the same few diagnostic possibilities and the same few procedures again and again.

Laura's response was typical. "I really loved surgery," she said with a lilt in her voice. "Surgeons are like opera singers, or conductors in the amphitheater—tremendous narcissists—it was just a lot of fun. And I was good with my hands, and surgery is so clean. A surgical procedure is pure and beautiful in a way medicine never is. And it seemed so easy." She smiled. "Do this one thing and never see them again, and meanwhile they love you forever."

She became serious again. "But it's like fixing cars or doing carpentry. It's very concrete, and the processes aren't themselves all that interesting. Even in medicine I didn't find the mechanisms we called on particularly exciting. I could be totally involved in saving my patient, but I couldn't work up any interest in electrolyte balance per se. Physiological explanations never fascinated me the way psychological processes do."

Michael Silberman is a dynamic, tough-looking psychiatrist in his early fifties, in private practice in Manhattan. His face is round, with broad Slavic cheekbones, his nose wide and flattened, his lips thin. In his rumpled suit, he seems to care little about his appearance, and he is strikingly competitive, ready for argument. His parents fled Hitler's Germany, and Michael grew up on Manhattan's Upper West Side. He is twice married, with one child from his first marriage and two from his second.

When I asked Michael about his choosing psychiatry as a specialty, he said, "I'd always been drawn to basic questions of the mind. I minored in philosophy in college and would have gone on with it if I didn't expect to support a family. And in medical school I turned to neurology in part because I thought I'd be able to ask questions of metapsychology there. But I found neurology to be arid and mechanistic, concerned essentially with reflexes and wiring diagrams: 'If the patient loses the ability to distinguish unfamiliar faces, it is an indication of focal damage in the right cerebral hemisphere.'" He took off his jacket and loosened his tie. "The larger issues—how we think, the nature of memory, how we create a sense of self, what is the actual relationship of the physical brain to the mind, what do we even mean by mind—nobody talked about that. We didn't know enough about how the brain worked to even ask those questions in a way that could get answers." He pursed his lips. "In any case, they were outside the scope of clinical neurology. I turned to psychiatry at least partly because I decided that must be the specialty that asked the big questions."

Now his tone became self-deprecating. "I started with metapsychology, and I have to admit I haven't been bored by psychiatry, but it certainly hasn't turned out to be such an intellectual pursuit. Clinical work is rough-and-ready thinking, more like detective work or chess, or many kinds of problem solving, whereas my feeling was I'd be a philosopher-doctor thinking profound thoughts."

No one I interviewed had ever considered the specialty practices of proctology, or gastroenterology, or cardiology, whereas practically everyone had seriously considered neurology or internal medicine, the most intellectually demanding and least routinized of the medical specialties.

Several were board certified as internists; one had not only passed internal medicine boards but had done a year's fellowship in oncology. All of them had also been exhilarated by the challenge of the emergency room and the intensive care unit (ICU).

"I considered emergency room medicine or working in an ICU when I finished internship," Laura said. "When I was a resident, I used to moonlight in the ER of a local hospital, and it was the best part of my day. It was exciting, I never knew what was going to happen next, I made a lot of diagnoses, and I had to think on my feet." She frowned. "Of course, psychiatry was a lot like that too, except that I knew what I was doing in the ER, while I was barely competent as a psychiatrist. And the ER didn't drain me emotionally."

Like emergency room medicine, psychiatry provides constant challenge, a lack of routine, and the need to be always on alert. But psychiatrists are attracted not only by excitement, but by those aspects of medicine having to do with human relationships, and psychiatry provides the chance to work intimately with another person. Like John Hames, with his vision of the Norman Rockwell family doctor, psychiatrists want to know their patients more fully than other specialties allow, and they are unwilling to be limited to a largely technical role. "When I was in med school, I dated a psychology grad student for a while," John said, "who kept telling me that I was nothing but a glorified plumber. You might say that to a surgeon. You can't say that to a psychiatrist."

In fact, the psychiatrist's concern with human relationships is thought to have deep and personal roots. Certainly, most of the psychiatrists I've known have been raised with a parent or sibling with disabling depressions or exceptionally peculiar behavior. Several also had a parent die while they were children; others had a parent desert them; and all but a handful of the rest had a member of the family who was physically disabled, often blind or deaf. I also have the impression that psychiatrists who specialize in "difficult cases" are particularly likely to have come from terrible homes themselves. In fact, several psychiatrists told me that they were told by their own analysts that their childhoods were far worse than those of the vast majority of their patients.

The bare outline of Steve's story, for example, is far from rare. "My mother suffered major depressions," Steve said baldly, his handsome face expressionless. "Although she was never hospitalized for depression, my father had to hire a housekeeper many times to cook and run the house. . . . There were weeks at a time when my mother wouldn't even leave the bedroom. Often I'd come home from school, and she'd be sitting by the bedroom window in the same nightgown she'd worn for days. . . . I felt I had to go in and talk to her, and tell her about my day, as if that would help, but she wouldn't answer. She just looked past me, out the window. As if I weren't there."

I thought of his mute patient, Carole, and murmured her name.

Steve raised one eyebrow impatiently. "Of course," he said.

And there is Laura. "I adored my father, but the reality is that he was hardly ever home. He was a surgeon, and he lived his life at the hospital. And my mother was an alcoholic. We had money, and I went to private school, but there were days when no one picked me up in the afternoon. I was so ashamed, I made up stories about my mother being too sick to come for me, but, of course, they knew. Sometimes I waited for her until five o'clock." Her oval face looked vulnerable in the afternoon light, despite her fashionable clothes. "One of the reasons I love New York is that I can always take a taxi home."

Or Gary. "My mother had her first break a few years before I was born, and from then on she went into the hospital every couple of years. She checked herself in when she felt she was getting delusional or suicidal, and they'd give her electroshock, and she'd come back after a few months. And my father was chronically enraged, feeling trapped but unable to bring himself to divorce her. He beat us both, and once he broke my arm." He ducked his head and looked away. "If I'd known where I could go, I'd have run away from home."

Or John. "My father became blind when I was four. So he stayed home, and my mother went to work. But she worked the evening shift, from four to midnight, so I never saw her once I started school. Except on weekends, and then she'd always be doing laundry. Or we'd go to the supermarket together. And no one ever acted as if this were strange. That she was never home and I was raised by a blind man." He hesitated. "I loved my father. I loved him a lot, but I not only had to watch out for me when I was four; I had to watch out for him."

Or Michael. "After my father died, I had lunch with another psychiatrist, and I told him that my father had been crazy. Really crazy." He smiled lopsidedly. "And he said to me, 'Of course I believe you. Would you like to know the diagnosis on my father?'"

Those in charge of residency training have the impression that almost everyone who trains in psychiatry is drawn at least partly by a lifelong, although often unconscious, puzzlement about human relationships that stems from their own peculiar childhoods. Indeed, they may still be trying to understand and master a family situation that was inherently unreasonable.

As Laura said, "Apart from being alcoholic, my mother was a rather paranoid woman, and my choice growing up was either to believe in her view of reality and ignore my own perceptions, or learn to ignore hers while still having to live with her. But it left me with a tremendous craving to know what really went on in people. In training, they don't talk much about the need to know, because that craving to understand is useful. They want to encourage understanding. But I think it motivates so many of us. So many of us came from homes where there were serious problems with a parent or a sibling, where we really had to struggle to understand people of tremendous significance to us.

"When I began psychiatry," she continued, "I didn't realize all this. I had no feeling for how personal my interest was until my own analysis. But I'd read Freud's *Introductory Lectures* in college, and I'd fallen in love with the way he wrote, his incisiveness, and the world he opened up. I thought he was a hero, to explore the mind as he did."

Other factors that shape psychiatrists apply more generally to doctors at large. Among the most consistent findings is that there is a link between the choice of medicine and the need to do useful work, to help other people, and to relieve suffering.[2]

Laura said, "My father was a surgeon, and he was hardly ever home. But he was a hero to me, almost a kind of god, doing the most important work in the world. He saved lives.

"It never occurred to me that we were rich when I was a kid," she added softly. "We lived the way everyone else I knew did. But all the other kids' fathers were only businessmen. They seemed to me to be playing kids' games, like trading comics. While my father mattered: When he got a call in the middle of the night and left for the hospital, it was because someone really needed him."

"I had a distant uncle who was a doc in Providence," John said, "and everyone in the family always treated him differently. When my mother had breast cancer when I was ten, she called him first. He told her who to see, where to go. He set up the appointments." He shrugged ruefully. "Of course, no one told me at the time what was happening, but I could see how they turned to him. Everyone else was wringing their hands and not talking, but he could *do* something."

In many cases, as in Laura's, a parent was a physician, and physician-hood itself expresses an early identification with the parent, in a kind of familial calling. Identification was a way of coping with the parent's frequent absences and preoccupation with patients, a way to overcome the rage of abandonment with idealization, and a way to keep Daddy or Mommy always present by taking him or her inside the growing self. Sometimes, such idealization and identification are thought to come into play even when the child had little sense of being abandoned, the outcome not of loss but of genuinely loving and being loved by a much admired parent. In any case, the fact is that a large proportion of doctors have doctors as parents or as important relatives. I am also reminded of an ancient joke within the psychiatric community:

> GUEST TO PSYCHIATRIST'S CHILD: And what do you want to be when you grow up?
> ANSWER BY CHILD: A patient.

Wishing to be the doctor is a far healthier solution.

Both in medical folklore and in case studies of physicians undergoing psychoanalysis, doctors also seem to be driven by an unusually intense fear of sickness and death that dates to their own early lives. Apart from the fact that a parent was often a physician, inevitably bringing discussions of illness home at least to some extent, future doctors were often seriously ill themselves for a prolonged part of their own childhood. Often, as well, someone they dearly loved was disabled, very sick, or died. Whatever the reasons, the future doctor seems to be unusually sensitive to issues of illness and death. And many physicians certainly remember specific experiences that were decisive in leading them to medicine.

"I had a dog," John said, "a mutt I'd rescued as a stray. When I was thirteen, he got out of the yard and was run over by a car. He died while I was holding him. I had no idea what to do, and all I kept thinking was that if my uncle were there he'd know what to do. I don't know whether he could have saved him or not, but that's when I decided to be a doctor."

Steve said, "I was fifteen years old when my grandfather had a stroke." He moved restlessly, eyes remote, drumming his fingers on the arm of his chair. "My father and I went to the hospital, and my father left me in the room while he went for a cup of coffee. My grandfather began to choke. I ran for the nurse, and they got some doctors up real fast and sent me out of the room, but it was too late. I didn't remember it until I was in psychoanalysis, but that was when I decided to go to medical school, because I really believed I could have saved him if I'd been able to act right then, as it was happening." He stopped, making a visible effort to back off, and cleared his throat. "Of course, I probably couldn't have saved him, not really, and he had cancer anyway, but it didn't matter. I was standing there watching him die, and I was totally helpless."

In the psychiatric literature the term "omnipotence fantasy" is often used to refer to the doctor's drive to defy illness and death, and to her unconscious fantasy that she can defeat them if she tries hard enough, a belief that training programs exploit to push her to her utmost efforts. In fact, the term refers to a wish we are all thought to bury deep within the unconscious, a more general and powerful craving for unlimited power that arises in reaction to our enormous helplessness in infancy and early childhood. In psychoanalytic theory, the wish for unlimited control begins in babyhood, with our absolute dependence on others for survival, for satisfaction of our basic needs, and for love. It becomes even more of an issue when, as infants, we begin to realize our separation from the inanimate world, for such separation carries simultaneously an experience of exhilarating selfhood and of terrifying weakness as we discover just how unresponsive to our efforts the physical world can be. (In this context, I remember watching my infant son discover one morning that the mobile over his crib moved when he pushed it. He gazed at his hand in wonderment, gazed at the mobile, gazed at his hand, pushed again, watched the mobile turn, and laughed out loud before repeating the process over and over for at least fifteen minutes. But the next day he found that pushing wasn't enough to make the horn on the mobile squeak. That mastery was to take another week or so of frustration, until he developed the coordination required for squeezing its handle.)

The craving for control becomes particularly acute around the time we begin to really perceive ourselves as separate beings, individuals with our own wishes whom others can satisfy or frustrate, hear or ignore, help or hurt. When as toddlers we begin to say, "I want," and "I don't want," and "No!" we become aware in yet a different way of the limitations on our autonomy, the innumerable constraints on our satisfactions, the demands others make on us, as well as the recalcitrance of the physical environment.

When Freud first began listening to patients, it was the concreteness of toilet training that he heard most, the struggle between the child's wishes to stay dirty (and in control of his own body) and the parents' wish that he be clean; and the struggle within the child between his wish to do as he wants vis-à-vis the toilet and his fear of losing parental love if he disobeys. Later analysts extended the domain of Freud's "anal phase," emphasizing the toddler's developing drive for autonomy, control, and self-control in all spheres of his life and his ever present need to maintain parental love while avoiding the despair that comes with surrendering to parental power.

We all make a variety of accommodations, accepting that we can't fly, or walk through walls, or safely play with matches; promising to stay dry and clean and out of mud puddles; agreeing not to hit or bite other children, not to make scenes, and to eat everything on our plate if we expect to get dessert. Essentially we do whatever we can to keep our parents' love; for without that, we are forsaken and lost in an empty world.

In psychiatric dogma, unconscious fantasies of omnipotence are universal, with the craving for God-like control the inevitable outcome of our need for love and for protection from hunger, pain, and fear in the face of our enormous helplessness and absolute dependence on the care of others. No one knows whether the future doctor's desire for control was greater to start with, or whether some unresponsive or scary aspect of her early life heightened the potential already within her. But while the omnipotence fantasy may make others wish to be president of the United States or the monied head of a major corporation, in her it takes the form of battling disease and death.

Rooted in the early years of life, these desires are operative before medical school or internship, but they are then fueled by the training itself, heightened and incorporated into the developing physicianly identity. Although not directly observable, they are inferred, like other such motives, from psychoanalytic exploration, from slips of the tongue, and from careful observation of physicians in action.[3]

"Doctors are the guiltiest group of professionals you can meet," Gary said. "That's why the best doctors are so often overworked. They can't say no to a patient. They can't say no to another doctor who wants to send them a referral." He unwrapped a sandwich and began to eat, explaining that he'd missed lunch because of an emergency. "Years ago," he said between bites, "after I missed my younger daughter's birthday party, my wife went through my appointment book, blacking out all my Saturday mornings and hours after eight P.M. She just put X's on every page of my book for the rest of the year, so that I had no choice: I couldn't say yes. And at first I was shocked at what happened afterward, because I'd agreed not to work those hours. I'd told her it was my decision too, and I'd not do it again, yet every few days I'd say yes to someone on the phone or in my office, and only when I discovered there was no room to write the appointment, that the space was crossed out, would I realize I'd done it again." He shook his head and gestured ironically to his sandwich. "I can't tell you how completely you're taught never to say no."

Because the omnipotence fantasy promises absolute control, any failure inevitably carries guilt; there are no excuses once you have total power. Certainly some of the extraordinary measures doctors take with patients, some of their unwillingness to admit defeat that to an outsider may look like little more than an uncaring and useless prolongation of a patient's agony, goes back to the need to avoid admitting helplessness: to win. And some of the arrogance for which physicians are noted, and their general air of authoritarianism, are also part of the same fantasy: control. For it is not that the doctor necessarily feels less anxiety; on tests, the death anxiety of the young physician, at least to the third year of medical school, goes up as training progresses.[4] She is simply defended from her anxiety by the artifice of wish and the actuality of training, for the more she knows, the closer she can come to the power for which she aches. On the other hand, she has less and less room for failure as she knows more.

"If you're really pissed off at another doc, you never tell him you're pissed," Steve said coolly. "You tell him how disappointed in him you are, how you'd been so sure he could do better. No doc can argue with that. It tears him to shreds."

The drive toward mastery over life and death and the fantasy of absolute control are remarkably accessible to many physicians' consciousness (although their deep roots in toddlerhood are not), and are even mentioned spontaneously by nonanalyzed nonpsychiatrists. Other motives that are less often acknowledged are generally discussed only in the psychoanalytic literature, where they may also be linked to the choice of particular specialties. These motives include sexual curiosity, sadistic impulses, a "maternal" need to nurture, and a "masculine"[5] drive toward activity and intrusiveness.[6]

Although medical personnel are unaware of the psychoanalytic literature, they certainly believe that different specialties attract different kinds of personalities. Surgeons are notoriously nasty and abrasive, neurologists cooly intellectual, pediatricians nurturant. And psychiatrists are the most clearly dualistic—simultaneously nurturant and empathic while probing and intrusive. But above all, psychiatrists must be comfortable with all facets of being human, for unless they find and accept these facets in themselves, they cannot accept them in patients.

LAYER

3

A MOST PECULIAR
RELATIONSHIP

8

Peculiar Rules and Lopsided Intimacy

The psychiatrist spends the bulk of his time listening, opening himself to the other person in the room, intruding as little as possible of his personal concerns and being. He sees himself as helping the patient discover her real wants, her real needs, her true wishes and beliefs.

The office is a refuge, a safety zone in which the patient can finally be the person she really is, no longer struggling to maintain a social facade. But the freedom to be genuine carries the inescapable burden of reaching for a higher level of functioning. The therapist constantly prods the patient toward self-awareness; while the patient is pitted against herself, struggling for growth against the inner forces pushing toward retreat.

Torn between the wish to stay the same and the wish to change, few of us would stay in treatment without the therapist's active encouragement and aid. Demanding that the patient use the freedom of the hour to explore the options of her selfhood, the therapist offers himself as companion, ally, and fellow traveler on a road that would otherwise be left eternally unexplored. Yet, all his help would be insufficient in a normal social setting. Psychotherapy is a world apart, with its own reality and rituals; and one of the weirdest aspects of the work is that a relationship designed to foster sanity follows rules that would be bizarre anywhere else, rules that at one and the same time foster tremendous intimacy and a peculiar distance.

"I was assigned the most orthodox Freudian in the clinic as my training analyst," John said. "When I was a boy, I had the fantasy of a perfect school in which I put questions into one end of a hollow log and had answers sent back from the other end. My analyst was so silent, I sometimes thought I'd gotten that hollow log. Yet my analysis was the most intense personal experience of my life. Every time he took a deep breath, I knew it; and every time I took a deep breath, he knew it. His silence and refusal to make our relationship into a social exchange had nothing to do with the reality of our total investment in each other during those hours."

Whether in classical psychoanalysis or in psychotherapy, a new patient is likely to notice oddities even at the opening meeting. From the first session, there is little small talk, no brief exchange about the weather. If the patient tries to make conversation, the psychiatrist may not even answer.

Gary said, "Sometimes I shake hands only twice in the course of someone's therapy: when I introduce myself initially, and when we stop at the end of the final session. Even if that's ten years later. The point is that treatment is not like other kinds of meetings: it forms one continuous whole in spite of the existence of apparently separate sessions."

Another psychiatrist said, "I never understand how psychiatrists expect patients to accept the peculiar rules of psychotherapy without explaining the reasons for them. If I hadn't answered a patient's question when I was an internist, if I'd just stared silently back at him, I wouldn't have had a practice. When I start treatment," he continued, "I tell patients our time together is to be focused on them and their problems, and that it's not a social meeting. And I explain that I don't generally respond to questions until they tell me why they're asking and what they imagine I might say. Because their thoughts are what really matter, and not my answers—and I might think it was a poor idea to answer even then."

John agreed. "Patients learn soon enough that when they come into the office I'm not going to say hello. I wait for them to speak. But it helps to explain why, that the goal is for them to follow their own thoughts, and that I don't want them diverted by anything I do or say. Not enough psychiatrists spell out the ground rules to patients, and I think it makes for craziness. God knows, it doesn't help the psychiatrist's reputation with other doctors."

A second convention of psychotherapy also becomes apparent to the patient at the very beginning, for she discovers in the initial interview that the amount of self-revelation expected of her is enormous, unmatched in any other setting. The psychiatrist will ask why she is coming for treatment, and why she is coming now instead of last week or last year. If the patient says she is depressed, the therapist will want to know how depressed. Is she sad all the time, does anything give her pleasure, can she get up in the morning? Does she think of suicide, and does she have a plan of action, and if so, what exactly?

Or if the patient says she's anxious, just how anxious is she? Is she anxious all the time or only under certain circumstances? What circumstances? When did the anxiety first appear? Exactly how does the anxiety feel in her body? What does she do when she starts to feel that way? Does she avoid situations that make her anxious, and how widespread is this avoidance?

And what is her social life like? Does she have friends? What about relationships? What is her husband or boyfriend like? Children? What about sex? Where has she gone to school? What was it like? What does she do for work, and how does she feel about work? What about drugs or alcohol? How is her health? What about her parents, brothers and sisters, her childhood? Any deaths in the family as she grew up? Serious illness? How was her health? What about divorces, moving, any other upheavals? What does she remember of childhood? How did she get on with her family? How does she get on with them now? What is she good at? What would she like to do with her life? And what does she hope to get out of treatment? This is not an exhaustive list by any means, and few psychiatrists get a complete history in the first session. On the other hand, many questions need not be formally asked, for often the patient volunteers the data spontaneously. How much the psychiatrist asks is also to some extent a matter of style. And sometimes the detailed taking of the history needs to wait.

"Sometimes patients arrive ready to spill over," John said. "But they may be ashamed to come back if they say too much at the first meeting. Or it may unhinge an already fragile balance, letting loose material that's too disturbing to them."

He took off his glasses for a moment, looking unseeingly at the elaborate bookcases built along one wall of his office. Then he nodded to himself and looked back at me. "A few years ago," he said, "an internist at the hospital sent me a patient of his for consultation, a very difficult and demanding woman with a number of vague physical complaints and no physical findings. He thought she might be depressed." His voice was subdued. "In our first interview, she revealed a complex paranoid delusion about her ex-husband's plot to kidnap their son, with both her downstairs neighbor and a nearby grocer in league with him. When I asked how she was so certain of this plot, she said the FBI had telephoned to warn her. If she'd begun treatment, I would have begun to examine the delusion with her, and I would have tried to have her agree to take antipsychotic medication. But telling me the story solidified her suspicions, and she tried to set fire to the grocery later that day."

I told John that her behavior seemed rather extreme. He frowned slightly and said that it was sometimes impossible on first meeting patients to know how they'd react to the initial interview. I waited again, and he said, "A few months ago I asked a new patient, a married man, about his sexual life. His answer was curt, and I didn't press for more information because it wasn't essential immediately. All I really needed to know was the degree of his depression." He leaned forward intently. "Afterward, he told the psychiatrist who'd referred him that I was an unfeeling bastard. The consultant referred him to someone else who eventually found out that the marriage had never been consummated." John's dark eyes glinted behind their lenses. "To me it was a routine question—and I was willing to wait until we knew each other better once I saw his reluctance to answer. Even so, he experienced the interview as profoundly intrusive."

Once the patient's history is taken, sessions usually focus on what she brings spontaneously into the hour. But the psychiatric session is still intrusive. Even if this intrusiveness is balanced by the psychiatrist's empathy and legitimized by his genuine need to know, the patient's self-revelation is the name of the game. In other situations, one is supposed to keep a stiff upper lip, or at least a decent amount of reserve, and simply never share the bulk of one's inner life with anyone. Furthermore, normal sharing is always reciprocal: I tell you a secret; you tell me a secret. But in treatment, the entire focus of the session is on the patient, and on the patient's psyche. It is not a time for social balance. During the hour (which normally lasts forty-five or fifty minutes) she is expected to reveal her inmost secrets without regard to any of the normal social rules of politeness, reciprocity, or even simple self-protection.

"When people think of psychotherapy," Laura said, "they often think of secrets—of shameful memories, or humiliations, or events they've longed to tell someone all their lives but never dared reveal. That's one reason the psychiatrist must come across as an ally from the very beginning. And once treatment begins, patients also have critical thoughts about the psychiatrist. Some people are afraid to express these thoughts, and so they have a new set of secrets. And since the thoughts are recurrent, the inability to reveal them interferes with treatment." She looked down at her hands and frowned slightly. "To the psychiatrist," she said, "of course, it's all grist for the mill. Most of the time the thoughts soon lead away from the psychiatrist anyway. They really have to do with other people in the patient's life—and his past." She smiled briefly. "And that's always easier to say when you're not the patient." And then she told me an experience from her own analysis.

"My analyst's office was in his apartment," she said quietly, "in a large co-op on the West Side, and one day I came up in the elevator with his daughter—and to my eyes she was terribly homely. I stewed over this for weeks, unable to tell him but unable to let it go. And finally one day I confessed that I couldn't help it, I had to tell him that I'd seen her and was surprised at her ugliness. I said that I felt sorry for him, that I knew it must be terrible to have such a homely daughter, but I wasn't supposed to keep thoughts from him, and that was the way it was. And then I all but bolted out of the room.

"He didn't say anything, and for weeks afterward I thought I'd made a terrible mistake," she added. "I was afraid of retribution from him, and I felt guilty too. I told myself I should have shown some common sense and kept my mouth shut. Then one night I dreamt of a doll carriage, in which a man reached in and replaced a homely dark-haired doll with a blonde long-haired doll and wheeled the carriage down the street. When I told him the dream in our next hour together, I realized the street was the one his office was on. I'd been angry with him for some time and not wanting to acknowledge how much I longed to be his daughter, how I envied his real daughter." Laura laughed, her whole face brightening. "Only then did I realize that I didn't even know if his daughter was homely or not. My feelings were so intense, I could easily have misjudged her looks. In any case, my responsibility in that hour was to my treatment, to exploring my associations, and not in protecting him from such possible realities as having a homely daughter."[1]

Generally patients are even more reluctant to confess love or tenderness for their therapist than anger, and they may be aware of loving feelings for the therapist long before they're ready to admit to them. Patients are afraid of provoking rejection, or a sexual overture. Sometimes they're afraid of the intimacy itself.

Gary said, "Some people are caught in an impossible bind: they want desperately to snuggle up and be close, but their experience has been that closeness is dangerous, because they never really existed for the other person. Whoever took care of them when they were children didn't really register them or their needs, only their own. And the very intensity of their desire to be close is itself terrifying." He stretched his legs and leaned back in his armchair, hands characteristically clasped behind his head as he gazed at the ceiling. "And so these patients deny their warm feelings toward you and—if anything—express even more contempt and hatred whenever a loving impulse rears up from their unconscious.

"They tell you how stupid you are and how ugly your office is for session after session," Gary continued. "A woman I saw today walked in, sat down, and said, 'Well, I'm ready to waste more of my money on you.'" I gasped, and he shrugged. "Sometimes patients project their feelings onto you. Instead of insulting you, they accuse *you* of demeaning them." When I asked for an example, he picked up his pen and began doodling on a yellow pad. "A man I saw yesterday said, 'I know you think I can't stay in college. I know you expect me to fail,' when the reality is that I think he's too smart for the school he's going to.

"The issue with these patients is the same: They're afraid of being close to another person, and they have various [usually unconscious] ways of protecting themselves. It's more naked in my office, but they do it outside too, and it makes for chaotic relationships."

The prime rule of treatment is, Hold nothing back. Patients are told to say whatever comes to mind, however embarrassing or painful it may be, however loving or insulting to the therapist, and however meaningless or stupid. In analysis, of course, the demand for self-disclosure is strongest; all thoughts are to be accepted as equally important, however irrelevant, pointless, or gratuitously unpleasant they seem. But analysis and other kinds of psychotherapy aren't so different. While people in less analytic treatment may talk in a more focused and straightforward way, sometimes even presenting a kind of agenda for discussion at the start of a session, they are still expected to drop the social mask. Even if treatment is limited to a preset number of sessions (as in managed care) or a particular area of difficulty, they are expected to resist self-censorship. All psychotherapy demands that patients be open and honest.

Yet many people have to learn how. They are not only self-protective and afraid of reprisals; they may also have no experience attending to their mental lives, and even less in expressing their thoughts and feelings. Many people don't even have a vocabulary for emotions, using a general word like "upset" to cover everything from rage to grief. This is not resistance but genuine ignorance, and it means that they need to learn a new vocabulary and a new way of attending to their mental processes. Some of this lack of fluency may relate to the patient's diagnosis; another factor is social class.[2]

"In general, the middle-class person is more likely to believe that talk treatment has value," John said matter-of-factly, "that talking about feelings has a point or can change what happens. He's also more likely to be ready to think in terms of motives and have the verbal skills to express his internal experience. Lower-class upbringing promotes action instead." He sat back, looking bemused. "I grew up in a blue-collar Irish neighborhood, and I fought all the time—everyone did. My kids went to a nice middle-class suburban school, and when I'd ask why they didn't punch someone who pushed ahead of them on the playground, they'd look at me as if I were a barbarian."

Furthermore, a lot that comes to mind during the session seems simply pointless. "When you really allow yourself to attend to every thought that passes across the field of consciousness," Steve said, "you discover what disorganized and fleeting impressions appear, how much is fragmentary thought that you don't even have time to express before another appears. You also discover how much is simply an awareness of the physical machinery of your body, of a slight gas pain, or tension in your neck, or pressure in the bladder. Somehow you get a feel for when it may be important, of psychical relevance. Otherwise you learn to let it go by."

To some extent, fleeting half-thoughts and sensations seem to dominate consciousness whenever we pay close attention to how we think. (In the late nineteenth and early twentieth centuries, the Introspectionist School of psychology explored the phenomenology of consciousness in depth;[3]

and the psychologist William James characterized the moving "stream of consciousness" in 1890 in his remarkable book, *Principles of Psychology*.[4])

Moreover, anxiety and certain kinds of depression can make the stream of consciousness even more chaotic and fragmented. Or the patient may narrow free association down to the same repetitious thoughts or to a pre-occupation with trivia, engaging in what is actually a form of unconscious resistance, a way of seeming to use free association while actually blocking the exposure of important material.

Laura said, "If you allow it, some patients will give you every detail of a meeting, every word of who said what to whom. They will bore you to death with whether the meeting started at 2:02 or 2:03, and they will focus on these trivia in order to avoid every possibility for experiencing feelings about what went on. Until they begin to change, you have to keep asking how they felt at that moment, digging for the emotion. And sometimes the person complains and says they're just following the rules and telling you whatever comes to mind.

"Freud used free association as a window into the unconscious," Laura continued, "a way of slipping past our unconscious censorship. What he then found, what we all find, is that everyone *still* blocks or consciously suppresses material. Because no one says everything they think. Even in the strictest analysis you only come near the ideal toward the end of treat-ment." Her smile was impish. "It's even been said that the whole point of analysis is to get you to the point where you *can* free-associate...because that's the sign of not needing many defenses." She laughed aloud. "When I was in analysis I had a dream in which I had a dream that was very im-portant. And in the dream I then dreamt that I forgot it. And I woke up laughing, thinking it was the ultimate resistance dream."

After a moment, she added a coda. "In one form of resistance your mind may go completely blank, while in another nothing may appear in con-sciousness but a stream of obscenities, or a volley of jokes—and sometimes they turn out to be important too. In general, you definitely ought to say anything you feel like sweeping under the carpet. The desire is itself a clue to resistance and to the likelihood it's important. And it's only in the saying that you begin to explore what it means, and what about yourself you've been hiding from awareness. From my side," she continued, "the trick of therapy is for me to see when I encounter resistance by the change in the patient's behavior, by a change in voice tone, or breathing, or position, and by my asking what they're thinking or feeling at just that moment."

In treatment, the patient discloses aspects of herself revealed to no one else (and often, until that moment, outside even her own awareness). In return, the psychotherapist gives his undivided attention, unequalled in any other sustained relationship. The therapist listens with total concentration, as if for the moment only the two of them existed in a universe reduced in size to the room they share.

Michael sat very straight, his hands flat on the polished desktop. "Even in once-a-week psychotherapy, that hour is unique. It is probably the first time in your life that you're given permission—no, a directive—to think only about yourself. It's neither selfish, nor self-centered, nor lazy. Instead, you're told that attending to yourself is work—the work you're supposed to do in that time." He drummed his fingers on the desk as he gathered his thoughts. "In as work-oriented a society as the United States still is, this kind of permission is often a first in your life. And furthermore, you have another person, a highly trained expert who is totally committed to you for that hour. No one else matters. Nothing else is supposed to interfere."

During the session, the therapist is riveted on the patient. He asks only that she be as honest as possible. But the third and most basic oddity of the relationship is its peculiar lopsidedness. While the psychiatrist knows the other person intimately, he reveals little or nothing of his own problems, hopes, and outside-of-the-office life. His attention may be fixed on the patient, but for all the intensity of his concentration, it is not romantic love; it isn't even paid friendship. It is nonreciprocal and imbalanced, a professional and bounded exchange in which one party opens her soul to a largely unknown other.

To some degree, the imbalance resembles the usual asymmetry between doctor and patient. The physician, after all, is given authority over both body and mind and routinely asks questions about the most personal matters while examining the naked flesh. Yet the physician is much less intrusive than the psychiatrist: Little that he does touches our inmost selves. And he may, on his side, volunteer at least a bit more of his personal life: I know my doctor jogs, for example, and likes to sail, and I know he saw an Ibsen play just before my last appointment.

Psychiatry is different partly because the patient reveals more and is told less, but the real distinction is more profound. The skewed relationship of patient and psychiatrist is neither a detail nor an accident, but a defining characteristic of treatment. Most psychiatrists in the United States believe that treatment works only if the therapist remains a shadowed figure, with his beliefs, attitudes, and feelings in large part determinedly kept secret, for what the patient knows of her therapist has ramifications that go far beyond the actual small talk they exchange or the facts the patient knows of the therapist's personal life.

The less the therapist reveals, the less likely he is to distract or unduly influence the patient. "You have to remember that you're terribly important to your patients," Laura said. "Whether they love you or hate you, they always react to you, to everything you do and say. So you're obligated not to intrude more than you must for the purposes of therapy. You can tell someone you don't allow smoking in the office, and you can pursue the self-destructive aspects of their smoking because that has therapeutic value, but you have no right to tell her how you feel about your husband's smoking, or how your uncle died of lung cancer when you were fourteen."

The therapist becomes a central person in the patient's life. The patient comes to see herself in part through his eyes, in terms of what he defines as her significant motives and fears, strengths and weaknesses, as he asks leading questions, points out the consequences of her actions, and makes innumerable connections between unconscious conflicts and the tangles of her daily life. Ultimately, the patient sees herself through the mirror of his reactions much as she once learned to see herself through the reactions of her parents.

But all of the therapist's efforts are in the service of helping the patient to find her own path, her own choices, and not his choices for her. Since all of his responses have influence, he tries to limit personal reactions that would impose his own values and beliefs. His own opinion of marriage or the role of men and women in the modern world, of politics or religion, of a book or movie—all would be disturbing intrusions of himself into the treatment hour. Of course, some of his values leak through inevitably; it is almost impossible not to have some of his feelings about marriage, for example, or divorce, or raising children affect the treatment when these become prominent issues in the therapy, particularly if he strongly agrees or disagrees with the patient's views. But to a surprising extent, the empathic bond allows the therapist to frame issues in terms of the patient's needs, with the therapist's personal convictions and biases remaining irrelevant. (The self-knowledge demanded of the therapist by the conjoint need for empathy and nonintrusion is one reason for the therapist himself to seek intensive psychotherapy or psychoanalysis.)

The therapist has to keep a low profile partly because the patient is affected by everything he does, by his mildest words, by the flick of an eyebrow, by a momentary frown. Moreover, the patient develops intense feelings about him that have little to do with reality, unconscious distortions that the therapist depends on for understanding her and promoting her growth. These "transference" distortions (discussed in the next chapter) play a crucial role in all psychotherapy, and the more the therapist makes use of them in treatment, the more likely he is to say little about himself. For the less he reveals of his real-life circumstances, the freer the patient is to go with the flow of her own feelings, expressing whatever wells up from her past and unconscious needs.

Gary said, "You don't put your wife's picture on your desk. It makes it harder for the patient to express fantasies about your being single or homosexual. As treatment continues, the patient can manage to ignore almost anything he knows about you, but there's no point slowing the process down by giving him unnecessary information about yourself."

The "transference" distortions, coupled with the enormous influence the therapist wields as part of these very distortions, means that everything he says—and does—in the hour reverberates with meaning for the patient. So the psychiatrist is taught to stifle simple friendly responses, not volunteering the name of the charities he gives to or the candidate he votes for, avoiding direct answers to many questions, and not asking his own questions without more excuse than simple curiosity.

How little of himself the therapist actually reveals depends on how close treatment comes to a classical five-times-a-week-on-the-couch-Freudian-psychoanalysis, in which, ideally, nothing is volunteered. He may, in fact, reveal a good deal, but zero is the standard against which he measures his disclosures, seeing himself always as at least in part a mirror, a distorted glass in which the patient reads his own reflections. Although few American psychiatrists are strict Freudians, their opacity is one bulwark of treatment they generally maintain. While Freud himself saw patients in an office cluttered with personal belongings, American psychiatrists usually have offices that are rather sparse and unrevealing, and they maintain a standard of opacity to which Freud himself, in fact, never quite adhered.[5]

9

Ghosts from the Past

Modern psychotherapy was born out of psychoanalysis, and psychoanalysis was both a revolutionary theory of the mind and the first purely psychological approach to the cure of mental disorder. Moreover, no one before had seen just how crucial the patient's feelings for the therapist were, and in particular how important were the "transference" feelings. Yet the revolution owed its initial conception to the treatment of only one woman, a patient Freud himself never even met.

The patient was Anna O., a beautiful, intelligent, twenty-one-year-old who suffered from paralyses, amnesia (although she lived in Vienna, she had forgotten her native German and spoke English), disturbed vision, phobias about eating and drinking, and moments in which she seemed to exhibit another personality. Diagnosed as a hysteric, she has to the modern ear a much sicker quality than we associate with hysteria.[1]

Joseph Breuer, a well-known physician and a colleague of Freud's, treated Anna with the experimental technique of hypnosis from 1880 to 1882.[2] Observing the changes hypnosis evoked, he offered a brilliant hypothesis, suggesting a psychological link between hysterical symptoms and emotions not known to the conscious mind. For he found that Anna O. improved once she relived with full emotion the events occurring at the moment her symptoms initially appeared. In reexperiencing the terror she felt at her father's deathbed, for example, Anna became able to move the arm that had become frozen in the position it had held in those traumatic—and repressed—hours.[3]

Freud was very impressed by Breuer's results, and in 1889 he tried Breuer's "cathartic method" for himself, after he too began to see patients with hysterical disorders. In a joint paper in 1893,[4] the two doctors suggested that all hysterical phenomena—all their patients' paralyses, spasms, tics, hallucinations, and sensory disturbances—came from powerful emotions pressing for expression in the absence of conscious memories and manifesting instead as symptoms; that there had been a "conversion" of buried emotion into a physical complaint.[5] And recall of memory led to cure: "For we found, to our great surprise at first, that each individual hysterical symptom immediately and permanently disappeared when we had succeeded in bringing clearly to light the memory of the event by which it was provoked and in arousing its accompanying affect, and when the patient had described that event in the greatest possible detail and had put the affect into words."[6]

Jean-Martin Charcot (with whom Freud had studied from 1885 to 1886), and his student Pierre Janet,[7] had suggested that in hysteria there was a splitting of the psyche into conscious and unconscious compartments, but these brilliant neurologists believed the cause of hysteria to be a physical weakness of the brain. Once Freud began treating hysterics, he and Breuer revolutionized the discussion of the disorder by suggesting that the splitting of the psyche was also a psychological defense: the deliberate, although unconscious, shutting out of ideas that provoked tremendous anxiety. "The hysterical patient's 'not knowing' was in fact a 'not wanting to know,'" Freud wrote (with Breuer) in 1895.[8]

In the course of the next decade, Freud expanded on the image of turmoil within the unconscious as he developed the psychoanalytic theory of mind, depicting a seething mix of unconscious memories, impulses, and feelings all pressing on the ego for conscious expression. Moving far beyond Breuer, he also wrote that all neuroses, not just hysteria, seemed to be connected with anxiety over sexual matters.

Breuer had terminated treatment with Anna O. in 1882, once he recognized his wife's (understandable) jealousy of his unending preoccupation with his patient. But his saying good-bye to Anna precipitated a crisis. Breuer was called back to her house that night to find her in the midst of hysterical childbirth, delivering an imaginary baby, with Breuer her fantasied lover. Anna had never as much as mentioned sex before, and Breuer was not only shocked by her passion, but panic-stricken.[9]

When one of Freud's patients confessed her desire for a kiss from him,

Freud reacted not with shock but with disbelief that she was really attracted to *him*. Taking another major theoretical leap that was soon to put the patient's feelings for the analyst at center stage in treatment, he hypothesized that his patient's passion—and Anna's—really had nothing to do with him or with Breuer. It had been displaced, unconsciously transferred to them from their original, and forbidden, sexual object. Like hydraulic fluid, repressed emotions exerted pressure and could flow down a path of lesser resistance. In the psychoanalytic treatment he was inventing, they were displaced, or "transferred," to the analyst.[10]

Freud first described transference as a "false connection"[11] in which repressed sexual desire was shifted away from someone unacceptable to the patient's conscious mind—usually a parent—and displaced instead onto the analyst. Later Freud broadened the idea of transference to include not only sexual desire but the whole range of positive and negative feelings for the analyst (and also to account for many of our reactions and feelings toward others in everyday life). Since Freud, therapists assume that the patient at times feels about them as he once felt about the most significant people in his childhood—although he has no awareness that what he is feeling is a reexperience of feelings that stem from early life. Usually the therapist feels like a parent, but she may also stand in for a sibling, grandparent, nursemaid, or anyone else important in the patient's upbringing. Who she represents changes in the course of treatment, sometimes from session to session.[12]

The most striking quality of transference, Freud emphasized, was its unconscious and repetitive nature, both in treatment and in the patient's outside life: "There are people in whose lives the same reactions are perpetually being repeated uncorrected, to their own detriment, or others who seem to be pursued by a relentless fate, though closer investigation teaches us that they are unwittingly bringing this fate on themselves."[13]

Since Freud, psychiatrists view transference as permeating our lives. Because the significant people in our childhood had power over us, transference is omnipresent in our relationships with those who have power over us now; and our need to please, to placate, or to rebel may reappear in inconvenient and unrealistic ways in our dealings with teachers, bosses, police, doctors, or the bank officer who has to approve a loan. And in marriage, men see in their wives the woman who married dear old dad; while women see Daddy himself (although in fact it's more complicated, and we really see bits of pieces of both parents). Many of our transference reactions were popularized by Eric Berne in his 1964 best-seller, *Games People Play*.[14]

The power of transference comes from its unconscious quality. If a transference reaction is unusually intense, or remarkably inappropriate or rigid, we may notice that something peculiar is going on, but even then we're likely to have trouble changing our feelings. Because the connection from the present to the past is out of our awareness, our reaction feels like a direct response to the other person in the here and now. Some therapists even believe that most adult relationships are largely transferential, that everyone we love, or hate, is in part a phantom, a stand-in for the important people in our early life. For these therapists, much of what we do in later life (unless thoroughly psychoanalyzed) is to repetitiously reenact our infancy and childhood. But most therapists believe that transference is generally only one component in our relations with the outside world. If your father was domineering, for example, you may react more strongly to a domineering boss than you otherwise would, but you can usually distinguish a domineering boss from one who isn't. If you can't make this kind of distinction, you may find yourself in trouble.

☜

The therapist fosters the transference by revealing little of herself. She encourages a more accurate perception of herself as she really is in the hour when she chats with the patient, however briefly, about a mutual interest, takes part in back-and-forth exchanges during the session, sits in sight across the room and not invisibly behind the couch, and shows some emotion. But people bring transference distortions into the treatment no matter what the psychiatrist does. In fact, the strength and quality of the distortions is one measure of illness.

Michael said, "I look for transference anytime the patient has an intense reaction to me right away. Patients may take an immediate liking to me or not, and, of course, I hope they'll see me as capable. But when they immediately love me or hate me, or have some kind of weird expectation of me, I take that as a warning of the kind of difficulties we're going to run into."

He leaned forward aggressively in his chair, his feet planted wide apart, shifting his weight to his hands with the palms pushed against his thighs. "Just this morning, a woman called my emergency service but left only her first name and telephone number. I told my service to call back, find out who she is, and tell her I wouldn't be free until the afternoon. And it turns out that I've never seen her. I have no idea who she is. Meanwhile she's already called back twice. Her not leaving a last name suggests that she believes I know her when I don't. And the number of calls suggests that she feels I'm a very important—and powerful—figure in her life. My guess is that she has some fantasy about our relationship, a preexistent transference." He pursed his lips for a moment, his jaw jutting forward. "I'll speak to her, but I doubt we can work together. I'd have an uphill fight bringing any reality into the therapeutic relationship."

Emily Mandelson, the elderly white-haired psychoanalyst we met at the end of chapter 6, described the more typical form of transference that occurs early in treatment, the "honeymoon phase," in which simply entering treatment arouses feelings of relief—dating from infancy—at being taken care of by a parental figure. Almost eighty years old, Emily was meticulously dressed in black, a single strand of pearls showing through the silk shawl draped around her thin shoulders. She spoke with her habitual dryness. "Often people feel magically better after the first meeting or two, well before I can be of any realistic help. They are so relieved to be in the hands of a caretaking figure that their symptoms simply drop away—as if I were mother and they were babies once again, being soothed and protected." Her mouth turned up at the corners. "If you want to insult another psychiatrist's work, you say he's only getting a 'transference cure.'"

Indeed, some positive transference is essential, just as it is when a physician is treating a physical illness. But reality and transference are a constant mix, shifting in the most unsettling way from session to session and minute to minute.

John spoke slowly, taking off his glasses once again. "The therapeutic relationship is very complicated. The room is filled with ghosts and phantoms you and the patient both bring in. First of all, there's the legitimate expectation the person begins with—that you're the expert and you're there to help him. Then there's a realistic perception of you, in the session, as really listening to him, as really working with him on his behalf, and as sometimes missing the boat, not catching something or coming in late, or even forgetting an appointment."

Laura said, "Patients can be very accurate about some things. They know if you're not interested in them. You don't have to yawn or forget an appointment. And sometimes a person's sense of you is extraordinary."[15] She added softly, "But there's always some distortion. You're a parental stand-in and the target for everything they've ever felt growing up." She frowned, her finely arched eyebrows drawing together, and repeated something she'd told me several times. "In fact, if you never hear anything negative, you're not doing your job."

She added, "And some patients will idealize you as the 'good' parent for a long time. They may expect you to know just what they're thinking and be genuinely surprised when you explain that you can't read their mind, that they have to keep you informed. And they often put you on a pedestal, sure you're never irritable, or tired, as if you weren't human like them."

She smiled in reminiscence, revealing the faint dimple in her cheek. "A few months after I started seeing my analyst, he was sick during a session and had to keep leaving for the bathroom. I was stunned that he could have diarrhea." She giggled. "Another time one of my contact lenses popped out. And the two of us ended up searching the rug for my lens. I'd never pictured him doing something so trivial. And as I talked about it in the treatment, it led to a wealth of associations to my father and to seeing the ways I idealized his remoteness and unavailability to save myself from disappointment and anger."

Many patients will leave treatment still idealizing the therapist, in part because it is so comfortable for both parties to leave those feelings alone. As one psychiatrist said, "I look for the transference right away if a patient tells me he hates me. But I may believe him when he tells me that I'm wonderful. It's a hell of a lot more pleasant believing I'm really a great guy and a great therapist than asking myself who the patient is really talking about."

Several other psychiatrists commented that they usually tried to bring themselves off the pedestal of idealization. "By the time the person finishes treatment," Gary said, "they generally know I'm human like them, and not some idealized fantasy. And they feel appropriate gratitude, and also an appreciation of the treatment as a mutual effort, with both of us working as hard as we can.

"But the more supportive the therapy, the less I interpret the idealization of the positive transference. It helps the treatment go in the first place. And it's often helpful all through their lives—long after treatment ends—for them to have the idea of me always in the background, larger than life, and caring for them in the special way they never quite got as kids. People often do no more than send me a Christmas card each year—and I answer—and that's sufficient to give them the feeling of a safety net."

✍

The core of Freudian doctrine is so revolutionary that we're still struggling to accept its basic tenets, for none of us wants to believe we're ruled by wishes and impulses we don't even know we have, and none of us wants to believe that we largely see the present through the prism of our past. Freud's conclusion was as revolutionary as his doctrine: gain freedom from the past by reshaping the personality. And he suggested using a particular trick that is, in fact, the defining characteristic of psychoanalysis: bring the person into the present by encouraging the transference and by examining everything the patient feels in treatment in terms of that transference.

Only the orthodox Freudian analyst doing an orthodox Freudian analysis makes transference the absolute center of treatment. But most American psychiatrists continue to feel transference has a major role in all psychotherapy, even if it is only observed by the therapist without commenting on it to the patient. Therefore they accept the need to keep themselves relatively hidden and their relationship with patients profoundly skewed.

Of course, psychiatrists can remain in shadow only in a large city; in smaller cities or towns, therapists and patients have too many natural points of contact. Most psychiatric patients in long-term treatment are middle or upper class, verbal, and well-educated. They often belong to the same organizations as the psychiatrist, live in the same parts of town, send their children to the same schools, and know many of the same people. Also the psychiatrist, particularly outside of the large city, may even see patients in an office located within her home. Even if she wanted to remain unknown outside of the session, she often can't, not only because of any natural overlap of her social life with her patients, or because of the information they have access to without effort, but because patients are intensely curious and particularly during certain stages of treatment may ferret out every bit of information they can get.

"During my analysis, I looked my analyst up in the directory," Gary said. "I already knew where he trained because he hung the diplomas in his office, but I wanted to see where he lived and if he was married or had kids. I even had lunch with another psychiatrist in analysis with him so we could compare notes. And I got to hear stories about him from other candidates he supervised at the analytic institute." He grinned. "I acted just like any other patient. The only difference was that I could find out more."

"A lot of people look you up in the biographical directory," someone else said to me. "Or drive by your house if they know where you live. One of my friends had a patient of his enroll in the pottery workshop his wife teaches. And a patient of mine who works as a door-to-door salesman came to my apartment and tried to sell my wife a vacuum cleaner—although that's an extreme example."

Transference feelings in therapy can be extraordinarily powerful. They also feel utterly real—not an artifact of treatment, but solid and genuine, no different from the emotions people feel in their current outside-the-session life. If there is any difference, it's that feelings toward the therapist may be stronger. Nor does anyone see these feelings as in some way displaced from their real objects, carried from childhood and suddenly, and inappropriately, transferred to the therapist.

"Last week," Steve said, "a very attractive woman that I see stood up from her chair and told me she wanted to make love, right there, right then. She knew I'd say it was transference, she said, but she knew it wasn't. She really loved me, and she didn't care that I was married. She wanted to make love."

Steve paused and rubbed his chin with the back of his hand. I was very aware of how good-looking he was, and how sexually appealing. "People who've never been in intensive treatment can't believe this really happens," he went on, "that patients really try to seduce you, and that their feelings are really hurt when you turn them down. As far as she was concerned, this was a real issue between us."

I asked what he'd said, and his answer made clear why his actual physical appeal was irrelevant. "I told her that I wouldn't argue with her about the meaning of her behavior, but she was my patient, and it was unethical for me to even consider having sex with her. And then I turned it back to the transference by asking her to consider how it was that she could insult me by asking me to break my professional oath." His blue eyes were unblinking. "But outsiders can't believe this kind of stuff. They can't believe how intense the feelings are that get generated."

In some sessions, a patient loves the therapist with the passion of a two-year-old, and in others he hates her with the same undiluted intensity. At times he idolizes the therapist as all-loving, all-knowing, all-good; as mother, father, and God in one compact package. At other times, he feels she is a boring nonentity, hardly worthy even of contempt, and may even remark on his surprising indifference to anything his shrink might think or say.

But the person in treatment doesn't experience any of this as transference. It all feels real, immediate, and justified. He wants to know more about the therapist, therefore, not because he knows so little, but because the feelings toward her are so central to his life. Although he might deny it, his curiosity has some of the quality of the small child eavesdropping on the grown-ups from the hallway stairs, trying to hear the secrets they won't reveal in front of him, and the feelings they won't say to his face.

"People don't have to be crazy to be totally caught up in what you're like," John said mildly. "Particularly in long-term intensive treatment, they relive with you their growing up. In reality, you already are like another parent to them in many ways. That *is* your role, to rework their past by substituting yourself in a new and reparative relationship. But in saying they relive the past we mean they experience the present moment through the distortions of transference. Patients react to you *as if* you were the parent even if they don't consciously realize it, and therefore you seem to become as important and central to their lives as their parents were. So everything about you matters, not only what you think of them, but what kind of tie you wear, how you keep your office, what you do for relaxation."

In less psychoanalytic treatment, the psychiatrist discourages the development of an intense transference toward her by talking more and by focusing on the relationships in the patient's outside life. In such treatment, the emphasis is not on the patient's transference in regard to the therapist but on transference in regard to people in the patient's regular life. But the transference to the therapist is still present and always plays a major role in every kind of psychotherapy. Sometimes the positive transference is the background state that allows treatment to go on at all, particularly in the beginning or in more painful phases; it is certainly what most patients bring to any medical doctor's office. But the importance of transference goes much further, for it is one of the primary sources of information in psychotherapy, telling the psychiatrist things about the patient she couldn't otherwise know.

"One of my patients always kicks her chair to turn it away from me," Steve said. "Last week she pulled the chair around with both hands instead of kicking it. She spent the rest of the session in silence, and even though I hadn't fully registered what she'd done, I knew something had been different, and I had an overwhelming impulse to ask if she was feeling sexually threatened by me. When I did, she said that she had felt threatened because of her own desires to sit close to me, and she'd tried to counteract the wish by pulling the chair away from me.

"This woman has always been fearful of intimacy and afraid of humiliation if she revealed her yearning for closeness. But most of our work has been at the preoedipal level, around issues of autonomy and separation that predate true genital interest. . . . What the layman means by sexuality. Yet I'd noticed that she'd begun to dress more carefully for sessions, that she'd begun to use lipstick and eye shadow, and that she was in a subtle way more desirable than she'd ever been before. She didn't have to talk about it. She was acting on it in the transference." After a moment he added, "In retrospect I can say that she had kicked the chair in earlier sessions much like a small child acting tough, and that moving it with both hands had an older quality to it, even a sensual quality. But the reasoning came later. All I knew at the time was that sex was in the air between us."

"In some ways, I know my patients better than I know my wife," Gary said. "I know things about them, about their past, about what they want and what they're afraid of, that you never learn any other way. But what they say about themselves is sometimes less revealing than what they do." Gary continued. "People wonder sometimes how you can treat someone without meeting their wife or husband, how you can believe what they say. They're sure you need external information to verify what patients tell you. In fact, I like to meet with the spouse. They often tell me things I'm not going to find out otherwise. But that's because I've missed a cue or because it would take too long.

"The patient eventually brings his whole world into my office. It's not what he tells me that's so important—that's the least accurate information I have. It's *how* he treats me, and how he feels I'm treating him. I know how he acts with his girlfriend because he acts that way with me some of the time. And I know what goes on with his boss or his kids in the same way."

So the therapist stays low, trying to be a neutral target for the distortions. Meanwhile, she is totally engaged in the exchange, thinking about the issues for the patient in that meeting. She is never the mere object of the patient's monologue: The communication is addressed to her, and both she and the patient expect her to make a relevant response. In this sense, a real relationship exists. The therapist is an expert offering help—empathically listening, trying to understand, and using all her skills to relieve pain and promote growth. Yet the paradox remains. Because of the transference, patients have incredibly intense feelings toward someone they know little about. Furthermore, these feelings may have so little to do with the psychiatrist's experience of herself that the very intensity of the emotions can make her feel like a ghost.

But a real person sits behind the neutral face so maligned in fable and cartoon, and the real person feels not merely the limited and acceptable emotions of professional concern and warmth, but far more complex reactions that must not be directly expressed. Behind her professional calm, the therapist reacts to everything the patient does and says; the main paradox is that both the patient's intense feelings about her and her own intense responses occur while she feels herself to be in some ways invisible.

Freud wrote that he preferred to sit behind the couch because he couldn't stand being stared at all day.[16] By contrast, some psychiatrists will comment on feeling like a phantom, a figment of the patient's imagination, an object acted on with little regard to who they really are.

"When I was in training," Gary said, "I'd feel so drained by the end of the day I'd sit in front of a blank wall trying to get back my own sense of myself. Even now I start to wonder who I really am sometimes. I get treated as if I'm a son of a bitch so much of the time there are days I have to remind myself that my wife and kids really love me, and I can't be such a bastard."

These distortions of transference contribute enormously to the oddness of the therapy relationship. When the patient says his therapist is unpredictable and nasty, he is convinced of the reality of his perception. "Any idiot can recognize a sneer," the patient says. But the therapist knows perfectly well that she's not sneering; in fact, at the moment of the accusation she may be pleased that the patient has openly expressed a fear he's been leading up to for months.

Transference is a major tool of psychotherapy, and it constantly transforms the relationship between patient and therapist into something very different from what it seems. The emotions displayed in sessions are frequently irrelevant to what has actually occurred, or they are sparked by an interaction much more trivial than anyone watching the explosion could guess. Whatever the feelings that are generated in treatment and however intense these feelings are, most of that intensity is false; the love, and hate, felt for the therapist has mainly to do with people who never appear in the flesh in the office, phantoms of the past who live only inside the patient's head.

Transference is the patient's reexperience of feelings he had twenty, thirty, or fifty years ago. Even if his parents are alive now, even if he has a reasonably good relationship with them in his current life, the emotions of transference are neither recent nor adult, for he brings to the session his experience of his parents as he comprehended them way back in childhood and infancy. His fear of police has nothing to do with his father now. It has to do with his fright when he was five, or four, or even younger, when his father loomed over him like an ogre in a fairy tale, his hands the size of his son's head. In the office, much of what one transfers to the psychiatrist is not even an adult's distortions, but the limited comprehension of a child.

Not only is the psychotherapist seen as someone she is not; she is seen through the prism of a youngster's mind—as wonderful or terrible, loving or nasty, in the black-and-white, either-or way of children. As Gary said, "Sometimes I'm Superman, sometimes I'm Luthor. But I'm hardly ever seen as me."

10

The Psychiatrist's Strange Loneliness

For all its intensity, the relationship to the psychiatrist is limited, sharply bounded by the confines of the office and the hour, the transference fantasies never to be lived out. Still, the relationship has two parties within its boundaries, and the psychiatrist, too, is deeply engaged at all levels of his being. Yet psychiatrists are often bothered by a sense of isolation and loneliness within the very intimacy of the therapeutic relationship.[1]

Perhaps this experience contributes to the peculiar bunching of psychiatrists near one another, within a few states, within a few cities in those states, even within the same few neighborhoods of major cities. In 1988, for example, there were about forty-four thousand psychiatrists in the United States.[2] But they were concentrated in urban areas, with the majority in California and along the East Coast from New England through the Middle Atlantic states.[3] Even then, most of the psychiatrists in Massachusetts were in Boston, and most in New York State were in Manhattan. As one psychiatrist said, with minimal exaggeration, "If you drive thirty minutes from the George Washington Bridge, there's nobody there."

Psychiatrists as a group are city people, relatively intellectual and interested in the arts, but they bunch together not primarily for this reason but because of the nature of their profession. To a small degree, the reason is also economic. Psychiatrists generally set up practice near the hospital in which they were residents, and the distribution of major training centers is itself geographically skewed.[4]

"Although you've been taking care of patients for years, you don't really feel like an adult until you set up practice," Steve said slowly, his blue eyes intent and guarded. "You've always been in school, with someone watching over you, even in the residency. . . . And you've been given a salary." His voice dropped, and he spaced the words out deliberately. "And now you have to pay rent on an office, and *maybe no one will show up.*"

"Of course, you don't pick up and move," Laura said tartly. "The only people who know you are with the residency program, and without them you're afraid you'll starve. Patients aren't going to wander in off the street. Anyway, you're scared. You're going to be alone with any patients who do show up. You're finally on your own. You need to know there are people within range who care about you."

In the last few years, more psychiatrists have been interested in part-time salaried positions in hospitals or community mental health programs,[5] at least partly so that they'll have some guaranteed income in the face of increased competition and the rise of managed care. But the lure of salary is only one aspect of taking a job; for established psychiatrists a part-time job may even involve a drop in total income.[6] In fact, psychiatrists routinely leaven private practice with unpaid teaching or supervisory posts, usually at hospitals (about eight hours a week that is added to a paid work week averaging forty-eight hours).[7] Although the psychiatrist's nominal workweek averages over forty-eight hours, only about two-thirds of that is spent with patients; the rest is spent in consultation, teaching, administration, or research,[8] because all jobs, paid or unpaid, keep them from total isolation.

If we're not responded to, if we get no return from other people, we feel less alive. Solitary confinement, after all, is considered an extraordinary and brutal form of punishment. For the psychiatrist, one issue is simply this lack of feedback, the absence of what Eric Berne popularized as the normal "strokes" of social exchange in *Games People Play.*[9]

Michael motioned me into his tiny office while he made a cup of coffee with quick, economical movements, his solid, muscular body dominating the narrow space. "Private practice pays best," he said rapidly. "But everyone volunteers a few hours a week for teaching or supervision. You have to balance your time or you start resenting your patients. You have to get out of your office and do something less demanding than therapy, but it's more than that; you need some time during the week to relax and be with colleagues. Although we talk *about* patients, we're not talking *with* them. We're talking to each other." He smiled with sudden charm. "Another psychiatrist knows what it's really like to sit here all day—and he has no illusions about me.

"A friend and I have lunch together each week," Michael added. "We supervise each other on troublesome cases, but we also talk about research ideas and theoretical issues. This man knows me better, at least in the context of my work, than anyone else in the world, and he sees me with the least distortion." He poured the coffee and sipped it black and steaming hot. "Although I love my work, those two hours at lunch are the emotional center of my week."

As we grow up, our identity is formed in the crucible of reflections from other people as to whether we are good or bad, competent or foolish, trustworthy or undependable, or any other characteristic we name. In a sense there is no objective reality to our self-perceptions; they grow essentially out of our sense of how we were seen by the significant people around us.

Even in adulthood, our sense of ourselves depends on daily exchanges with other people. At the least, social interactions provide recognition of our existence as a particular human being, as in the courtesy of a greeting. But this is precisely what the therapist tells the patient to deny him. From the opening moments, in which the patient is expected to launch into a recital of her own state of mind, the therapist says in myriad ways that the bond is far more intimate and intense than any mere social relationship. But it is one in which the therapist's needs must be totally submerged—even his needs for normal human acknowledgment and recognition. He is remarkably alone amidst the therapeutic intimacies, for he must not expect or ask for the normal human responses of sympathy, concern, or idle chitchat.

Gary said, "We learn so early to say, 'Hello, how are you? I'm fine, how are you?' And you even give up that. You not only don't say, 'Shit, my back hurts, and my car had a flat this morning.' You don't get the chance because you train patients not to even give you an opening."

The lack of normal social exchanges may seem strange to the patient; to the therapist, it is a multifaceted deprivation. The lack of even minimal social exchange is only one aspect of his deprivation; even more pervasive is the fact that he is at work every moment of the hour, with no break for a casual remark, or a figurative—much less literal—slipping off of his shoes.

Rosemary Seiden is in her early fifties, her thick brown hair short, straight, and heavily streaked with grey, her figure full and matronly. She wears good but nondescript dark dresses appropriate to her professorial rank, and no jewelry beyond her wedding band. Married to another doctor for many years, she has two grown children. She is also an expert ceramicist, and a number of her pots decorate her office.

"The issue is that I am always doing more than the patient knows," she said serenely, her voice low-pitched and musical. "Although it is completely automatic, I am monitoring everything I do and say in terms of my concept of what the patient is ready to hear, whether an interpretation is useful at this moment, whether it's time to analyze a resistance, whether I ought to respond at all or wait to see what's coming. Eventually one's responses are so automatic, one seldom thinks about it, and it certainly feels spontaneous—but it's hardly the same spontaneity I feel having dinner with friends. Because the issue is always, What does this person need at this moment to further his growth? Not, What do I feel like saying?"

She walked unhurriedly to one of her hanging plants, felt the soil for moisture, and reached for a ceramic watering jug. Without looking toward me, she said, "Last week a patient called to tell me his sister had just killed herself. I felt terrible hearing it, worse because I'd met her, and I was very open with him that it was awful, a tragedy." She moved gracefully around the room, watering plants here and there. "We talked about the therapist she'd been seeing, and wondered what had happened and why, and I told him my thoughts about her therapist and how badly I felt. And I didn't think I was very different than I would have been with a friend." She seemed almost to be talking to herself, but once she returned to her chair she looked at me squarely. "In that first moment, I didn't ask to explore what it meant to him, or how he felt. I could be simply human because that's really what was needed: not distance, not silence, not interpretation, but someone there who really cares about him and his sister." She leaned forward composedly, her elbows on her desk. "But the difference is there. I'm not a friend, and it will come out later, when we talk about the whole range of feelings he will have as he grieves."

Gary put his feet on his desk, his long angular body almost storklike as he stretched out in relaxation. He indicated the photographs on his wall with a quick glance. "If a friend asks me about a photograph, I can talk about where I shot it and what I was trying to do. I can't legitimately do that with a patient with the same spontaneity, because the critical issue is always what their question means, why they've asked, what they're fantasizing.

"And the real meaning of the question is often hidden behind the apparent content, out of their awareness. My job is to listen for the underlying connections in everything they say." He searched for an example. "This morning a writer I see complained of being stalled on his book. A few minutes later, he commented that all the photographs on my wall were crooked. I felt both statements reflected some feeling about treatment that wasn't yet fully conscious." Gary smiled, his face alight with remembered satisfaction. "So I asked him if the crooked photographs had anything to do with a feeling that treatment was going awry, like his work. It was like a lightbulb going off for him, and he said that was exactly the point. And then we got down to business." His hands behind his neck, he stretched and arched his back. "In that moment, when the connection became conscious for him, we were genuinely together. But much of the time I have an awareness of a hidden agenda the other person isn't ready to admit to consciousness, and for all our closeness we inhabit two worlds." Grinning, he added, "Freud said that sometimes a cigar is only a cigar, and that's true too. But not in most sessions."

Another aspect of the psychiatrist's isolation is the lack of professional feedback. Gary said, "Only the patient and I have any idea what goes on between us, and the patient is seldom in a position to judge me. Even if he has some feeling for the kind of person I am, and of his own progress, he can't know what I know. "No more than I can be sure about other therapists," he added. "I may have an impression of them, but I haven't seen their work. When I make a referral, I have to depend on how good a resident someone was, or go by how they did with the last patient I sent them." He stopped himself and backtracked. "And I usually don't know more than what the psychiatrist himself tells me. Sometimes the patient calls me once or twice. Or I hear about them from a friend or relative in treatment with me." He flicked a hand dismissively. "It's not much. Even if someone teaches at the hospital, I don't know what really goes on in the office, when they're alone with patients."

He took a Swiss Army knife from his desk drawer and began to methodically peel an orange. His tone was thoughtful. "When I started in practice, I saw a rather disorganized woman—an artist—who insisted that her previous psychiatrist had sex with her. I didn't know him myself. But he was a respectable, reasonably well known clinician with good credentials. And he supervised at a major teaching hospital." He spoke more slowly than usual, with many pauses. "Because she was so insistent, and didn't seem psychotic, I asked around about him. At one point I even called him. Of course, he denied everything—and I had nothing but her word. But after a year of treatment I became reasonably sure that this was no delusion, and I told my patient to report it to the Board of Ethics [of his local chapter of the APA]." He removed the peel in one single spiral and offered me a segment of orange. "About five years later, he was forced to resign after several more patients complained about him, but if they hadn't, I'd never have had more than my judgment of her word against his. I had no way of knowing what had happened in the privacy of that office."[10]

We shared the orange companionably. After a bit, he said, "I've been burnt so many times making referrals for friends or members of my family that I sometimes wonder if anyone but me practices psychiatry as I've been taught it. I'll be told someone who supervised me as a resident is always late with his own patients, or doesn't remember what he's told, or is just plain insensitive." Then he smiled wryly. "But I've had patients—who weren't psychotic—accuse me of falling asleep, or of deliberately missing an appointment.

"When two people show up for the same hour, I can look in my appointment book to see what went wrong, but when someone comes in on Columbus Day for their regular Monday appointment and later swears I never told them I was taking the time off, I can't always be sure that my memory is accurate. And those are matters of fact, not nuances of voice tone or expression. So I also know how impossible it is to go by someone else's report of another psychiatrist."

In A. A. Rogow's book, *The Psychiatrists*,[11] psychiatrists reported that most of their dissatisfaction centered on isolation: vis-à-vis patients, vis-à-vis other psychiatrists, and vis-à-vis the medical community to which psychiatrists are still largely peripheral. They also talked about being misperceived and misunderstood, by patients and by other physicians, and caricatured as either all-knowing superiors with x-ray vision or incompetent idiots touting a nonsensical set of beliefs.

Yet the most striking finding was that psychiatrists as a group were happier with their specialty, for all its drawbacks, than were most other medical doctors. Although the common wisdom in the field is that psychiatrists suffer burnout, they are actually more likely than other doctors to continue to love their work. One explanation is that the ongoing revolution in psychopharmacology has made so many previously refractory patients treatable. But mostly the sense of fulfillment has precisely to do with the nature of the therapeutic relationship, in all its inherently paradoxical qualities.

For all the one-sidedness of the relationship and the distortions of the prism through which patients see the therapist, and despite the need therapists have to maintain their own emotional distance, the best psychiatrists are intensely, extraordinarily involved with patients, enamored of the intimacy of the bond, and elated by the total involvement and commitment that each session calls for. Some of their involvement has its roots in early experiences of their own, deeply imbedded in their own consciousness, although presumably dissected and brought under control in the course of their own analysis. But beyond these specific childhood underpinnings, psychiatrists also have a desire to know fully another person, to enlarge the boundaries of their own skin, to appreciate the uniqueness of another, and another, and another.

John said, "Laymen always wonder if the shrink gets his kicks hearing about people's quirkiness. But that's not where the high is. The draw isn't titillation but the chance to finally find out what goes on in someone else's head."

Many of us played doctor with our friends when we were little, trying to find answers to the mysteries of male-female differences. Psychoanalysts believe that doctors chose medicine in part because they carry within them a five-year-old still trying to resolve those questions. In fact, orthodox psychoanalysts believe that all curiosity is rooted in early sexual befuddlement—and that medicine is one of the few fields allowing direct examination of the issues. Whatever the role of simple sexual curiosity, however, psychiatrists in the course of their own psychoanalysis generally unearth a child within themselves who is driven by broader questions about human relationships as well, that part of themselves that is still hoping that everything could be resolved if only they could listen in on the grown-ups' secrets. Yet even this is too narrow a view of what motivates the psychiatrist.

"I have no doubt that some part of me is still listening to my parents through the wall," John said, "and still hoping to rescue them too. But getting out of my own skin and entering someone else's goes far beyond those issues.... When I was a kid, I wanted to do everything and be everything, and no matter how I stretch it, the reality is that I have only one life to live.... That's why people read biography or fiction, to stretch the limits of one life."

Listening to patients allows the therapist an inside view of the stockbroker's world or the model's, allows him for the hour to change sexes or generations, social class or ethnic group. The experience goes far beyond voyeurism to an expansion of his own possibilities and humanity. Beyond that, therapists gain something they seldom talk about or discuss with patients: an enrichment of themselves that comes simply from being allowed to really know and appreciate another human being.

Some of the therapist's reward lies simply in perceiving the richness of the tapestry we each weave about our psyches: the imagery of our dreams, the humor, the intelligence and creativity we reveal when we are least guarded. For people are hardly ever truly dull—even if they seem that way on the surface. Dullness is merely an attribute of illness, part of the defensive constriction of the frightened inner child, and dullness vanishes in the course of good treatment. Dullness is the cloaked greyness of the rider in enemy territory, and one of the therapist's great pleasures is in helping the patient unmask.

Gary said, "Certain kinds of patients use dullness as a defense, and they'll drive you crazy if you can't penetrate that defense. Obsessionals, for example, always see the trees instead of the forest, because they're afraid of losing control if they allow themselves to register the emotionally relevant issues. So you find that between the endless details of how they got up in the morning, and brushed their teeth, and took a shit, you never get to hear the fight they had with their wife. When I get a patient who can only see me at ten minutes of two on Wednesdays or five minutes after four on alternate Tuesdays, I know I'm in for a lot of dead hours. But that's not because they're boring people underneath; it's their particular armor against anxiety."

Laura said, "I don't mind obsessionals; it's hysterics who set my teeth on edge. Hysterics look lively at first, with lots of shouting and crying and melodrama. But it's a façade, a way to avoid facing the real feelings underneath. Hysterics lose all the relevant details in the emotional storm, so that it takes forever to find out what actually happened, but the drama is ultimately boring because it's not real." She ran long fingers through a wayward strand of auburn hair, pulling it back from her face in an unconsciously elegant movement. "When someone thinks his craziness is what makes him interesting, he has it totally wrong. Because it's the craziness that's most repetitive, most alike from patient to patient. There are only so many ways to be paranoid, or hysterical, or obsessional. It's when you get behind these defenses that people become unique.

"People are always surprising, richer than they seem on the surface," Laura concluded. "And as they become well, their possibilities only increase." She frowned, deepening the fine line between her eyes. "When I interned I saw the worst in people. I was at a city hospital, and I treated too many knifings, and chronic drunks, and twelve-year-olds with syphilis. My mother was an alcoholic, and between my background and the internship, my respect for the human race bottomed out....Except when I had a chance to really speak to patients, like some of the hypertensives I saw again and again in the ER. And then my own analysis turned me toward psychiatry. And as a psychiatrist I've found most people to be extraordinarily resilient, with reserves of strength and humor and creativity that go far beyond what our society assumes. I am often awed by my patients."

11

Passivity and the Surrender of Control

The oddities of psychiatry make for a peculiar mix of intimacy and distance in the doctor-patient relationship that is unique in medicine. The relationship must also accommodate profound changes in the physician's authority and control.

The medical doctor has learned to be authoritative: decisively issuing orders, incisively taking charge of situations and patients, prescribing in minute detail what the person in her care must do in order to be helped. She is active, even intrusive, casually assuming the right to information allowed no one else. She is physically invasive as well, free to use all the technology of medicine to penetrate with complex instruments those areas she cannot directly touch. Taught that death and disease are her personal enemies, she has been granted her medical degree on the assumption that she will leave nothing undone, fighting to the patient's final breath—or beyond—even in situations where others might say that the more humane course is surrender. If patients don't wish to be resuscitated after a cardiac arrest, if they don't want a life-support machine and feeding tube, they'd better make arrangements in advance or risk the doctor's sense of moral obligation to keep them alive no matter what.[1]

While some of these characteristics may develop from the doctor's unconscious omnipotence fantasies (as psychoanalytic theory says), some are also basic to medical indoctrination—inculcated at considerable personal cost to the student and as much a part of her professional identity as her knowledge of physiology or pharmacology. Tampering with these qualities shakes a persona that has become a most satisfying part of herself, a persona that protects her from feelings of anxiety and helplessness while simultaneously making her a more effective physician.

But psychiatry demands renunciation of the active role of rescuer. In many ways, the psychiatrist must lean instead toward deliberate passivity, receptively opening herself to patients' needs and desires while relinquishing the right to control patient's actions. In this new role, the psychiatrist is even supposed to be physically inactive, renouncing the freedom of movement that might distract patients from their obligatory self-absorption. While other physicians stand up and move around in the course of examining patients, the psychiatrist is restricted to the chair, every movement constrained, her face largely smoothed of commentary. In fact, one of the most annoying aspects of psychiatry for her is simply this experience of confinement and impassivity in the face of the patient's verbal assaults. Back problems, chronic back pain, and back surgery are astonishingly common among psychiatrists, an occupational hazard of work that is not only profoundly sedentary but filled with emotional turmoil that must not be expressed; often taking its toll in tensed and spasmed muscles.

"I have a chronic back problem," Gary said. "If I don't swim almost every morning, my back hurts. And I end up flat out in bed." When I told him I'd heard this from other psychiatrists, he said, "I know at least four besides me who've had disc problems, and three that have had surgery."

Steve sounded wistful. "I played competitive squash in college, and I still play twice a week. If I didn't have some physical outlet, I couldn't last a month in psychiatry. It's so sedentary your body deteriorates in the chair. . . . Sometimes all I can think of in a session is how much I want to get up, that I'd do anything to be able to walk around the room a couple of times, or go out in the hall."

Laura focused less on physical constraints than on having to keep her face relatively blank. "By the end of the day, I sometimes feel my face is fixed into such calm that I wouldn't blink even if I found a roach in my coffee," she told me, "I know two women psychiatrists who take aerobic dancing two or three times a week, not just for the exercise, but to get a chance for some physical expressivity."

Another aspect of medicine has always been the independence of the doctor—her ability, within the limits set by a full waiting room, to use her time as she likes, keeping one patient longer whether or not someone else has to wait, fitting in an emergency, or taking an occasional long lunch. Psychiatrists, on the other hand, don't have even that prosaic freedom. With the session's length fixed at forty-five or fifty minutes and each patient arriving on the dot for his session, psychiatrists can come to hate the clock, the punctuality with which sessions must begin and end, the fact that coming in ten minutes late means that they will be late for every session for the rest of the morning, that a five-minute emergency phone call may mean a host of angry and resentful patients, each of whom is paying for a session that ought to have begun five minutes sooner, all of whom fear that only they have been deprived of time they know to be theirs.

"If you piss too long, you know you'll be late for the next hour," Steve said, in deadpan exaggeration. Without acknowledging my smile, he added awkwardly, "What really gets me is the inability to attend to my own concerns. When I was getting my divorce, my lawyer would call ... and of course I couldn't talk during the hour. I had only the time between sessions. If we needed more than that, it had to wait for the end of the day. ... Once I schedule sessions, I have almost no elasticity."

Gary gave an even more specific example. "Last year my younger daughter was hurt in a gymnastics class, and my wife couldn't reach me because I don't pick up the phone during sessions. My daughter was all right in the end, but she was paralyzed from the neck down for a week, and that first hour I could as well have been on Mars for all the good I did her." His long face was somber. "My wife's complained for years that I can't be reached in an emergency, and after that I finally installed a second phone line just for her. Now I can't believe I did without it so long."

Of course, the degree of physical constraint expected of the psychotherapist depends on the kind of psychotherapy being practiced. The analyst in particular is supposed to be a blank screen, "opaque,"[2] as Freud wrote, to the patient. When Freud said that he sat behind the couch because he couldn't bear being stared at, he had more than his own discomfort in mind. In a less often quoted passage, he added that it was necessary for him to allow his own thoughts to float with the patient's, in open receptivity, and that therefore his own face expressed all sorts of transient emotions from moment to moment which would interfere with the patient's free flow of associations if they were seen.[3] And to get up, to move around, to smile, to frown, to—unimaginably—talk on the phone, would all be even greater intrusions of the analyst's own distinct selfhood, a distraction and interference with the work of treatment.

In the modern world of psychotherapy, very few people get psychoanalyzed, and in most treatment the therapist is less physically passive than the analyst must be. Although as limited by the clock as the analyst, many psychotherapists doing other forms of treatment feel comfortable answering the phone, at least some of the time, and they may express at least some emotion. And, of course, they face patients who are sitting in a chair facing them, so that some of their emotional responses are necessarily incorporated into treatment. Yet the paradox remains: Good psychotherapy is aimed at helping the patient reach greater autonomy, but within the session, the patient's autonomy develops to some extent at the expense of the therapist's.

In the deepest sense, almost all psychotherapy requires an extraordinary surrender of physicianly activity, an abandonment, at the most profound level, of efforts to control the course of the patient's illness by controlling the patient. Except in emergencies and in the prescribing of medicines, the psychiatrist is no longer in charge in the way that the doctor is in cases of physical disease or trauma. In reality, of course, the ordinary doctor doesn't have total control of her patients either. If she did, diabetics would keep to their diets, no one would smoke, and everyone would take whatever medicines were prescribed for as long as the doctor said. But the transition from medicine to psychiatry takes place at a deeper level entirely, for the psychiatrist must, in principle, renounce her authoritarian role.

John Hames may couch his interest in psychiatry in terms of Norman Rockwell's benevolent family doctor, but the underlying image is godlike and authoritarian, a childhood vision of big daddy coming to the rescue. Yet psychotherapy patients can seldom be passively cured by a rescuer, no matter how competent, for patients are not merely objects for the psychiatrist to work magic on.

"When I was stationed in Nam," Steve said tersely, "my job was keeping soldiers alive. When I breathed someone long enough for the surgeon to take over, when I tied off an artery torn by shrapnel, the issue was only my competence. But in psychiatry, you can't ever say that the operation was a success even though the patient died." His voice was edgy behind the midwestern easiness. "No matter how good your technique, psychiatry isn't a solo performance; it's a duet."

"Last month, one of my patients OD'd on aspirin," Michael said in his abrupt way. "She called after she took the pills, and I phoned the police, and they took her to the ER, where the intern intubated her, and pumped her when her heart stopped, and generally did great medicine to keep her alive. But even in the hospital she can't stay on suicide watch[4] indefinitely. And once she's off watch, she can always find a way.... Last year someone threw themselves down a flight of stairs." He made a sudden movement with his hand, slicing sideways. "I can't even commit her indefinitely. If she really wants out, she can insist on a court hearing every few weeks. Eventually a judge will decide she's competent—or the hospital administration will stop fighting to keep her. And once she's home, I can't force her to stay on antidepressants, or have her guarded while we work out her feelings of hopelessness. She can jump in front of a bus, or out a window. She can slit her wrists on a piece of broken glass." His mouth twisted. "She can drown herself in the kitchen sink if the impulse really overtakes her. It isn't just a matter of what *I* do. *I* have only limited control."

John told me a doctor's joke, one of the few that aren't simply gruesome, and one that conveyed the essence of omnipotence fantasies. "A doctor died and went to Heaven." John smiled. "When he walked through the gate, he saw God striding around in a white coat. 'What's He doing?' he asked St. Michael. 'Oh,' St. Michael said, 'sometimes He likes to play doctor.'"

When I laughed, John sat back in satisfaction, his round face kindly, watching me through his thick glasses. Quietly he added, "The doctor is supposed to be all-powerful. And the psychiatrist is Svengali, reshaping the patient with the wave of his hand. Of course, it's nonsense. If you're really good, you have an amazing amount of power, but you have to work every inch of the way, and ultimately you can do nothing unless the patient is working at least as hard as you are."

Modern psychiatry is a medical specialty, but its practitioners must move away from the authoritarian underpinnings of medicine in order to do psychotherapy. Even though today's psychiatrist has an arsenal of effective medications to prescribe, many patients refuse to take them—or discontinue medication without informing the doctor.[5] And even when medicines work dramatically and are taken as needed, they're not the cure-all they are sometimes claimed to be, for almost every patient has residual problems that medication won't affect. If he stays in treatment, the patient is inevitably faced with the slow work of psychotherapy, in a process of psychological growth that can't be prescribed or forced.

John said, "If I give a person with a mood disorder the right medication, his acute symptoms go away. His delusions, if he has any, vanish. And his mood, his speech patterns, his sleep, what he thinks about—all that normalizes. But I can't ignore the fact that he's had to cope with inexplicable and profound changes in himself that he's had no control over. By the time he comes to me, he's often had a number of episodes of mood swings, and his character, his personality, his life circumstances, have all been affected."

He sat back, absently rubbing his chin. "I've just begun to see a businessman who's had inexplicable rage attacks all his life. He's found excuses for the rage so as to feel less out of control, ways of interpreting what happens that puts the blame on others. And he's learned strategies of coping— that he can't work for anyone else, that he has to run his own business, that he'll never be close to his wife, that he has to accept that his kids are uneasy around him. When he began treatment with me, I put him on an antidepressant, and the rages vanished. But meanwhile his work, his marriage, everything in his life has been damaged."

John continued earnestly, his voice troubled. "This man is forty-three years old, and he has a sense of himself, of who he is. He may not like everything he sees, but it's all he knows. And rage is only one component. He's also someone who has times of high energy when he accomplishes more than any other five people he knows, and times when he can do nothing, so that he's learned he can't count on being able to work steadily at anything. He knows he wakes at three in the morning, going over his accounts in his head because he's afraid of going bankrupt, or lies in bed thinking about dying. That he often feels as if the world has no color, that everything is grey or muted; that all his experiences have a kind of distance, as though a pane of glass separates him from other people."

John shrugged and spread his hands palms up in a gesture of emptiness. "These are all manifestations of a lifelong depression—just like the rages—and I expect them to vanish with medication.[6] But the residual, the effects of living with himself as he's been, is his whole life. An antidepressant like Prozac may eliminate the rages, the distance, the energy swings, the sadness, the worry, the sudden shifts of mood that he's never understood. But the mold's been set. He's stuck with the choices he's made, and with the identity people know him by, and at the same time he's missing all sorts of skills he'd have if he'd been medicated way back. It's going to take time and effort to work out who he is now, and what he can and can't do with his life, and how to integrate into himself the experience of being so changed."

Steve said, "Even one episode of illness has a profound impact if it's disabling—the common story of the college kid who suffers a really bad depression (or a manic break),[7] and has to come home for intensive treatment, or even go into the hospital. Usually these are high-functioning kids, bright, with friends and the ability to do well in school, who until now, whatever swings of mood they've had, have basically felt the world was their oyster, their future was open. And now they're scared, really scared, because suddenly and mysteriously they really came unglued: they overdosed, or slit their wrists, or decided their roommate came from outer space, something bad enough that they were packed up and brought to the college infirmary and from there to a hospital, or sometimes home and to a private psychiatrist. On one hand, they still have residual feelings that are part of the original episode—the depression, the despair, the total lack of energy, or a kind of suspiciousness and distance from others, whatever. But beyond that, they now have to come to terms with being genuinely different from most of their peers, different in a way that is incomprehensible to their friends *and* themselves, something they've heard happens only to other people. And they feel profoundly vulnerable, perhaps for the first time in their life—and they are—and they also feel vulnerable in a way that they are inevitably going to feel as shameful weakness. They want to hide under the bed just for those reasons, and on top of that they still feel lousy. . . . Even if the medicines eliminate the majority of their symptoms, they don't have the bounce, the resilience they're used to. At the beginning, even deciding what to have for breakfast is a major decision, much less issues around going out and resuming any of their usual activities. And the medications they take have side effects. People are often sleepy, or jittery, or have problems remembering what they study, or have muscle tremors, or can't stand up suddenly without starting to black out—those are the commonest ones.

"Even one break, one period of complete inability to function, leaves major scars. It's never enough to medicate, because the patient has to come to terms with a new fact about himself, a very real vulnerability that does mark him off, and that he has to make accommodations to as he returns to his life. And I can only help. I can offer connections. I can make interpretations. But he has to hear them, and then he has to go out into the world and use them. *Not me, him.*"

This kind of work requires yet another change in the doctor's role— the deliberate cultivation of a wait-and-see attitude. As a physician-pharmacologist, the psychiatrist prescribes drugs for a particular diagnosis and specific set of target symptoms, with her focus sharp, relatively narrow, and action oriented. In contrast, the psychotherapeutic role calls for her to listen without automatically classifying the material unearthed.

"Any category is a simplification," Laura said, "in any part of life. Any doctor knows that no pneumonia is exactly like any other, but it doesn't matter as long as penicillin gets all his patients well. But I have to think beyond a patient's symptoms to his total personality. And in that context, categories are not just simplifications; they are falsifications. In categorizing, you lose the details and uniqueness of the total pattern. You reduce the richness of each person's inner life to stereotype."

The psychiatrist can't help but think in terms of the classifications she's learned, because she'd be totally overwhelmed by the complexity of the individual if she didn't. Scientific progress depends on generalization and simplification, and the use of medication requires giving patients diagnostic labels. At the same time, the psychiatrist is aware that no one is ever a textbook type; people are always mixtures of contradictory features that in totality create a one of a kind. So the psychiatrist must try not to put patients into boxes. She must empathically listen while suspending judgment about the meaning of what she hears. She must deliberately cultivate a kind of cognitive passivity.

In that context, the psychiatrist's own free associations can be used as a tool to sidestep her desire to jump to conclusions, a means of deliberately cultivating the ability to listen without imposing categories on the data. Freud wrote, in 1912, "... [T]he most successful cases are those in which one proceeds, as it were, without any purpose in view, allows oneself to be taken by surprise in any new turn in them, and always meets them with an open mind, free from any presuppositions."[8] An impossibility, of course, but an approach in polar opposition to the physicianly skills of diagnosis and prescription.

In the psychotherapeutic mode, understanding is always provisional, new data always erupting. Beyond that, therapy is seen as a process of the patient's continuing growth, with the meaning of the data and the apparently relevant themes of treatment evolving as the person changes. In doing good psychotherapy, the psychiatrist looks beyond the resolution of discrete symptoms to deep (and unpredictable) alterations in the patient's ways of being in the world. Remaining open to new information and new possibilities, and aware that nothing in life is permanently settled, the psychiatrist must never allow herself a final summing up of the patient's limits.

Gary shook his head ruefully, talking about how hard it is to maintain a truly open mind. "I find it hardest with people who begin seeing me when they're very sick. It's impossible to wipe out the memory of what they were like when we began. And it's difficult to register the enormous difference between their initial functioning and what they become. After a few years, they're not the same people."

His expression was shrewd, the angular planes of his face sharpened. "No matter how I try, I tend to impose my memories of them on what they are now and to see them as far more limited than they are, to see them as fragile in a way that is no longer true. I've learned to send anyone I've seen three or four years for a consultation, and I don't tell the evaluating psychiatrist how the patient thought I was a Martian when we started, because I want him to see them in the present moment, and without the biases I inevitably carry.

"Patients don't have to be psychotic for immense changes to occur," he added. "If I see someone for four or five years, they may marry and have a child, or graduate from school, or change careers, and I'm going to be exploring different themes with them. People bring up different themes in the course of living, and I can never type them or predict the limits of their growth at the start. We agree on provisional goals at the beginning of treatment, goals that make sense at that time, but the patient brings in other issues along the way. If treatment goes well, he experiences more change than he ever expected, changes he didn't even put on a wish list. On the other hand, there's almost always a particular problem that brought him into my office, and when that's taken care of to his satisfaction, he's generally ready to stop—even if I see other issues remaining."

I asked for specifics. Gary nodded and went on almost instantly. "If someone comes to me because he wants to get married and doesn't know why he can't meet any desirable women, that's the focus of treatment. But once we begin work, we find a variety of unconscious feelings that have relevance not only to women and marriage but to commitment, and self-esteem, and beliefs about what he deserves from life, and a potpourri of issues that is different for each person." His voice lightened. "And as we work on them, he's going to find himself different at work: more assertive, or cooperative, or creative, or ten other things. He may decide to move to an entirely different part of town. He may change the way he dresses. He may go back to school, or take a course he's always wanted. He may start a new career entirely." He smiled. "In fact, his friends may tell him he's so different they can't believe it, but until he meets a woman, he's not going to feel he got what he came for. And he hasn't. While, conversely, none of these changes are what he asked for, or may even have wanted, when he arrived at my office. So as the psychiatrist, you have goals that you and the patient have agreed on—and the patient may bring in new ones in the course of treatment—but you also know something the patient doesn't, which is that he's going to get a hell of a lot more than either of you bargained for."

Once the focus of treatment shifts from the patient's illness to his evolving growth, the psychotherapist moves even further from the paternalistic attitudes of medicine. As with raising a child, the psychiatrist not only has limits to what she can impose on her patient; she has to stand back and see where he goes.

"With very sick patients, of course, or someone in an acute crisis," Laura said, "you must take on some of the traditional physicianly role. If a patient tells you he's going to kill his boss because the voices tell him to, you have to talk him out of it. You may even have to hospitalize him against his will. You're also likely to give a more disturbed patient advice or tell him what he can and can't do—whether you think he's ready to leave home or marry or have a child, whether you accept his judgment about

changing jobs, letting him know your opinion on issues of major importance. You have to set limits, provide information, offer your judgments
on these decisions, because if you don't, he may screw up some facet of his
life in a serious or irremediable way." Her voice was sharp and emphatic.
"You have a parental responsibility toward the sicker patient much as you
would to a young child.

"But you don't intervene if you feel you have a choice," she said more
softly, "even with patients with very serious difficulties. If your role includes
fostering his autonomy, you must be open to him choosing his own path
even if you have qualms about his choices. Not unless you're convinced not
only that you're right, but that the issue is so important that you have to intervene even if that means you're interfering with his autonomy."

Later in the interview, Laura said with some hesitancy, "This may strike
you as odd, but I often think of myself as not very different from a garage
mechanic. I have certain expert skills, that's all, and I think some of us take
ourselves too seriously. Someone pulls into my garage and tells me all sorts
of things are wrong with his car, and I say, 'Well, I can fix that, and that,
and that.' And then he tells me which part of the job he wants done."

I asked her about the patient who has a car towed in, collapses over the
hood, and says, "Help!" To that she said, "In that case, I tell him exactly
what needs to be done to get the car drivable. If he expects me to fix it,
that's what he has to work on. If he says no, I tell him he needs another
garage."

Some of the therapist's most difficult decisions revolve around this balance between protecting the patient from harm and respecting his autonomy enough to let him make his own mistakes. "It's often a judgment
call," Gary said. "No one grows without false steps and errors of judgment. The trick is to minimize the damage. Sometimes you realize you
want to intervene because, in a personal way, you don't like the directions
the patient is moving in—and, of course, then you keep your feelings to
yourself. The difficult decisions occur when you're trying to judge if the
potential damage is worth the potential growth.

"One of my sicker adolescents," Gary continued, "wanted to take this
past summer in Europe with a bicycle club. I thought he didn't have the
social skills for a sustained tour, and I thought he might fall back into
psychosis under the stress of being socially isolated, away from home, and

in a foreign country. He's only a year out of the hospital, with very shaky self-confidence—another setback would do him enormous harm. On the other hand, he felt my lack of confidence as another of the many put-downs in his life, one more of the manifold ways he's been treated as delicate, or sick, or weird. In the end, he insisted on going, and he came back with an enormous increase in self-respect and self-confidence. But I've had other patients collapse under similar circumstances." Gary rubbed his neck tiredly. "You win some and you lose some, and most of the time you can't guarantee in advance which it will be."

John said, "When you function as a physician, you write orders and tell patients what to do. If they don't comply, it's their business. You've done your part. Most of the time the therapeutic relationship is totally different. The patient makes the final decision, but the two of you together try to understand what's going on." He took off his glasses, his eyes no longer magnified by the thick lenses, and looked across the long room without seeing. "It's not that you're neutral. You're always allied with the healthiest part of the patient against the regressive forces within him. But you can't tell someone what to do when all you have is an educated guess as to what will happen 'if.' Because whatever people think, you're not a magician, you can't read the future, you can't even pretend to play God with their lives."

12

The Real Relationship

Freud made interpretation of the transference the core of treatment, with cure achieved by the analyst's dispassionate and meticulous uncovering of the patient's feelings toward him.[1] In a well-known—and misleading analogy—Freud compared the analyst to the surgeon: "I cannot advise my colleagues too urgently to model themselves during psycho-analytic treatment on the surgeon, who puts aside all his feelings, even his human sympathy, and concentrates his mental forces on the single aim of performing the operation as skillfully as possible."[2]

In this scenario—which became the prototype not only for psycho-analysis but for most conventional psychotherapy in the United States—the psychiatrist was a "blank screen," unrevealing of himself, his very colorlessness what allowed patients to fully explore their beliefs and fantasies about him and their relationship. Here Freud wrote, "The doctor should be opaque to his patients and, like a mirror, should show them nothing but what is shown to him."[3]

Yet as psychotherapists after Freud have stressed,[4] the image of the surgeon-psychoanalyst falsifies the reality, because it leaves out the bedrock on which all treatment, of whatever kind, depends. All psychotherapy presupposes the creation of a new—therapeutic—relationship that is different from those that shaped the patient in the first place. Within this relationship, which is intimate, intense, and supportive, the therapist substitutes to a great extent for mother and father in a rerun of the patient's growing up, giving her the chance to come to a new understanding of herself and other people, and creating a new model of what it means to be human.

Whatever the peculiarities of the treatment situation, two real people are sitting in the room, and they have a real relationship. One modern master of psychoanalysis, Ralph Greenson, gives a wonderful example of failure in this underlying relationship in his book, *The Technique and Practice of Psychoanalysis*, in a story involving a young psychiatrist seeing a new mother in psychoanalysis. Soon after beginning the treatment, the woman told him—weeping—that her baby had become terribly ill the night before. The psychiatrist said nothing. At the next session she sat down and cried through the hour without speaking. The psychiatrist still said nothing, asking only from time to time what she was thinking. The next week the woman came in, told him he needed treatment more than she did—and walked out. Greenson comments that she was right.[5]

If the psychotherapist were as cold, emotionally withdrawn, and determinedly colorless as Freud's analogy to the surgeon implies, the patient's experience within the session would be little better than her experience outside it. In fact, Freud himself was nothing like this.[6] The truth is that a real relationship is always created during therapy, a relationship that is separate from the transference. It is founded on the therapist's empathy and concern, but it always includes more.

The psychiatrist is a man or woman with a particular ethnic, class, religious, racial, and regional background. Certainly neither sex nor race can be hidden, but neither can many other identifying characteristics. If nothing else, the therapist reveals his ignorance when he asks for further information to clarify aspects of the patient's background that may be totally different from his own, and he is likely to betray a certain familiarity with areas the two of them share, even if only by his increased understanding.

John said, "I'm the major referral for a theological seminary in New York, so I treat a number of very devout Catholics. In this group, sicker patients often can't tell that I was raised a Catholic—and they explain points of doctrine to me. But less disturbed patients can generally tell that I was raised within the Church. And they can also tell that I'm no longer religious, and that I don't feel strongly about it one way or the other."

The therapist also dresses in certain ways and has particular speech patterns. Most of all, he reveals something of himself in the office furniture he's chosen, in the pictures on the wall, and in the ornaments and books that fill the office shelves. In fact, none of the offices I saw were anonymous. One had a wall of nature photographs the psychiatrist had taken during vacations. Another office was cozy, with hanging plants in hand-made pottery bowls. A third was book-lined wall-to-wall, with esoteric volumes on religion, comparative linguistics, music, and literature in addition to psychiatry. Another was relatively bare, with throw rugs scattered on the hardwood floors, and large, very modern paintings looking down on patient and psychiatrist alike. Each office was revealing in some way of the therapist's interests, of the kind of room he made his home for half his waking hours.

Gary explained, "The reality is that I spend as many hours in my office as I do at home. It has to be comfortable for me, I have to have something to look at besides the patient, I need a sense of space and light, I need a room that feels in tune with me. In fact, my office reflects my taste and needs more than my home does because I don't have to accommodate to anyone else's wishes." He gestured toward his closet. "I don't put my wife's picture on my desk because that would interfere too much with patients' fantasies about me, but I keep a scrapbook of photos in that closet. And I hang up photographs of places I've been because I enjoy them every day." He smiled wryly. "And it reminds me of an existence outside this office when I might otherwise feel I was being swallowed up."

I asked him if he was aware of how sensual his photography was. "How could I not know when I'm the one who took them?" he answered. "I expect patients to use them as jumping off points for all kinds of fantasy." A moment later he added, "On a more overt level, most patients are also going to realize that the outdoors and outdoor life mean a great deal to me, and a number of people pick up that I'm not at core a city person. Some people feel closer to me for that, and some more distant." He smiled. "One very competitive man accused me of narcissism, of showing off my photographic skills, and then proceeded to point out all the technical faults. I used it as a wedge for examining his competitiveness and anger toward his rather overbearing father, but I also knew he had a real point. I won a prize for one of those pictures."

Patients always learn more about the therapist than the therapist intentionally reveals, and what they observe has all sorts of meaning for them. But the most essential information comes from direct interactions—from what the psychiatrist says and how he acts from the first telephone contact.

Gary said, "One of my patients had seen a psychiatrist who didn't charge for missed appointments or vacations as long as he received twenty-four hours' notice. In the second year of her work with him, this woman was admitted to the hospital with acute appendicitis. She'd never before missed a session without notice, and her husband phoned her psychiatrist from the emergency room. At the end of the month, he charged her anyway, saying that was his rule, and it wasn't his responsibility that she missed the hour." Gary grimaced with distaste. "He'd also preserved what I assume he felt to be psychoanalytic neutrality by not phoning her in the hospital. As a result, she felt that all her beliefs about his coldness and rigidity were confirmed. And she never forgave him. Their alliance was ruptured.

"This woman has recurrent depressions, so she saw a second psychiatrist some time afterward. His rule was that patients paid for all sessions, no matter what, including vacations that didn't coincide with his, explaining that he felt the hour to be hers no matter what she did. Although she wasn't earning more than before *and* now had to plan vacations around the psychiatrist, she told me she wasn't bothered at all the same way—that this rule seemed consistent rather than rigid. And the idea that the hour was really hers, *no matter what,* carried an extraordinarily powerful message about this psychiatrist's commitment to her."

Some issues, like those about payment for missed hours, involve the ground rules of treatment, and others address the general environment created in the office. Does the therapist, for example, call back quickly when phoned? Does he talk softly or emphatically? Does he seem unruffled no matter what happens? Does he remember what you said about Aunt Martha two weeks ago in passing, or does he ask you to explain who Aunt Martha is again? Does he seem filled with suppressed energy? Does he look healthy? Does he have a chronic cough? Is he overweight? All of these details provide information about him, which in part feed the transference but are at the same time part of the actual relationship.

"I happen to have an excellent memory," Steve observed. "And I can generally remember something a patient said casually even a few years before.... You have no idea the impact it has when I remember that Norah was someone's best friend in the sixth grade, or that they had trouble with calculus in their freshman year of college. It conveys in the most powerful way that you really listen and keep track of what the patient says. Just as there are few things more deflating than having a therapist not remember something important." Steve paused, his eyes narrowed. "In fact, forgetting is generally a signal of something wrong, either the eruption of counter-transference on the therapist's part [that is, just as the patient has a transference to the therapist that is rooted in feelings toward the significant figures in the patient's early life, the therapist has countertransference feelings toward the patient. See discussion in next chapter.] or a sign that he's ill in some way. Part of training is learning how to remember the details of all your patients' lives.[7]

"Everything about the therapist forms part of the real relationship and part of the transference," Steve added. "I'm an active, physically healthy man. Most patients find this reassuring. It gives them the feeling they're not overburdening me, they don't have to worry about me, and I can handle anything they throw at me. They also identify with it as something good, something to have themselves.

"Patients will react any time you're sick, particularly if you have to miss a session. And although they may feel concern, they're generally angry and hurt at some level—all kinds of issues of abandonment may arise. But with chronic or serious illness, the issues are infinitely more complicated, because many patients have a profound need to protect you then from their own anger at feeling you're less available to them ... just as they once protected an unavailable or incompetent parent. Treatment can become stalled because they're so torn between anger, resentment, and fear of hurting you ... apart from their truly caring about you and feeling useless. When I was out for some minor surgery last year, a patient told me she just wanted to bring chicken soup to the hospital, even if she left it anonymously ... that it was terrible not to be able to do something."

Another psychiatrist said, "The worst is when the psychiatrist is really sick and won't admit it, and the patient is sure he's sick and needs him to confirm it, and he won't. Those are treatments that drive the patient crazy." When I asked for more detail, he said, "I was recently called in as a consultant on a case like this. The psychiatrist was desperately ill and entirely unable to admit his condition, much less discuss it as a treatment issue. He'd done wonderfully with this patient in the past but was literally making him crazy again by his denial. I told him that his patient had to see a new psychiatrist."

To some extent, the patient carries expectations about therapy and the therapist to the first session. But these transference reactions are inevitably interwoven with the real interactions that occur. For while the patient generally arrives expecting help, she must also see evidence of the therapist's desire to help her. She must feel safe, she must feel that she will not be judged, she must feel that the therapist will not be overwhelmed by her fears or by her illness, and she must feel that the therapist is competent.

When I began talking with psychiatrists about the real relationship between therapist and patient, I had a strong bias. I had heard too many horror stories, sometimes from these same psychiatrists about their own treatment, about therapists who seemed to lack the most fundamental of human responses, and I was all too aware of how easily the analytically oriented attempts at dispassionate neutrality could be unintentionally caricatured.

Laura said, "When you're first learning to do psychotherapy, you feel a terrible conflict between what seems like a natural human impulse and your belief that you mustn't intrude yourself unnecessarily on the patient. It's worse in an analytically oriented residency training program, as mine was, because the implicit model then is always psychoanalysis."

Misapplication and caricature of psychoanalytic techniques are most common near the beginning of a psychiatrist's training. They were even more common in the past when more psychiatrists went on to psychoanalytic institutes.

As Gary said, "You got very confused [when you began specialized psychoanalytic training] because your physicianly impulse when somebody said they were desperate was to do something, to act, to intervene. But you felt your analytic supervisor standing over your shoulder, and you were afraid of reporting that you'd done anything but interpret the feelings." Gary went on: "So you'd hear about analytic candidates who had a suicidal patient but didn't respond with active intervention. . . .

"When I worked in the emergency room as a resident, I saw a patient who'd made a serious suicide attempt while being psychoanalyzed by a candidate at the analytic institute. When I phoned the psychiatrist, he told me he'd realized that she was decompensating [that is, getting worse as her defenses crumbled] and had just begun to medicate her, but he hadn't told his supervisor because he was afraid to admit he was breaking the rules. It was clear he would never have waited so long if he wasn't seeing her as part of his analytic training, and he certainly wouldn't have kept her on the couch." (When medications first appeared that were effective against such symptoms as depression and anxiety, using them was frowned upon in psychoanalysis and in psychoanalytically oriented psychotherapy. This psychoanalytic candidate knew that his supervisor would say that medications would simply suppress symptoms and in so doing make unavailable for treatment the necessary upswelling of emotionally relevant material from the patient's unconscious and, in the long run, harming her. These beliefs are discussed in later chapters.)

People undergoing psychoanalysis are expected to be healthy enough to tolerate the deprivations of psychoanalytic treatment. But most patients need more cues from the therapist than analysis provides, or more supportive psychotherapy, or even medications. As one psychiatrist said about his own analysis, "It still feels incredibly stupid to me that I was supposed to lie there talking to someone who almost never answered. How could that offer a corrective emotional experience when I grew up with a chronically depressed mother who hardly ever answered me?" He sounded really angry. "There was no way to work through my feelings, many of which dated to a time before I could even speak, when I was working with someone who refused to bend from a rigid psychoanalytic position. As far as I was concerned, his silence and general lack of response was just a repetition of what I grew up with."

Moreover, beginning psychiatrists are so unsure of what they're doing that they tend to try the same pseudoanalytic approach with all their psychotherapy patients, including those who need a much more supportive, nonanalytically-oriented treatment. Even nowadays, psychiatrists doing psychotherapy may be confused about the meaning and applicability of psychoanalytic neutrality, particularly because, as residents, they may still have supervisors for whom psychoanalysis is the model of treatment.

Gary said, "It's tremendously difficult to learn to modulate your response, particularly, I think, because it goes against the grain. You really want to be more active. And so you get paralyzed, and you do a parody of psychoanalysis. Of course, there are some people who've always wanted to be analysts, who find an excuse for that kind of passivity very appealing. I think most of them have no judgment at all. They're just doing what they want without any regard for the patient. It's pseudoanalysis, not analysis."

Laura said thoughtfully, "Even if it's entirely inappropriate for your patient for you to stand back, you're much more neutral than you're likely to be when you're more experienced. But you always face a tension between your desire to nurture and the patient's needs at that moment. And the balance varies from patient to patient and across time.

"One person may feel much closer to you if you offer him a hot drink on a bitterly cold day; while someone else may feel overwhelmingly guilty because they'd been angry at you the session before. And someone nearing termination may simply see your offer as a reasonable human response and normalization of what has been until now a highly idiosyncratic relationship. And eventually you come to do whatever is most appropriate without even thinking about it. I'm sure that's why therapists from different training bases become more alike as they develop experience."

A real relationship and transference distortions always coexist, even in the strictest psychoanalysis. Moreover, formal psychoanalysis is rare today, and few patients are expected to tolerate the deliberate deprivation of the classical analytic relationship. These days most therapists acknowledge both the inevitable existence of the real relationship and its importance to the treatment. Meanwhile the stereotype of the analyst behind the couch, silent, detached, and seldom offering advice or information or warm emotional support, exists mainly in books or movies. But this change in models makes the psychotherapy situation even more complicated. The relationship of patient and psychiatrist may have a "real" component, but only within oddly limited boundaries.

Steve made a design of the paper clips on his desk as he searched for an example. "A few months ago, one of my patients was caught in a storm on her way to my office and soaked to the skin. She was shivering, and I wrapped her in some towels from my bathroom. Since then, she's told me several times that this was a turning point in her treatment." His voice was sad. "She'd been severely neglected as a child, and she never expected me to take care of her when she reached my office...."

He looked up soberly, and his blue eyes darkened. "My response was a therapeutic one—by definition—because it was so exactly right for her, ... and as a simple human gesture it was also reflective of a real relationship. But I often have to stifle the indulgence of simple human impulses, because I'm not there to offer a social relationship in any ordinary sense of the word. I don't go to the movies with patients. We don't play squash together. And as glad as I am when a patient gets married, I don't normally go to their wedding—and patients certainly weren't invited to mine."

Gary said forcefully, "Everyone likes the idea of the kindly therapist with whom you have a solid, 'real relationship,' the therapist who gives you cookies and milk and wipes away your tears. The desire for a loving and supportive parent is enormous in all of us, and particularly for most of us who need treatment.

"The problem for the psychiatrist is the impossibility of knowing when to draw the line. It's pouring outside, and your patient has no umbrella. Your impulse may be to offer him an extra you have, but you have to think: Does this foster his dependency? Isn't this someone who never wants to take responsibility for his actions? Or is this someone who's going to see your offer as implicit criticism, the kind of criticism he was constantly exposed to as a child: Why didn't he think ahead, why didn't he plan better, why wasn't he organized like his older brother? Or is he going to see your offer as an intrusion, an imposition of your will? Maybe he likes walking in the rain." He paused. "With some patients, particularly women who've had incestuous experiences, any move on my part may carry a sexual connotation for them."

As his words continued to unroll, I saw that he'd been leading to this point all along. "Of course, that's where the rules about appropriate therapist behavior are most necessary—when you get into the arena of physical contact. I have many patients I've had the impulse to hug, or to hold when they've cried. I'd like to offer comfort on that primitive, intensely human level as much as they'd like to receive it.[8] And I've been in the patient's chair, too. But with the best will in the world it's easy to go too far."

Now he was completely caught up in his words, obviously thinking aloud. "Holding someone in distress can easily degenerate into a more sexual response, and hugging can end up kissing. And if you respond to pain by touching someone, what do you do when they say they're hopelessly unattractive, and no one can ever love them? Or that if you made love to them, then finally, for the first time in their life, they'd feel loveable? People *do* say that to you—fairly often. And many therapists who admit to sexual contact with a patient argue that they were only offering what the patient needed, that the patient was lonely, or desperate, or required that kind of physical reassurance."[9] His voice was firm. "It sounds simple to say, 'Be more human,' but I feel it's safest for the patient to have some hard and fast rules that you don't break. You don't touch. You don't hug."

13

Feelings for the Patient

Freud wrote that analysts could never be truly neutral, for they wish the patient to get well. Still, he believed the analyst should strive to work for the patient's recovery without any personal stake or emotional involvement. Emotional responses, of whatever kind, were shameful, to be analyzed and eradicated as quickly as possible.[1]

Later writers modified Freud's position.[2] They recognized that even an exhaustive psychoanalysis couldn't erase all the therapist's emotional responses. The issue is that her responses and desires, no matter how "normal" or expectable, ought not to be allowed to interfere with the treatment.

Gary said, "Where I run into trouble is in liking a patient so much that I don't push hard enough for material that's going to get them feeling angry at me. The transference is always ambivalent and they always have mixed feelings toward me, but there are times when it's just so nice meeting with someone that it's very easy to let pass clues to their having more negative feelings. I'm human, too, and I like having a patient smile at me, or say thank-you at the end of an hour. Most of the time I get so little thanks it's an enormous temptation to sit back and bask in the warmth when it's offered."

"I treat a number of models," Steve said, "and there's no way in the world I couldn't have a sexual reaction occasionally." His voice sharp, he added, "But it helps to remember that their seductiveness toward me has nothing to do with *me*. It's transference. They might find me attractive if they met me at a party, but first of all, many of them wouldn't, and secondly, they wouldn't find me *that* attractive." He was quiet for several seconds, looking out the window. "Actually, I felt most tempted with a patient who wasn't beautiful, someone I genuinely would have gone out with if she weren't in treatment with me. We had a lot of interests in common, and a lot of shared feelings about things. But I had to accept that my interest and desire couldn't be acted on. The taboo is absolute: you don't have sex with a patient."

He paused again. "Everyone in the business knows of a famous analyst who told a patient she was too attractive for him to treat her, sent her to someone else, and eventually married her." Steve's voice was earnest. "I've had two women patients ask me why I couldn't do the same with them. After all, it was quite a precedent. But I think that story has scared a lot of people. The idea that it's ever possible to break the taboo, even after sending the person to someone else, is very frightening. The therapist is supposed to be absolutely above temptation—just as with the incest taboo. The taboo may be broken in reality by some people, but the idea of breaking it *is, and should be,* revolting."

He hesitated. "With the woman I liked so much, I thought for a while that I might have to send her to someone else, but I didn't want to tell her even that I was having that kind of problem with her. I thought it would be too damaging, so I paid for supervision of her case[3] for several months, and while this was happening I met Barbara, my second wife. Once I met her, the problem receded, and ultimately it vanished. I had someone I was happy with. The fact that I found my patient attractive, that we would have been lovers if I'd met her under other circumstances, became just a fact, not an intrusion on the therapy. In fact, at that point my finding her attractive could be more clearly communicated to her, and it added immensely to her self-esteem."

Steve added, "The truth is that I have to be careful whenever the patient and I have something important in common. I treat someone who has a passion for cars. Well, I spent half my teen years under the hood of a Mustang convertible, and sometimes I just want to ask him to say more. I'd enjoy the conversation. Or last year, when I was buying a new car, I really wanted to ask him his opinion... because he undoubtedly knows more than me. I'll be able to do that when we're nearing termination. I'll want to introduce more reality into our relationship then. I'll want him to get me off the pedestal he has me on right now. I'll want to equalize our positions. And even before we reach termination, there will be times when asking him about cars will increase his self-esteem enormously. But in a general way, I don't see anything like that as part of the therapy hour, because that hour is basically his to use in whatever way is important to *him* at that time. My intrusion of my own needs is just that, an intrusion, and one for which he's paying. And it's even a kind of extortion, because there's no way he'd feel in a position to tell me not to waste his time."

Gary said, "It comes up whenever the patient is a person you'd really like to have as a friend. Because you can't. Whatever the legitimacy of your feelings, the patient is caught up in a mix of transference and reality in which the transference dominates. The two of you can't be friends, because they'd be going out with a fantasy, and you'd never untangle the mess you'd made of treatment." He paused. "This is entirely different from the rare times you offer a patient something to drink or even eat, because those are clear therapeutic interventions where it's important to actually fill in a deprivation. These aren't moves you make because you want to—and you don't make them lightly either."

In an ideal treatment, neither therapist nor patient oversteps the boundaries of the therapeutic relationship: The therapist always acts in accordance with the patient's needs, and the patient doesn't make demands the psychiatrist finds unacceptable. But many patients do go beyond the acceptable limits of behavior. Some break the rules by phoning the psychiatrist at all hours of the day and night, or by paying late or not at all. Some break agreements about not drinking or taking drugs or cutting their arms. Others lie about taking essential medication that they've agreed to take. Occasionally, a patient follows the psychiatrist home or threatens her or her family.

The more unacceptable the behavior, the more it complicates the therapeutic relationship. In these cases, the psychiatrist has emotional responses that must be acknowledged. She must allow herself to become aware of her anger, resentment, or fear. She also has to tell the patient how she feels, and discuss the behavior in sessions. If the psychiatrist doesn't acknowledge the problem, she is all too likely to treat the patient with covert resentment or even to terminate the treatment in anger.

Michael said, "It's necessary to tell someone when they're doing something you find unacceptable. And you don't have to hide your anger either.

It's a piece of reality the patient can incorporate and make use of to understand what goes on between normal people.

"The other night a patient left a message with my service that he had to speak with me urgently. This is a depressed man, not someone I normally think of as a suicide risk. But I could always be wrong. So I spent several hours trying to reach him." He pursed his lips. "The kicker was that his line was busy. I called the operator because I thought he might be talking to friends, but it turned out he'd taken his phone off the hook. When I spoke with him the next morning, he said he'd gone to sleep, and I told him I was furious, that he had no right to leave an emergency message and then make it impossible for me to get through. I said he'd taken up my whole night, I was worried, he had a responsibility to me to be available once he said it was an emergency.

"Some psychiatrists wouldn't have felt comfortable showing they were angry, but I see no reason not to. It's appropriate, and appropriateness is part of what the patient has to learn from me. And far better I tell him what he's done than risk having my resentment spill over in the treatment. And once I told him I was angry, we could talk about how he mistreated me, acting helpless and vulnerable while exerting tremendous control over me—manipulating me. But I want to be clear. I didn't yell at this man, and I didn't go on for ten minutes about what he'd done to me. I just told him openly and with feeling that I was angry and that I felt he had no right to treat me as he had. And then we could examine his behavior in treatment." He eyed me narrowly, his tone blunt. "I don't want you to hear me saying it's all right at times to express anger as a license to abuse the patient. He's still the patient, you're still the doctor, and your obligation always remains to behave responsibly and with restraint."

Ideally the therapist is like a sponge, soaking up the patient's very essence and responding empathically to his needs, hearing his inner voice and saying precisely what will be most useful to his growth. Obviously, psychotherapy can never be continuously at this level. This is a fantasy even the most dedicated therapist can't live up to. However empathic she may be, the therapist is only human. As one psychiatrist said, "Empathy is exquisitely sensitive to any disturbing influence. Fatigue, a cold, a new love affair—any of them can interfere with the ability to let go of your own concerns and put yourself in the patient's shoes." The psychiatrist also comes to the session with her own quirks and style, inclined to irritability or withdrawal under stress, or to be too ready to jump to the rescue. No one can always respond with the patient's best interests in mind.

In the early years of the psychoanalytic movement, therapists were expected somehow to be free of any interference from their own wishes and needs. Once the impossibility of this was acknowledged, however, their feelings became viewed as one more tool of treatment. Whatever the kind of psychotherapy being provided, sophisticated therapists nowadays are marked by the ability to decode their own responses as well as patients', treating their feelings during the hour as neither meaningless nor irrelevant, but as signals that point to something the patient is calling forth. Some of these feelings are expectable human responses that are largely independent of a given therapist's specific life experiences; and they are sometimes referred to as "counterreactions."

Even more important to the treatment, however, are those feelings that *are* rooted in the therapist's own particular life experience and childhood. In this sense, her own transference feelings (from her past onto the patient) are an inevitable part of treatment, for even the thoroughly psychoanalyzed psychotherapist continues throughout life to respond in part to other people—including patients—as if they were significant persons of childhood, feeling herself cared for or rejected, approved of or criticized, understood or misunderstood, and responding to those feelings in characteristic ways.

In treatment, "countertransference" refers to an upswelling from the psychiatrist's own unconscious of such feelings, coming from her own past and transferred now onto the patient. The more thoroughly she knows herself, the more realistically in the present her reactions are likely to be in the treatment hour, the milder are those countertransference responses that do occur, and the easier they are to spot. But the truth is that the attempt to keep reality and illusion in *entirely* separate boxes is impossible, and in practice the boundaries between realistic perceptions and unconscious distortions blur for therapist as well as patient. The critical issue is that countertransference can be useful if it is monitored by the therapist and an interference in the treatment if it is not.

"When I was in psychotherapy," Gary said, "the psychiatrist I was seeing had a nasty, sarcastic sense of humor. My father used sarcasm as a weapon, so I'm very sensitive to it—and I don't think it's legitimate with any patient. You have to be careful using humor at all, because patients are so vulnerable, they easily see themselves as the butt when you don't intend it. And in retrospect, I'd say that his sarcasm during the session was a countertransference response when I was particularly depressed or in turmoil. I still remember one time, I was really upset, I was crying, and I said, 'You're just sitting there. You don't do anything.' Now there are lots of ways you can answer that. I know that now, but what he said is branded on my brain: 'Somebody in this room has to keep his head.' As if I had no right to feel frightened about the way I felt. It wasn't reassurance; it was rejection. And I'd say in retrospect that he felt over his head, and he was particularly anxious because I was a psychiatric resident."

Each therapist is likely to have a particular array of countertransference responses (for example, anger, sarcasm, attempts at control, overprotectiveness) that are likely to be triggered when the right buttons are pushed, and even the best therapists may be unaware of countertransference while it is happening.

Looking back on events, Steve talked about the countertransference issues that surrounded his divorce. "No matter how 'amicable' the divorce, it triggers whatever feelings you have about being rejected and unloved," he said. "You feel an immense sense of loss, of grief, of abandonment, of failure, and of anger at the other person for doing this to you, . . . and it's all muddled with your other experiences in life, particularly those as a child. Given my mother's chronic depression, and my feeling that I was the least-loved child in my family anyway, I had to overcome enormous feelings of worthlessness and fury.

"And afterward I realized that throughout this time I was not only too impatient with patients' demands on me, but much less supportive to most of my women patients than I normally am, and much more inclined to look for ways in which they were at fault, like my mother. And part of my defensive reaction also involved a kind of hardness, a 'What the hell do you need anybody for anyway?' that left me very insensitive to people's needs for love. I really pushed patients toward independence that year in a way that often disregarded other issues." He stopped for a minute. "I was seeing one man who had three young kids, and rather than try to assess more clearly what was happening between him and his wife, and whether they could be reconciled, I encouraged him—I see that in retrospect—to leave the marriage." He spoke slowly and reflectively. "The issue with countertransference is precisely that it's out of consciousness. You learn to look for cues to its existence, particularly for anything unusual you do with a particular patient or at a particular time, any change in routine, or how you act, but it's all too easy not to look, particularly when your own life is in turmoil."

Laura, too, talked about how insidious countertransference could be. "Anytime you find yourself thinking about a patient more than you normally do, you have to ask yourself about it. As soon as they become special, worth more of your energy and commitment than someone else, it's either that they're really in serious trouble and you'd better figure out what's gone sour in the treatment, or it's countertransference."

Laura then told me a story that illustrated not so much countertransference as what seemed more like an enormous need to feel powerful, in control, and even invulnerable, what has been described previously as the omnipotence fantasy. She said, "A patient walked into my office, sat down, and said, 'You're working too hard.' Without even thinking, I said, 'No, I'm not. Why do you think so?' And he said it was something about my bodily posture when I stepped into the waiting room to greet him. Then at the end of the hour I told him I'd already given him his bill, he denied it, and I suddenly realized I hadn't. I'd only billed the patient before him. So I told him he was right, I *was* working too hard."

When Laura told me this story, I burst out laughing, because she was still leaving out the most relevant fact. She saw this patient just before she went on vacation, and she had already told me that she was so tired she wasn't sure she could make it through her last day of work. Yet she couldn't admit her fatigue when he called her on it. She could only use an error of billing as a signal after the fact that he was right. Here the patient responded to an aspect of their real relationship, only to be met by her denial of vulnerability.

In fact, I was shocked by the number of psychiatrists I spoke with who seemed unwilling to admit vulnerability or other unpleasant realities of their work. One man is known particularly for his ability to treat unusually difficult adolescents, yet he told me with a straight face that most of his patients weren't particularly "sick," that they had merely "made messes of their lives." I called him on it, and he ended up getting out his appointment book to show me. Then he was shocked: "manic," he read, for one patient, "schizophrenic" for another, "attempted suicide" for a third, and so on down the page.

Several psychiatrists, not just this man, swore that they saw few difficult patients, although they have reputations for working with people most therapists find untreatable; one told me she never tolerated abusiveness when the very voice of the patient coming into her office after our interview was so filled with contempt it made my skin crawl. Others said they'd limited their schedules, although I know they often saw patients back-to-back for hours, or before seven in the morning, or after dinner, or on weekends. But the most appalling denial has to do with the potential for violence.

"I know of only one psychiatrist who sees dangerous patients as a regular part of his practice," Steve said with disarming reasonableness, "and I've been told he keeps a gun under his chair. But anyone can get threatened occasionally. It's an inevitable aspect of the work. And no one hears a threat to themselves or their family with complete neutrality, particularly if the possibility of danger is real." He looked relaxed and sure of himself. "But patients seldom pose a serious threat in a personal way. I know that so-and-so is going to make me the target of his rage and hate at some stage of treatment, but I count on the affection that's developed between us, and on his knowing that hurting me will cost him his treatment. And because we have a relationship of trust, he's likely to tell me his dangerous impulses well before he acts on them. So that I have a genuine opportunity to resolve the issues peacefully, . . . and to protect myself if I need to."

"I'm much more troubled by threats to my family than to myself," another psychiatrist said wryly, "although I'm aware that some of that is a neurotic feeling of my own omnipotence and invulnerability, and some of it has to do with my training."

Then he added: "One of my friends had a patient tell him she was going to kill him so that the two of them could go to heaven together. He warned her to forget that idea and keep in mind that he'd never speak to her again if she killed him. And he wasn't too worried until she called to say she was leaving town to buy a revolver. At that point he called the police, but it took a week to trace her, and he moved his family to a motel to

wait it out. The cops eventually picked her up at the airport, with a revolver, and she was jailed prior to a commitment hearing." He explained
that a number of his friend's colleagues convinced him that he owed her a
final visit at the jail. "When they met, she pulled a knife from her bra and
stabbed him. And his colleagues still felt he was right to see her."

The story fascinated me. For however one analyzes this as masochism,
grandiosity, omnipotence fantasy, and—perhaps—terrible judgment in the
name of physicianly responsibility, it was not just one psychiatrist's error
but a communally agreed upon value within this psychiatrist's peer group.

Harold Searles, the brilliant psychotherapist of chronic schizophrenia,
wrote an essay that seems relevant, entitled "'The Dedicated Physician' in
the Field of Psychotherapy and Psychoanalysis." He says:

> Typically, to the extent that one feels bound by the traditional physician's
> role, one feels wholly responsible for the course of the patient's illness, and
> feels it impermissible to experience any feelings toward the patient except
> for kindly, attentive, long-suffering, and helpful dedication. The psychiatric
> resident, in particular, relatively fresh from the dedicated-physician atmos-
> phere of the medical school and general internship, is often genuinely un-
> aware of feeling any hatred or even anger toward the patient who is daily
> ignoring or intimidating or castigating him, and unaware of how his very
> dedication, above all, makes him the prey of the patient's sadism. It has
> been many years since a young schizophrenic man revealed to me how
> much sadistic pleasure he derived from seeing a succession of dedicated
> therapists battering their heads bloody against the wall of his indifference,
> and I have never forgotten that.[4]

Few patients are as obnoxious as those we encounter in some of Searles's
writing. (I always have to remember that Searles is legendary for his specialized treatment of intractable—and usually unmedicated—schizophrenic patients.) Still, the young (or not so young) therapist may have a
need to save the patient that overpowers all other concerns. Some of this
need is sanctified in the physicianly role, and some of the need has its roots
in the omnipotence fantasy. The need to save the patient is also one of the
most ubiquitous of countertransference phenomena, rooted in the psychiatrist's past. This rescue fantasy stems in large part from the therapist's own
unconscious drive to save someone close to her in her own childhood,
usually a parent and sometimes a sibling.

"There are a few patients you feel you have a special relationship with,"

Laura said, "patients you feel especially connected to and whom you feel you can help when even the most experienced therapists have failed over and over again." She frowned in concentration. "And the truth is that sometimes the patient evokes that response in you precisely because there *is* a match between them and someone very important in your past, so that you really do understand them in a special way. *And* because you also put out a superhuman effort, you sometimes work a miracle."

Almost everyone I interviewed had one patient, maybe two, almost always at the beginning of his or her career, who called forth the most extraordinary efforts, efforts no one could manage more than a few times over the course of professional life. In looking back, all of these psychiatrists said the motivating force was the rescue fantasy.

The effort they had put in is unimaginable to an outsider. When the treatment worked, it was also in part because these psychiatrists communicated an unshakable conviction that they could help. Their patients mobilized their own efforts, too, because they knew that this was probably their last chance: If they couldn't do it with that psychiatrist, they were really lost. On the other hand, no therapist can allow the rescue fantasy to propel her too many times without risking total burnout.

Laura continued. "On the whole, the feeling that you can do what no one else has been able to manage should be taken as a cue to reconsider, to realize that you're in the midst of countertransference, and that you can't trust what you feel. What it means is that this person reminds you of your mother, or your father, or whoever's craziness got you into this field in the first place, and emotionally you're back in the past trying to hold them up or put the pieces back together."

Steve said, "Beginners sometimes do so extraordinarily well when experienced therapists have failed... not only because they have a special connection with a particular patient, but because they're motivated to put out everything they have.... As you undergo your own analysis, you're likely to become suspicious of these cases and much less likely to act on the feeling." He shifted his weight in his chair. "In fact, you become completely drained if you respond to many patients so uncontrolledly.... And these are often disastrous treatments anyway. Because they're based on countertransference and not on a realistic assessment of the patient. To the extent you really do understand them, that's fine, but often you're wrong. You just think you do. And you're also putting an enormous burden on them to get well for your sake."

When I asked John about the rescue fantasy, I expected a disclaimer. Instead he agreed on its ubiquity. "Most psychiatrists I know have the impression that we come from families with considerable pathology, like mine," he said. "That we're drawn to the field by an unconscious wish to save the parent or sibling or whoever it was who was so important and in need of rescue." He looked tired. "Why else would I be willing to spend my working day listening to craziness?"

But Gary was the one who spoke most clearly about his personal experience. The pain was still evident in his voice. "I've never lost the response completely. It's one reason I treat such difficult patients, but Maureen called it forth full-blown. Partly because I hadn't been analyzed yet, so I didn't even know what was going on. I had no idea why I was so totally obsessed with her.

"I was my parents' only surviving child," Gary continued. "But my mother had a stillborn daughter a year before I was born. When I was in analysis, we explored my guilt about surviving my sister—at replacing her—and I discovered how much of my enormous commitment to patients came from my continued need to save her for my mother's sake. In the course of seeing Maureen I began dreaming about bringing my sister back to life, breathing her mouth-to-mouth, and offering her to my mother alive and well. And sometimes I dreamed the baby *was* Maureen. And that was the drive, my identification of Maureen with my sister, and my unconscious craving to finally make right what I'd never been able to do in my real life.

"By the time she taunted me about my mother's death, I'd resolved most of the rescue fantasy. But I didn't fully disentangle Maureen from the identification with my sister until that moment." He paused. "I'd never known that baby. I only wanted to save her so my mother wouldn't be depressed anymore. Once my mother died, what residual fantasy I still carried became even less powerful—it was simply too late. And when Maureen screeched that she was glad my mother was dead, it wasn't just her inhumanity to me that I resented; I finally saw Maureen as herself. The cord was cut. My sister was gone."

Countertransference can be a problem in any treatment that's going badly, even in the absence of the rescue fantasy. Gary said, "I still find that the most difficult patient for me is the one who isn't doing well. If they've been in treatment with me for a year, and nothing I've tried has done them significant good, I feel guilty even now, after twenty years in the profession. For a while I'm likely to redouble my efforts, but if I still feel I'm failing, this is the patient I'm likely to be late for, or whose appointment I'm likely to forget." He looked at me sharply. "Unless you've been in treatment yourself, you have no idea how wounding it is when a therapist doesn't show up to see you or books someone else into your time.

"And that's what I really have to watch out for: how I can turn on a patient who's disappointed me, not even just in screwing up a meeting but in really hating them, in catching myself thinking about deliberately not returning a phone call, in hearing myself make nasty jokes about them to colleagues, or even stopping treatment without thinking it through. I know, in retrospect, that I didn't stop with Maureen just because I no longer identified her with my sister. I was furious with her, and I acted on my fury by refusing to treat her anymore. In reality, I couldn't continue to see her. She'd really used up all my ability to work with her... but at that moment, I also couldn't stand the sight of her. It wasn't *dis*interest; it was hatred.

"Anytime you screw up an appointment, or overbill a patient, or find your attention wandering, you have to use that as a cue to examine what's happening. Particularly if the treatment isn't going well." Gary was quiet for a moment. "And if you can't disentangle yourself and see what to do differently, you have to ask for a consultation and see what the consultant recommends."

The beginner and the unanalyzed therapist are particularly vulnerable when treatment goes poorly—or with a patient who is particularly demanding or abusive. Feeling helpless, guilty, and unable to set appropriate limits, these therapists often come to hate the patient.[5]

Michael said, "The hardest thing to teach residents is to keep from being stepped on all the time. Not only that they don't have to rescue everyone no matter what, but also to set limits... to say, 'You don't call my house, and you can't sit here for an entire hour and insult me endlessly.'" He spread his hands. "It's not that patients can't say what pops into their heads, that's a necessity, but it can't stay at the level the patient often begins at [without destroying the treatment]....I see this as a sleight of hand. The patients will say something, and I'll say, 'Now, I don't agree with that at all,' and they'll look very interested and say, 'But I thought I was supposed to say whatever popped into my head.' And I say, 'You are, but I'm equally free to disagree totally with what you say. I didn't say you shouldn't say it, but on the other hand, this is our life here, and I'm giving you *my* thoughts.'"

Michael's voice was dry. "I'll tolerate an enormous amount of abuse from a patient, where I feel they're too ill to incorporate anything I say. But if a healthier patient says, 'You have the ugliest office. It sucks. You have no taste, no sense,' I answer, 'Let's take a look at it. You're not so deeply into aesthetics [that] it can keep you going a whole hour. It's obviously something else.'"

Gary said, "When I was starting out, I'd be much more thrown for a loop by patients insulting me, but now I'm fairly disentangled from this kind of thing. The issue is that they're doing to me what they always do. My job is to reframe it so that we can get at the real underlying feelings. Not to take it personally." He paused, looking at one of his photographs on the wall, dunes and a winding trail through high grass. "On the other hand... when the patient who's doing well goes on and on about how they're not making any progress, I feel quite able to cut in: 'Wait a minute, last month you got a new job. You're going out with a woman now. What the hell do you mean you're not better?' Because I owe it to myself—and my patient—not to walk out of here at the end of the day wanting to slit my throat. If the work gets too burdensome, and I really feel like shit, it's going to reflect in poor treatment. Better I call the patient on it immediately, with full awareness of what I'm doing."

He swiveled his chair and put his feet on the desk, speaking more slowly now. "Sometimes when I call in a consultant, they'll tell me that I'm screwing up the treatment, that I've missed something important. And for me, that usually means I've allowed the patient to abuse me: I'm not setting limits on telephone calls or on how much they insult me, or on the fact that they don't pay their bills unless I beg them. And that in doing this, I've gotten hooked in, and I'm engaged in some behavior that matches something in their own past, rather than standing back and interpreting it to them dispassionately.

"I treat a young woman who never pays me on time," he went on. "Although she comes from a very rich family, I have to nag her for each payment, and she is always late by several weeks or a month. Of course she *is* a very difficult patient. She's insulting and contemptuous and very demanding, with a lot of emotional storms and phone calls. But I realize periodically that I fall into a countertransference bind with her again and again. Yes, she's difficult, but it's my choice to treat her. I could tell her I won't work with her if she doesn't pay on time. The real issue is that I'm willing to put up with her abuse to the point of getting furious at her. Once I disentangle her behavior from my own willingness to be victimized, I can point out the contempt behind her stringing me along, and connect it to the way she treats men in general. Even my fury is relevant because this is a woman who—before her treatment with me—would pick men up in bars and get beaten up."

The more sophisticated the therapist, the more likely she is to catch countertransference reactions and the less likely they are to interfere with the treatment. If she feels that her reaction needs a comment (as part of the "real relationship") but is essentially irrelevant to the patient's own problems, she can simply say that she was tired or distracted or just made a mistake. But sometimes deciphering her response may be critical to understanding the patient.

Laura gave an example. "I've been seeing someone for five years, three times a week. The second session after my vacation she was silent, and finally when I got it out of her, she said I'd ended the prior session a few minutes early. I was really angry, because I've put in years of work with her, and also because for a moment I felt the way I used to when my mother would accuse me of rushing out the door to get away from her. And I don't even think I let her go early; we compared watches and hers was a few minutes slow. But I was able to use how I felt, and tell her how she focused on these few minutes, one hundred and twenty seconds, rather than the five years of our work together. And we also talked about her other feelings, of my not being there, like her parents, because of my vacation. And so although she came in not seeing me at all, within twenty minutes the whole transference was right there, out on the table for us to look at." She smiled. "It ended up as one of the most rewarding sessions we've had, and it wouldn't have happened if I hadn't been aware of how angry I became, and able then to relate it to what she was doing to me."

In talking about countertransference, Steve returned to his experience with Carole, the mute teenager he saw at the beginning of his training. "I got to the point where I'd anticipate that glassy look of hers when I'd wake up in the morning. My heart would pound walking into her room, and I'd feel queasy, and I used to think about whether she'd answer me if I hit her over the head with a hammer. I'd say the stupidest things, trying to encourage her, things like, 'I guess you find it hard to talk to me'—really stupid statements. And sometimes I'd talk about the weather, or a book I'd read, until I ran down, and once I yelled I was going to read the newspaper if she wasn't going to talk to me.

"Searles writes that our humanity is validated by the people around us. If it's not validated, we experience ourselves as things. And sitting with Carole, I shared her experience of being a thing. And then I had that dream, in which I was a piece of furniture, a table, and my supervisor put his feet on me and said, 'At least he's good for something.' And I finally brought it all into supervision and understood that my feelings toward her had meaning for the therapy. That's what they meant by 'using the countertransference.' And I stopped being so angry at her. In fact, I came into our meeting—I remember it was a rainy March day—and I told her my dream, and she looked up at me, and she *spoke*. And she said very sympathetically, 'It feels awful, doesn't it?'"

Essential clues to the important themes of treatment, countertransference reactions are often intertangled, hard to unravel, and largely out of consciousness. It is particularly frightening to beginners to have feelings toward patients that are so strong, so unphysicianly, and so irrational. These feelings are the most disturbing a therapist experiences. It takes a while to learn that even the most lunatic responses may be valuable countertransference cues for treatment.

As Gary added, "The worst is sitting with a patient and feeling that you're going to suffocate if they don't stop talking, or finding yourself thinking about murdering them, or starting to yawn uncontrollably, or getting a hard-on. Those are messages from your unconscious, direct responses to the patient, cues you need to respect and use. But those kinds of reactions can really make you feel you're losing your mind.

"When I worked with Maureen," he went on, "I'd sometimes get very embarrassing erections and find myself thinking about what she'd be like in bed. That still happens to me sometimes with very ill people, but it took me years to realize it was a cue to me that I was denying how ill my patient was, and in particular that I was feeling hopeless about her at that moment. I finally learned that my response means the patient has gotten worse and I'm trying not to know it. I still don't feel entirely comfortable with it, but I accept it as part of the way my mind works."

LAYER

4

THE HEALING BOND
AND BRAIN CHEMISTRY

14

Medicines

Freudian thinking overtook American psychiatry because it looked useful. When effective medications were discovered in the 1950s for schizophrenia (and for other disorders creating psychosis) and for depression, and in the 1960s for manic-depressive disorder, medicines became the first line of treatment, at least for hospitalized patients. Since then, many more medications have been found and proven effective not only for the most disabling mental illnesses but also for less serious depressions, anxiety, and other problems usually treated in an outpatient setting (for example, panic attacks and obsessive-compulsive disorder).

From our vantage point now, it is hard to remember how miraculous the first medicines were—or what discouraging places mental hospitals had been before the advent of these wonder drugs. During the years between 1930 and the 1950s, there were really only three choices for very sick patients, and none of them were terrific: electroconvulsive shock therapy (ECT), insulin coma therapy, and brain surgery.

In ECT the patient was strapped down (for her own safety) and sent into a kind of epileptic seizure by passing electric current through her brain. The treatment itself looked barbaric. Moreover, it made patients amnesic for the days or weeks surrounding treatment and could cause disorientation, speech hesitation, and other symptoms of organic brain syndrome (such as drooling) for some time afterward, particularly if shocks were given over several weeks—which was common practice. Although ECT is more effective than medication for some conditions even today, and is now done in a way that results in few side effects (and apparently no permanent ones),[1] it went out of favor in the 1970s. In Berkeley, California, it was even outlawed.[2]

"It's very difficult to get patients, or their families, to consent to ECT anymore," Gary said, "and the myth has arisen that we don't need it anyway. It can be tragic because the reality is that most medicines need weeks to take effect; meanwhile everyone chews their nails and hopes the patient doesn't make it out the nearest window in the meantime. ECT works faster and for more people, particularly in the most severe depressions, and the way it's done now it has few side effects."

Before the discovery of antidepressants, ECT was the first avenue of treatment. The second choice, injections of insulin to produce a prolonged coma, was less effective, harder to control, and more dangerous. It was far too easy to cause permanent brain damage or even kill the patient, particularly in an overcrowded state hospital with few staff. And some researchers maintained that patients weren't really cured anyway, that insulin coma merely sedated people by destroying brain tissue through oxygen starvation.[3] The need for other treatments was so acute that surgeons in the 1940s and 1950s experimented with cutting out parts of the brain (lobectomy), or with slicing the connections between different areas (lobotomy or leucotomy). Thousands of people accepted such surgery in a last-ditch effort to make their lives bearable. Many had been chronically hospitalized, and most suffered such intolerable anxiety that they were willing to risk brain damage to be rid of it.[4]

Then came the medications: Thorazine, imipramine, lithium and their modern successors, Prozac, Tegretol, Clozaril (known generically as clozapine, it is an apparently miraculous medication for some people with schizophrenia), risperidone and others.[5] Between 1955 and 1992, the number of patients in state mental hospitals fell from 559,000 to 103,000—even though the U.S. population increased by eighty-five million during that time.[6]

As social policy, the reduction of the state hospital census was both unrealistic and insanely optimistic, because it ignored the fact that there were far too few outpatient programs in the community that could provide the continuing care most people with chronic mental illness needed. There was also little attention paid to the scarcity of affordable and safe housing for people who were generally impoverished by their illness. In the absence of inexpensive apartments, and without counseling, day-treatment programs, sheltered workshops, or any kind of therapy milieu, too many mentally ill people ended up living alone in filthy, dangerous, single-room-only hotels or wandering the sidewalks of major cities, to die eventually of exposure, disease, and malnutrition.[7] The best estimates are that at least twenty percent of homeless people have been in mental hospitals at some time,[8] while more than thirty percent have untreated schizophrenia, manic-depressive disorder or serious depression.[9]

On the other hand, medications themselves have been phenomenally successful, not only in the treatment of the most disabling illnesses, but revolutionizing the treatment of most psychiatric disorders, including anxiety and less serious depressions. They have become part of the everyday arsenal of psychotherapy. As Laura said, "The state of the art is changing so rapidly that it's impossible to tell where we'll be a few years from now."

Gary said, "The college kid, for example, who's always been a high achiever, with friends and a normal social life, the kind of kid everyone wants, who in the middle of his first year has to come home because he suddenly can't go on—he can't concentrate, he can't sleep, he cries all the time, he's failing half his classes; or maybe he's in his last year when he comes unglued, with the trigger his having to decide what he's going to do after graduation—five or ten years ago, he might have seen a therapist at the college who would *maybe* carry him through, or he'd have come home and lived in his old room—lying in bed, watching TV, and eating chocolate while seeing someone for psychotherapy two or three times a week.

And if he was lucky, after a year or two, his depression would lift and he'd come out of his room and begin to see a few friends again, and maybe even go out on dates, and maybe, just possibly, he'd go back to school—with all the sequelae of feeling he'd gone crazy and lost two years of his life. And if he'd had really good psychotherapy, he'd know a lot about himself and his psychological vulnerabilities that he didn't know before, including the kinds of stresses he was best off minimizing, and the signs in himself of oncoming depression. And he might have some better methods of coping with his mood swings and the different ways he reacted to the environment and other people as he became depressed. But he'd still be at risk for another depression like the first—and most people have at least one recurrence.

"And if he wasn't lucky, his depression might not lift after a year, or it might turn into a less intense but chronic state, and he could spend the rest of his life living with his parents, maybe getting a job way below the level of his original competencies."

Gary leaned back in his armchair, hands clasped behind his head. After a short silence, he said, "I began to treat a woman last year who'd gone to Brown on full scholarship, dropped out in her second year, and spent the next ten years back with her parents. As far as I could tell, they decided to bring her to me after her father had a coronary—I gather it finally occurred to them that she wasn't going to get better on her own—and they didn't know what would happen to her if they couldn't care for her." Gary's voice was sad. "If she'd had a course of antidepressants—or shock treatment—way back at the start, she could have been back in school in a few months and lived out the life everyone expected for her. Now her life is gone. She's thirty-four years old and too demoralized for anything but a day-treatment program right now, with no job skills, no dating skills appropriate to her age, ten years lost that she has to make up some cover story for, all her former friends married and career-building, with children of their own. And she's in mourning for her life and the opportunities lost, and at the same time she's enraged at what everyone else has, and angry and self-pitying. Here she is, smarter than most of the human race, as she says, and she's nowhere. So she tells everyone how much smarter she is than they are, until she falls apart because she has to go for a job interview as a bank teller, and every few days I have to make peace with the day-treatment program she goes to because she's so obnoxious to the other patients and to the staff. And none of it need have happened. With correct treatment she could have been over the original episode in three months."

In one popular myth, psychiatrists treat bored housewives. In their Park Avenue or Beverly Hills offices, they listen to the trivial complaints of affluent, spoiled women. Their patients don't really need them, but have an hour between tennis and the cocktail hour with nothing else to do, and going to a shrink has an odd kind of status at ladies' luncheons. Occasionally, a movie star replaces the bored housewife in the scenario, and sometimes an intellectual of some sort, indulging his ego with a fifty-minute hour in which he always plays the central role. But treatment remains a game of the leisured class, a modern example of potlatching.

In the other popular myth, the psychiatrist treats only crazy patients, disheveled and dilapidated people anyone could spot shambling down the street, people you'd never hire for a job or invite home for dinner. This used to be the dominant view of the psychiatric patient, and to many of us even now therapy carries enough of a stigma that treatment is something confessed only to close family (maybe) or a best friend—and certainly no one talks lightly about being hospitalized.

In the 1960s American society's flirtation with social activism became melded with psychiatry's newfound effectiveness to create a third myth in which psychiatry was envisioned as offering a cure for any kind of problem. Psychiatrists themselves were touting therapy as the royal road to universal self-fulfillment, marital bliss, and social justice, extending psychiatry well beyond its legitimate domain as they moved beyond the hospital and office to storefront clinics in Harlem and in Haight-Ashbury, to business corporations and remedial reading programs, and offered their services with equal aplomb to addicts and anxious suburban housewives. While many psychoanalysts remained immovable behind their couches, general psychiatry opened its arms with equal abandon to biofeedback, behavioral conditioning, EST, political activism, and Thorazine.

But after Vietnam and Watergate, psychiatry, like the rest of American society, retreated from massive social commitments and enthusiastic experiments in social policy. Unable to back up the promises of the 1960s, psychiatry was also becoming overwhelmed by trying to be everything to everyone, and beginning to recognize the impossibility of the attempt.[10] In the late 1970s, the basic role of the psychiatrist once again was defined in terms of the one-on-one relationship with a patient. But there was enormous disagreement throughout the 1970s over whether the therapist's role was essentially that of empathic psychotherapist or medicating physician.

Despite the widespread use of medication, many analytically oriented psychiatrists felt no need to modify their psychological explanations of mental disorders. The medical model of an underlying organic disease state was anathema to them, and they argued that medicines merely suppressed the symptoms of the basic psychological conflict while closing off the significant unconscious material that was the stuff of psychotherapy. Medication was a cop-out, they argued, a means for therapist and patient to avoid the real work of change, and even when these psychiatrists prescribed medication, they were likely to prescribe amounts too small to do more than quiet the most flagrant eruptions. On the opposite side were the psychopharmacologists, who argued that popping a pill was all that mattered if the patient felt better, and, furthermore, that the miraculous changes medication brought about in patients proved the irrelevance of complex psychoanalytic theories. In fact, for most of the late 1970s many psychiatry training programs were so enamored of psychopharmacology that they fell back into the reductionist view (oddly reminiscent of Freud's "Project") that all mental illness could be reduced to physical disturbances of the brain: Fix the abnormality and you need never speak to the patient.

"In the 1960s, when I was in training, inpatient care was still defined in terms of doing long-term individual psychotherapy," Gary said. "We used Thorazine for schizophrenia, and we were just beginning to try lithium for mania, and we had antidepressants like Tofranil, but they were seen as adjunctive to the basic issues of attaining psychological growth with talk treatment. Then we went through a period of tremendous doubt, where some psychiatrists argued that all you needed was the medicine, that psychotherapy didn't do much... if anything. And then came the many studies showing that you need both for maximum effectiveness. Meanwhile some training programs had fired half their faculty and replaced them with people mainly interested in psychopharmacology, and some programs still haven't caught on. They've so de-emphasized therapy that they graduate people who have really no idea of how to function as a psychiatrist. Some of these graduates come to me for private supervision on patients they're seeing in their own office. And they're furious at how inadequate their training was, because as soon as they have somebody who's not flagrantly psychotic, they're lost. They're like first-year residents."

But by the 1980s each side was coming to accept the other's importance, and now a new consensus is appearing: that many (and we don't know how many) mental problems are the outcome of an interaction between a biological vulnerability and environmental events, because the brain and the psyche are inextricably interwoven.

"In the 1970s," Gary said, "psychiatry became enmeshed in stupid arguments that couldn't be resolved because the questions were wrong. On one side, for example, you had researchers looking for essentially physical explanations of psychoses, searching for abnormalities of metabolism, say, or examining family histories and collecting cases of identical twins for evidence of the role of heredity. And then on the other side you had people who insisted that all the mental disorders, including psychoses, were essentially psychological. And even when a kind of compromise was reached, in which both kinds of factors were admitted, it was in terms of saying, 'Okay, it's twenty percent heredity and eighty percent environment, or eighty percent heredity and twenty percent environment.'

"But it doesn't work that way, because the genetics only provide a matrix of potentiality, a range of possibilities, just as the actual height you grow to, or weight you reach, depends on your environment—on nutrition, on exercise, on whether you get sick a lot, on the amount of stress in early life. Nothing develops in isolation, outside an environmental context, and that includes psychological phenomena. It's not heredity versus environment, or mind versus body. It's that nothing is expressed except as the dual outcome of both. That's the only game in town."

"I don't believe you can become really ill without a genetic contribution," Laura said. "No more than you can get diabetes. I see too many patients with all the environmental factors that should lead to disabling illness who have all sorts of problems, but not schizophrenia or major depressive disorder or mania. You have to have a very special quality to develop these disorders. Otherwise everyone who suffers a terrible life event would."

Michael said, "I saw a man for the first time last week whose wife left him for another man five years ago. His company's moved him twice since then, and he sees his kids only on vacations, and he feels his life is empty. He works hard, seven-day weeks, and when I asked what he did for pleasure, he looked vague and finally said he used to play baseball with his sons. He drinks two martinis with lunch and three shots with dinner, watches TV until two or three A.M., and takes barbiturates to sleep. He just got another promotion, and he's afraid that this time he's going to be fired, because he's felt out of his depth for the last year and doesn't know why no one else notices. He's sure that no one he works with cares if he lives or dies, and lately he finds himself waking at five in the morning dreaming of the coffin closing over his body. He hasn't dated more than a few times since his wife left, and not at all in the last two years. And when I asked him how he felt about his sons growing up without him, he started to cry.

"This man is chronically depressed," Michael continued, "with depressed mood, insomnia, feelings of inadequacy, social withdrawal, loss of pleasure. . . . I could read the diagnostic criteria right out of the handbook. Of course, there was a psychological trigger. He lost his home, his children, the friends and life they'd built together. And he was profoundly shamed by his wife's leaving with another man. But people normally recover from bereavement. They pick up the pieces of their lives and they rebuild. It takes a year, two years, and some of the scars never heal, but people do it. This is five years later, and the man is worse. He has a depressive illness, in which the depressive feelings are the psychological manifestation of some underlying biological disequilibrium that prevents him from taking the normal reconstitutive steps that other people with different constitutions can manage. With an antidepressant I expect to see his insomnia disappear, and then a return of his sexual interest, and an increase in general energy, and some move toward social contacts, pleasure, and a whole range of changes that seem to be mediated in some way by circuits in the brain.

"And he's also going to need psychotherapy to understand why his wife's leaving him was such an extraordinary humiliation for him, and because he needs to know how the hell it could have taken him by such surprise, because we need to know why she left him at all, and how he relates to women in general.

"This man is a rather rigid perfectionist who's never had a close adult male friend. And in some ways his ability to keep his depression so well hidden is an indication of ego strength." Looking suddenly grim, Michael raised his voice for emphasis. "But he's just the sort of person who could easily seek therapy with someone, M.D. or not, who'd use no drugs and try instead to analyze his obsessional defenses for the next five years. And until recently he's had the kind of chronic, relatively low-level depression that is endemic in our culture and all too often still seen as 'just the way Uncle Joe or Aunt Sadie is.' And it's tragic. These are illnesses, and they're treatable."

Michael glared at me. "If you're going to interview me, I have one condition I insist on: You must include what I'm going to say now, that medical care in this country is fairly lousy, but it's adequate. If I need to send a friend to an internist, I can find someone decent almost anywhere. But psychiatric care is abysmal. There's hardly anyone around I really trust to do right by a patient. And the list of sophisticated nonmedical therapists is even shorter. Patients with treatable illnesses are misdiagnosed and mistreated all the time, because too few people understand both drugs and psychotherapy—and there's simply no excuse for it."

Rosemary said, "It's not only the most disabling illnesses that are at issue. I have no qualms medicating any of my patients, even if they're in a formal analysis with me, if that's what they need in order to concentrate, and listen, and participate in the therapeutic process. I'd only be wasting my time and theirs if they're too agitated to concentrate, or too depressed to talk, if their thoughts are too scattered, if we can't work together for whatever reason of that kind, whatever their formal diagnosis might be.

"But I can't understand how anyone can imagine that drugs alone could do the trick. Drugs can take you out of mania, or deep despair and depression. Drugs can make your thought disorder come together so that you're able to be lucid. But how are they supposed to help you in the tremendous range of interpersonal relationships, with the judgments used in your daily life?"

John said, "About two-thirds of my patients have mood disorders, generally depression, sometimes depression with mania. And I medicate them all. There's always a psychological trigger, too. I can always find something in their lives that set the depression off if we really dig for it, but I see depression itself as the psychological manifestation of an underlying biological imbalance, and I medicate because my job is to help, to alleviate suffering—and it improves the therapy.

"Even in the seventies, when I was in training, some psychiatrists argued that you cut the motivation for psychotherapy if you medicated," John added, "or that you blanketed the relevant emotional material. But that's backward. First of all, you have a patient who's grateful because after a few weeks (or less) they're back to living. They're sleeping, they have some energy, they don't feel hopeless, they're interested in sex again, they're not wringing their hands and telling everyone the sky is falling. You've cemented the therapeutic alliance by really helping them, and they're much more willing to trust you and work at psychotherapy with you."

I asked Laura if she always assumed a psychological trigger. She said,

"You mean, do I ever see a patient whose life just falls apart around his ankles without there being any dynamic issue? Never." Then she added, "Of course, it sometimes takes a lot of probing on my part. You have to go back and really understand what happened at the time, not just take a history and think you know what it means but probe for what *exactly* was going on then and there, listening to the associations and being able to pick up on what seems odd or out of place, and then asking about it, because that's often a way into finding out what was really the problem."

And finally, one psychiatrist said, "It's like asthma. A child gets asthmatic because Mommie yelled at him, but the child couldn't get asthmatic if he had normal lung function. So you prescribe a drug to open the alveoli in his lungs, and you talk with him about what he feels when Mommie yells."

✍

Gary summed up his views of the interdependence of mind and body in the clearest explication I've ever seen of the subject: "Anyone who's raised kids knows you see different temperaments from the very beginning. Even if you're the same parent, you'd have a different relationship with each child because each one is different from the moment of birth, and you act differently in reply, and the whole gestalt changes. Apart from the fact that what really matters is not so much objective experience as the child's perception of his experience as it's altered by his temperament and intelligence and sensitivity. So that there's never a pure psychological universe. There are psychological possibilities that are sifted through the sieve of our constitutional readiness to react and perceive in certain ways."

He made a steeple of his fingers and looked through them. "I feel that most of my patients carry a constitutional vulnerability, a tendency to react to certain life events with an alteration of cell biology that disrupts normal brain function. Sometimes the environmental trigger is evident, sometimes it's not, but however it happens, the complex feedback loops that govern brain biochemistry get messed up, and the resulting disequilibrium manifests as panic, anxiety, depression, mania, thought disorder, obsessive-compulsive disorder...or some other set of symptoms. Our medicines have nothing to do with symptom suppression, but with correcting an underlying physical disequilibrium that's essential to regulating emotional response or thought...." He paused for several seconds.

"Constitution is really a shorthand way of talking about inborn cellular function at the molecular level, when we don't know the details, but the way I've come to think of it, our medicines alter the original molecular biases, and the result is that you're less prone to get terror stricken or manic or depressed or disorganized in response to the same psychological stress."

He watched me carefully to see if I was still following. "Too many therapists accept the psychoanalytic premise that we could always explain our feelings if we had enough data about their psychological meaning, and particularly by going back to childhood events—with no reference to biology. But it looks as though mental disorders fall on a continuum—the biological predisposition very strong in some of us, less strong in others, and sometimes minimal or maybe nonexistent. So some patients need medication periodically—even after they've explored the psychological meaning of the stressor in effective psychotherapy, because their biological vulnerability is just too powerful. They remain at risk because we have no way at present of permanently altering the biochemistry.

"And if the psychoanalytic observer chooses to call even the continuing correction of a basic neurochemical imbalance merely the suppression of symptoms, I not only disagree," and Gary suddenly grinned, "but I can argue that he's got it backward. He's the one who makes use of symptom suppression.

"In the original creation of the self," he went on mischievously, "the parent as perceived by the child is incorporated into the basic blueprint, bits of Mommy and Daddy taken in whole as primal ingredients. But in therapy you already have a self, however flawed it may feel, however much is missing or peculiar. And you can't easily integrate what you discover in therapy, in part because you already have this personality structure whose integrity you're going to defend from change. Long before you actually make the therapeutic insights truly part of you, long before they become integrated into the existent personality, the best anyone can do is a kind of role-playing, trying to imagine their therapist standing in their shoes: 'What would Dr. X do if he were here?' 'What would Dr. Y say?'

"Every therapist in town has patients who talk about carrying their analyst in their pocket, pulling him out when they need to feel or think the way he's told them they ought to. But I could argue that what they've really done is use the therapist as a new parent who 'suppresses' the natural response and allows the patient to temporarily make use of his viewpoint. Because it takes a long time before your sense of what your therapist would say or do is in any way experienced as part of your real self."

He leaned back in his chair, relaxing as he reached the conclusion of his argument. "As I see it, there's tremendous power in going back over events and reevaluating what really happened, what your own contribution was to a relationship or an interaction, and what happened in childhood, assessing the past differently as you reexperience it through adult eyes, borrowing the therapist's ego to look again at how you and others behaved. But there's only so much power to the process if you're trying to do this kind of work while buffeted by the same constitutional disequilibria that messed you up in the first place. If you're just as prone to panic or just as sensitive to rejection, or if talking about how you felt after your grandfather's death when you were three gets you as depressed now as it did then.

"Some of the great artists in the field are so extraordinary that they can somehow get through the most incredible distortions on the patient's part and help them achieve profound change no matter how intense the emotions. But for most of us I see medicines as modulators, something to use with any patient who's being torn by overwhelming emotions or a major thought disorder. Because it's almost impossible to reorganize your perceptions and beliefs in a really effective way, no matter what your insights, if at the same time you're at the mercy of overpowering feelings. That's how you get people into interminable treatment, patients who can recite chapter and verse on how they came to develop as they did, and who even know just what triggers the binge eating, or the repeated work failure, or why they can't sustain an intimate relationship . . . people who know all the explanations but still act the same."

15

Remedicalization and the Healing Bond

As adopted by psychotherapists in the United States, Freudian theory was purely psychological, a description of unconscious processes that operate beneath the surface of awareness, unknown to our conscious selves and forcefully denied. In these terms, a patient's failure to improve meant that more data were still buried in the unconscious, with the relevant material yet to be discovered or worked through. The first treatments were short, a year or less in general, but soon they grew to two or three or five years, or more, as psychoanalysts discovered deeper layers and went from curing specific symptoms to aiming at more global change in character.

Even in 1905, Freud was far from promising a cure-all for the human condition, writing:

> One should look beyond the patient's illness and form an estimate of his whole personality; those patients who do not possess a reasonable degree of education and a fairly reliable character should be refused. It must not be forgotten that there are healthy people as well as unhealthy ones who are good for nothing in life, and that there is a temptation to ascribe to their illness everything that incapacitates them if they show any sign of neurosis.[1]

And again, in 1912: "As a doctor, one must above all be tolerant of the weakness of a patient, and must be content if one has won back some degree of capacity for work and enjoyment.[2]

As he grew older, Freud became even more doubtful of the power of psychoanalysis to induce change. Ultimately, he valued it less as therapy and more as a research instrument for exploring the otherwise unfathomable human psyche. Some of his pessimism grew out of the pragmatic experiences of the growing psychoanalytic movement, but the devastation of

World War I was even more influential, leading him to hypothesize that the human mind contained innate, unchangeable, and overpowering destructive instincts. Indeed, he came to believe that a death instinct was buried in a species unconscious that went far deeper than any individual psyche.[3]

Freud's studies had been fueled initially by the driving need to relieve the suffering of patients. As the difficulty of reaching this goal became clearer, the aims of treatment began to shift for many psychotherapists who followed in Freud's footsteps. Expectations of change sometimes seemed to take second place to the process of endlessly probing the depths, and cure receded toward never-never land. However much pain the patient was in, the psychotherapist in this schema was essentially a guide on the path toward self-understanding. The goal of treatment became insight, illumination of the walled-off components of the self so that the person could finally grow up into a richer and multifaceted adult. But insight, which was originally sought as a means of provoking real-life change in otherwise incurable patients, too often became an end in itself. To many psychiatrists until recently, changes evoked in the absence of greater self-awareness were trivial, and self-discovery the only reality that counted.

"The whole thrust of the psychoanalytic movement was to find the secret psychological explanation," John said, "and therapists working in that tradition just turned their backs on medicine. They might have worried about missing a brain tumor, but that was the least of it. The whole complex interaction of brain and body got lost, the realization that our mental activity takes place in a physical context."

The discovery of Thorazine marks a defining moment in psychiatry's therapeutic approach, a divide that separates before and after. Now, once again, psychiatrists may think of themselves as doctors, pragmatically using whatever treatment seems to help, and insight is only one of several tools they use to help the patient toward recovery. Many of the hot issues in psychiatry in the last decade of this century involve the ramifications of this return to the doctorly role; the code word is "remedicalization." I have the impression that some of the rhetoric on the subject is polemical, an effort to stake a claim against psychologists (and to a lesser extent, psychiatric social workers). At the same time, I am impressed by both the passion and the logic with which the psychiatrists I interviewed claimed their role as physicians.

"When we first spoke," John said, "I said I saw myself as a doctor first, a psychiatrist second, and an analyst third. I've been thinking about what I really mean by that, and it seems to me that, first, I want my patients to suffer less, and that I'll use whatever means I can for that purpose—whether it's medication, or biofeedback, or an assertiveness training program, or making a contract that they start an exercise regimen or spend two hours a day doing something that gets them out of their apartment. And the second way in which I see myself as a doctor is that I do a medical screening all the time, not only at the first meeting.

"One man in analysis with me complained the other day about headaches and dizziness. Five years ago he had surgery for lung cancer. Metastases often go to the brain, and rather than assume he was showing symptoms of stress, I told him he needed a medical work-up, and spoke to his internist about taking a CAT scan."

John slowed for emphasis, his voice clear and earnest. "God knows that too many psychiatrists forget their training in physical disease. But there are even more nonmedical therapists who've never been trained at all. You have to remember that any psychological symptom can be the mark of organic disease. You can see euphoria with multiple sclerosis before any striking physical signs. You get profound changes in behavior with brain tumors. You get paranoid states with adrenal gland tumors, with lupus. . . . I could go on forever. Most psychiatrists lose their medical edge, but at least they've the training to hear that something doesn't sound right. Even if they don't do a physical exam themselves—and most don't—they should know to send the patient for a work-up."

Remedicalization also involves radical changes in diagnosis and a restructuring of the very categories and meaning of mental illness. The new approach is central to modern psychotherapeutic treatment and has been applied to every kind of emotional symptom from anxiety, depression, or phobia to psychosis. Just the first wave of revisionism post-Thorazine was relevant to everyone who might once have been diagnosed as schizophrenic—perhaps 3 percent of Americans.

Until the 1970s, diagnoses were often not made at all in the practice of psychiatry. When they were, the process was often intuitive, based on a general impression. In the treatment of psychoses, for example, people who hallucinated or were delusional were automatically labeled schizophrenic without regard to any more specific symptoms,[4] unless they showed clear signs of organic brain damage. But during the 1960s, it became apparent that hallucinations and delusions did not necessarily by themselves herald schizophrenia or anything more than a general state of psychosis, for Thorazine worked equally well for alcoholics hallucinating in delirium, people who'd become delusionally paranoid on amphetamines, LSD-users who thought the walls were swallowing them, or almost anyone else in a psychotic break from reality.

For decades, psychiatrists in other countries had said Americans used schizophrenia as a wastebasket classification for psychotic symptoms, and that many patients diagnosed as schizophrenics actually suffered from some kind of mood disorder.[5] Labeled schizophrenic, these patients might respond to Thorazine, Haldol, or another antipsychotic, but they didn't recover fully because they were being treated for the wrong illness and their real problem was manic-depressive (now called bipolar) disorder, or maybe even a delusional depression.

As a result, many patients went in and out of the hospital as if through a revolving door. In some studies—hard as this is to believe—people who had spent as much as twenty years in and out of mental institutions being inappropriately medicated for schizophrenia could leave the hospital and begin to resume their lives once they were appropriately diagnosed as manic-depressive and put on lithium—or later on other medications such as Tegretol or valproic acid.[6] *The tragedy is that decades after this work, some people are still misdiagnosed, and their lives are ruined.* In a recent survey by the National Depressive and Manic-Depressive Association, for example, almost three-fourths of the respondents had been originally misdiagnosed, over one-third had waited more than a decade for a correct diagnosis, and, on average, it took eight years for a correct diagnosis to be made.[7] It may also be that misdiagnosis is most common when the patient is black.[8] Every psychiatrist I spoke with had patients to whom this had happened—and everyone said it was still going on. It's only our ignorance that allows such untenable malpractice to continue.

Gary said, "If you go back and read many of the descriptions of schizophrenics treated by some very famous psychoanalysts, you'd diagnose them now as having delusional depressions or mania." He paused, "In fact, a very well known analyst referred several of his patients to me shortly before he died, and I diagnosed several as actually suffering from a mood disorder, not schizophrenia." He shifted heavily in his chair. "I had a hell of a time convincing them to change medications. He had a fine reputation, and they'd spent ten, fifteen, or twenty years working with him. How could they admit he was wrong?" He shrugged. "Two left in a fury and wouldn't speak to me when I called for a follow-up, but those that remained have never felt better in their lives. Of course, it hurts when they think how much time they lost, and I've told them that no one would have made the differentiation when he began working with them. That's the truth, but he never changed the diagnosis, and he should have."

Another psychiatrist, who is known for his pharmacological expertise, said, "It's better. The diagnosis of schizophrenia is made much more sparingly nowadays. But I still... find it very scary. I must have one of the most active practices in the city, so I see an awful lot. And I can't say how many patients I see carrying a diagnosis of schizophrenia, often hospitalized in some good places, who turn out to really have some kind of mood disorder—obviously not classical affective illness, but in that range. Or others who are brain-damaged, and I mean solidly brain-damaged, who are called schizophrenic.

"What's even scarier," he added, "is that many manic patients don't respond to lithium and then get labeled schizophrenic. Yet the state of the art has advanced way beyond lithium—Tegretol, valproic acid, calcium channel blockers, clozapine (Clozaril), even ECT. I've had some terribly refractive patients whom lithium didn't touch, who did well with these. Schizophrenia exists," he concluded, "but I think it will turn out to be an uncommon and real brain disorder, a real neurological illness."

While I was writing this book, a friend told me that her son, a wonderful young man in his first year of college, had been sent home after a psychotic break. As she described his efforts to rouse his dorm to fight off an invasion of Nazis, even I (without formal training) identified this as an episode of mania. Yet the initial referring physician was not so sure. He told the boy's parents that he might be schizophrenic because he responded to antipsychotic medication, and that he was doubtful about the boy's chances of ever returning to college. After a consultation with another psychiatrist, the boy was put on maintenance lithium for a manic-depressive disorder, along with a low dose of an antipsychotic agent.

Although he is still at risk for another episode of mania or depression, he has since graduated from college, had a successful course of psychotherapy, is currently off medication, and is living a normal life.

These are not arguments about the number of angels dancing on the head of a pin; they are diagnostic distinctions that determine someone's life. Schizophrenia, for instance, is a common, devastating, and very poorly understood illness, almost always misrepresented in books and movies, and widely ignored by the press. The disease usually appears for the first time in teens and young adults (between the ages of seventeen and twenty-five), and only one-quarter of its victims fully recover (although the numbers may go up with the introduction of clozapine and other new drugs). About fifteen of every thousand people become schizophrenic, and most are never able to leave home or support themselves, yet the disease is the most underresearched in the Western world.[9]

Depressive disorders are even more common. More than eight of every one hundred Americans will experience at least one serious depression in their lives, and most of them will have more than one.[10] Less severe depressions are even more common, and go untreated most of the time or are misdiagnosed as anxiety. In any given year, more than twenty-five million Americans have a diagnosable psychiatric condition that interferes significantly with their lives—not including drug or alcohol abuse.[11] In fact, many therapists think that a good deal of drug and alcohol use has its roots in untreated psychiatric illnesses, as people try to get relief however they can.

These figures sound unbelievable only because we don't recognize mental illness even when it stares us in the face. Most people never seek professional help, and 60 percent of those who do are seen by their family physician,[12] many of whom don't know very much about mental illness. In the 1970s, general practitioners handed out Valium (after 1986, it was more likely to be Xanax, which belongs to the same class of medication—the benzodiazepines—as Valium) like sugar water, diagnosing anxiety in essentially anyone who said he was blue, or who described insomnia, irritability, nervousness, or difficulty concentrating. When psychiatrists began paying attention to the milder forms of depression, they discovered that these symptoms were more likely to indicate depression than anxiety, and psychiatrists began warning other doctors to consider depression as a differential diagnosis. Since the introduction, in particular, of the antidepressant Prozac (fluoxetine) in 1988, sales of antidepressants have risen dramatically.[13]

About one-fifth of people with a diagnosed mental disorder see a mental health specialist for treatment,[14] but many others never receive an appropriate diagnosis or treatment in the first place. Whereas the psychiatrist may worry about missing significant physical diagnoses, the average internist grossly underestimates the presence of psychiatric disorder[15] (and doesn't send most patients on to a mental health specialist in most cases anyway[16]). There's nothing abstract about the furor in psychiatry over proper diagnoses.

John talked about another diagnostic differentiation—for panic disorder—that has generated enormous excitement in psychiatry in the last decade. As with most psychiatric disorders, more and more people have been diagnosed as the criteria for the disorder have been established.

"You get a thirty-five-year-old woman with two children who gave up a career when she married, and she's never been really satisfied with her choice, but she hasn't had the determination to make a major change in her life either," John said. "She's always been a bit shy, a bit unsure of herself, with poor self-esteem. Maybe mild chronic depression, but not enough for anyone to pay attention. And then one day she has a panic attack driving across the George Washington Bridge, and runs screaming from her car. Her pulse hits one eighty, she's gasping for air, she's shaking all over. She feels that she's dying, and she's so terrified, she's sure she's lost her mind.

"This is a full-blown panic attack," he said, "very different from an anxiety state, far more intense. It's the story the resident in the ER hears when someone has run out of a restaurant in the middle of a meal, and he says he's a businessman and shows his American Express card, and all of a sudden he freaked and thought he was dying and is he going nuts? Because that's what it feels like to him.

"People usually have no detailed recall of a psychotic episode, but the panic attack remains unbearably vivid. And even one experience like this is so traumatic that they make all sorts of changes in their lives to avoid being in the same situation ever again.

"But the attacks normally recur anyway, and they end up placing more and more limits on what they do. They become totally housebound, or need a companion to do something as simple as go to the supermarket." John leaned forward, his hands on his knees. "We have psychodynamic explanations having to do with separation anxiety, or repressed sexual impulses, or some catastrophic threat to the ego's defenses. And I believe these are always people who could use psychotherapy even if they didn't have panic attacks. But even in good treatment, in which the person grows and changes in a variety of ways, the panic attacks themselves remain largely untouched.

"What does often work is an antidepressant—often in low doses, with some form of desensitization training to the provoking situation. And I recommend psychotherapy to get at some of the underlying issues that make control particularly salient to this person. But basically I believe we're in a state with panic disorders that we were in with depression a number of years ago, just beginning to disentangle what phenomena we're looking at. And the same for a number of other diagnoses."

16

Where Do We Go from Here?

In the psychoanalytic mode of thinking that dominated American psychiatry until recently, the primary goal was understanding. Diagnosis of any kind was essentially irrelevant because the process of therapy was the same no matter what: The patient spoke as freely as she could, and the therapist listened, trying to understand what lay beneath the surface of her awareness. By following the course of his patient's associations, the psychiatrist would unearth her unconscious conflicts and the anxiety that drove her. All he needed to do was listen with an open-mindedness that paralleled his patient's openness of speech, and wait for the pattern of unconscious motivation to spontaneously emerge.

In this schema, diagnoses were a mix, in part dependent on the therapist's assumptions about unconscious conflicts and defenses, and in part based on observations of the patient's behavior. And such diagnoses were notably unreliable, since so much was based on inference and theory.

Rosemary gave an interesting example. "I was seeing an adolescent boy who was giving me a terrible time because he was so aggressive and filled with rage. My supervisor was sure the boy's fury was displaced sexual tension, and that the problem of treatment lay in my countertransference, that I was missing the sexual cues. Finally my patient attacked another boy and broke his arm. And at that time he was hospitalized, diagnosed as manic, and put on lithium. And all the rage he'd shown was simply incipient mania."[1]

Under the old systems, a person diagnosed as schizophrenic—or depressed, or anxious, or almost anything else—by one psychiatrist might easily get a different label from someone else. With the pharmacological revolution, psychiatry was confronted with the impossibility of continuing to rely on this kind of fuzziness, and embarked on a radical transformation of its approach to diagnosis, which ultimately evolved into DSM-III.[2] In this new approach, there was an effort to make diagnosis on the basis of objective criteria that different professionals could agree on, instead of depending on intuitive judgments and assumptions about particular unconscious processes. Even the term "neurosis"—which, by definition, refers to unconscious conflict—was eliminated except as a parenthetical addendum. It wasn't thrown out altogether because too many psychiatrists refused to surrender entirely to the atheoretical, observation-based nomenclature of the new system.

Although any creation of categories involves putting the raw data through a sieve of theoretical assumptions and biases, DSM-III represented a monumental attempt to eliminate as many theoretical expectations and biases as possible and to replace them with specific and concrete questions and a standardized pattern of signs and symptoms for each diagnosis. For the first time, psychiatrists could talk to their peers in other countries and be reasonably sure that they were describing the same kinds of patients, and research results from different sources could be compared, not only in the United States but around the world. With everyone following the same procedures from interview to interview, patient to patient, and psychiatrist to psychiatrist, studies from all over the world could be collated and new patterns found, whether the research compared different medications, kinds of psychotherapy, biological markers found through CAT scans, or metabolic measures; or whether the research examined the correlation of a particular diagnosis with childhood sexual abuse, parents' mental health, or school performance.

In the 1970s and 1980s, the field was in an uproar, for many clinicians were enraged at what they felt to be the gutting of psychiatry's soul. And certainly a large number of residents who were graduating at this time seemed to reduce patients to a diagnosis and a medical prescription. But psychiatry adapted to the new DSM system very rapidly. Nowadays psychiatrists can generally agree on many diagnoses—and on where the boundaries between diagnoses are still most fuzzy. And as these questions are sharpened, the categories of diagnosis themselves change. Not only has the differentiation between schizophrenia and mood disorder been sharpened, but a number of different disorders of mood have been distinguished; for example, organic affective syndrome; major depression, single episode or recurrent, with or without melancholia; bipolar disorder, manic or depressed or mixed; schizoaffective disorder; cyclothymic disorder; dysthymic disorder.

None of these categories and patterns are final—the whole point is that DSM-III (and its replacements, DSM-III-R and the most recent DSM-IV) have been as much research tools as aids to treatment, strategies for carving specific pieces out of the otherwise undifferentiated misery of mental illness. Since it is a work in progress, large numbers of patients don't conform to any of the DSM categories. A lot of people, for example, have a kind of mixed anxiety-depression for which there is no official slot as yet, but the importance of this particular pattern of symptoms only became clear after DSM-III had factored out a host of other conditions.[3]

In practice, the emphasis on diagnosis has led to other changes too. Offering a diagnosis is itself an intervention, giving a name to what is otherwise just a puzzling cluster of unrelated feelings and experiences. And naming is itself a relief.

"When I was in analysis," Gary said, "my analyst focused on the dynamics behind my anger or my fatigue, but he never told me I was depressed. I didn't fit the standard ways of thinking about depression then, and it never occurred to me that I was. I just knew I was miserable, that much of the time I didn't quite care if I was dead or alive. And I don't think it occurred to him either. He didn't think in terms of diagnosis." He paused. "But when I tell a patient that this whole list of symptoms is connected—all part of one thing that we call depression, or panic disorder, or whatever— it's like the lights come on, and they instantly feel better. It's not that I've cured them. But suddenly everything makes sense. They can say, 'That's why I've been withdrawn and self-destructive and anxious and worrying and not being able to go home at night.' I find just being able to start at the top, with a syndrome, and work down.... If you don't do that, nothing else makes sense.

"I also find it easier to say to a patient, 'When you start to need only a few hours of sleep a night, and you have ten projects you're working on at once, that's a sign of impending mania. Call me. Or when you start to think about how your father went bankrupt when you were ten, and how that ruined your whole life, that's another signal. Call me as soon as that happens.' It's much easier to talk with people about warning signs to use as markers for a particular diagnostic syndrome without regard to the underlying meaning. The meaning is for psychotherapy. It's a separate issue."

Still, making diagnoses clearer and more reliable doesn't transform psychiatry into medicine. In medicine a body generally gets sick because it is attacked and overwhelmed by an alien invader, and a simple physical test can often determine the nature of the invading agent unequivocally—a CAT scan for a tumor, a throat culture for strep infection. But in psychiatry nothing can be pinned down in the same way. It was, and is, impossible to point to any given person and say, "*This* is the cause of his illness, *this* germ, this abnormality of neural function, *this* anatomical abnormality of the brain, *this* abandonment by his mother when he was three, *this* school failure at five." No single agent can ever be dissected out of a larger context.

"All we can say now," John said, "is that our medicines act on target symptoms. We don't think they're all that specific as yet. As far as we know, they act on many different pathways, in different areas of the brain, in complex, interpenetrating ways. But they have effects we can see. A neuroleptic like Thorazine eliminates hallucinations and delusions. It doesn't make the withdrawn schizophrenic patient less withdrawn, but he doesn't hear voices. And an antidepressant normalizes sleep, and eating, and mood, and ability to concentrate.

"If you find that the same cluster of target symptoms generally disappears with the same drug, you have some justification for looking for a single underlying physiological abnormality—so that depression and panic disorder may be related in some fashion because they both respond to antidepressants. And when you take a history, you get other evidence of linkage, because you also find that many people suffer from both, and that both seem linked to loss or separation, and that the two run in the same families. But you can't simply lump panic and depression together. Because it's also true that medicines seem to act on more than one neurotransmitter and receptor site, and in many anatomical areas, so that any drug might well affect distinct and separate psychiatric syndromes— particularly at different dosages."

All of psychiatry involves an interaction between constitution and genetic factors, the current state of host vulnerability, and environmental stressors. But meanwhile psychiatrists work in the dark, trying to differentiate illnesses of unknown etiology by looking for subtle differences in epidemiology, symptoms, and drug response. And the hardest questions are only now coming up. As medications are found for more and more varieties of target symptoms, psychiatrists are beginning to question what is meant by "mental disorders" anyway. In the absence of causes, all they have are target symptoms.

"That's the most fascinating stuff," Gary said, "not treating clear-cut symptoms with medication, but the not so clear issues, changes in areas that we always thought of as character, that we think of as part of our real selves, who we've been throughout our life." He slowed his speech as he thought his way to his final point. "When I think about the extent to which medication can affect the whole person, I find the most striking examples to be in a few of my patients with minimal brain damage, dyslexia, hyperactivity, various cerebral dysfunctions.

"They've grown up with this. It's affected their lives in innumerable ways. It's made them feel stupid, and they've developed a lifestyle adapted to their disability. And some of them are amazingly changed after I prescribe Ritalin.⁴ They're forty years old, and suddenly they've learned to read, or can sit still when they never could before, and they can concentrate instead of jumping from topic to topic. And they come in and say to me, 'I thought I was just dumb.' And they really have to reorganize around this new perception of themselves, with a whole new set of possibilities open to them, and a profoundly different sense of who they are." He smiled widely. "Do I know which changes are direct manifestations of the drug and which are psychological reactions to underlying changes in their biology? No way."

"There are so many people with mood swings," John said, "where they bounce up and down. I see a lawyer who used to spend three months every winter in the doldrums. He'd be up at three A.M. with insomnia, he fought with his wife and hit his kids, and he hated his work. He had no sex drive, he sat in front of the TV without caring what he watched, his mind felt like mud, and he handled cases by remembering what he did when he felt normal. And by March he'd be back to himself. The sun was shining again, he loved his work, he made up with his wife, and he was a fantastic trial lawyer.

"He'd had three years of therapy when he was in his mid-twenties, and he'd resolved a number of underlying conflicts. And by now he's learned some methods of coping with his feelings, even to the realization that he becomes depressed every winter. And so he says to himself, 'If I wait it out, I won't feel this way in a month. These are my winter blues, so I mustn't file for divorce.' But the feelings didn't go away until I put him on an antidepressant. And then they just vanished." John shrugged. "Presumably there's something wrong with some of the neuroregulators in this man's brain. His trigger may even have to do with seasonal light changes and light's effect on the brain via the pineal gland.[5] In any case, an antidepressant normalizes him."

He hesitated, searching for words. "I don't know where we're going in psychiatry when I get a patient like this. He suffers from clearly diagnosable depressions, but he makes me wonder about all the people with the February blues. Is there one template for normal mood, or is there a range of templates? Is moodiness itself an abnormality? Or at what point is it abnormal? I know only that I don't believe in pain, and when someone comes to my office because he hurts, I treat him."

Laura said, "I find it extraordinary when I treat someone for a discrete depression who then tells me that all kinds of other things about themselves have also changed, characteristics they simply thought of as part of their personality, of who they are. And it frightens them, because they usually like the change—they don't want it to go away—but they don't know if it's the sudden surfacing of the 'real' them, or if what they're seeing is a drug-induced effect, more like the sense of relaxation, say, that you get after a couple of drinks. And meanwhile I sit and listen, and I start to wonder about those friends I have who are always just a little pessimistic, for whom the glass is always half-empty, who never have quite as much energy as I think a healthy adult should. . . . Like a very dear friend of mine who just bought a puppy, and was telling me last night how worried she was because the breed only lives about ten years, and she'd get too attached to it." Laura looked at me sharply. "You wonder, . . . what if I gave her this medicine? My friend? Would she stop picturing herself burying an old dog and be more able to enjoy her puppy? Would she finally get a decent haircut and buy some good clothes? Because that's what happens with my patients.

"These medicines aren't like street drugs," she stressed. "Cocaine, heroine, marijuana—any of the illegal drugs take you out of the normal range. You get high, or sedated, or speeded up. But an antipsychotic or antidepressant doesn't make you high; it normalizes you. And if you're not depressed, it does nothing; all you feel are the side effects, so that you're sleepy, and your mouth is dry, and your memory is lousy. It's nothing like smoking marijuana or snorting cocaine. It feels more like having a weight lifted that you didn't even know was there."

Laura continued, her face alight. "I find the most fascinating period of psychotherapy to be the weeks when I'm still trying to fit the pieces of someone's history together, watching his behavior in my office, listening to what he tells me about his life. When I'm trying to make a diagnosis, and when I'm trying to get some sense of what's biology and what's going to need psychotherapy."

Then she returned to her original line of thought. "Let's say I diagnose someone as depressed, but in the two to four weeks that we're waiting to see if medication will take hold, there's no point analyzing his nit-picking or his fearfulness of going out, or his compulsion to check three times if he's left the gas on in his apartment. Because all of these may vanish once the medication begins to work." She spoke reflectively. "And, unfortunately, the process can easily take two or three months because the fact that his depression doesn't respond to one medicine doesn't mean it won't to another. We have more than thirty antidepressants on the market, belonging to many different classes, and only a very unsophisticated psychiatrist thinks that lack of response to one or two is a reasonable treatment trial. But you feel like a damned fool waiting to see what happens when you have absolutely no way of knowing what in this person is going to change with drugs. Once he responds, at least you can say, 'Okay, let's forget that for now. After a lot of therapy maybe we'll know better why you have this symptom in response to this kind of stress, but I understand that all you really care about is that it went away, like a cough after penicillin.' " She frowned. "It's a complex problem, in part because many people feel demoralized when a symptom vanishes without any understanding of its meaning; while some people use these effects as an excuse to avoid working at psychotherapy: 'It's not me, it's my biology.' "

Gary had talked about changes in the intellectual profile of patients treated with Ritalin, and everyone discussed apparent changes with antidepressants in what might be called temperament, whereas Michael was fascinated by the effects of medication on what we normally think of as intention or will.

"There's an antidepressant called Anafranil that genuinely appears to work on obsessive-compulsive disorder." He drummed his fingers with a kind of nervous energy. "We have a great deal of psychoanalytic understanding of these patients, but they're extraordinarily hard to treat successfully. I see a number of obsessive-compulsives because I like the challenge. And I find them fascinating. I use all kinds of approaches, from psychoanalysis to behavioral desensitization to a kind of role-playing. And with some patients, people who may take two hours to dress every morning because their shoes have to be laced and unlaced ten times in just the proper order, or people who wash their hands fifty times a day so that their skin is macerated—for many of these people the compulsions just vanish on Anafranil. They just go.

"You see obsessive or compulsive behavior in mood disorders, too, and on antidepressants the patient's overwhelming need to keep the house clean, or the car washed, or the checkbook exactly balanced fades. I'm really talking about a generalized quality of rigidity," he said very thoughtfully, "where someone gets stuck on a particular track or detail and can't let go. . . . These look like disorders of will. Not mood, not thought, but intent."

Then he took the question to its limit. "I ask myself, at what point are we approaching the question of free will, of choice and responsibility? When the patient says the symptoms feel imposed upon him, we can see them as a derangement, but what about the patient who defends his obsessions or compulsions as reasonable? How extreme does something have to be for me to label it 'illness'?"

Steve's thoughts followed the same line as Michael's. "People have two kinds of problems of relevance to therapy," he said. "Symptoms and character. The complaints they bring in are usually symptoms, bits and pieces of malfunctioning machinery, usually things the person doesn't like about himself, and a sort of gloss on what he feels to be his real self—and symptoms are often relatively easily treated. On the other hand, character is what he sees as himself, aspects of his personality he is generally quite comfortable with. My experience with medication in the last few years has convinced me that a great deal of apparent character is often symptom, particularly mood disorder, but so long-standing that the person and everyone around him has come to label it 'him.'

"I have a patient with severe compulsions whom I put on Anafranil two months ago. And most of the compulsions—which felt alien to him—disappeared. But this is also someone who always has to buy a friend exactly the 'right' birthday present and ends up getting nothing or sending the gift six months late. Today he said he suddenly doesn't have to find the perfect gift, and how wonderfully free he feels. . . ." Steve gave me a piercing glance. "This man has also had a lifelong fascination with pornography . . . and that's vanished too. Abruptly. He has no explanation, nor do I." He leaned toward me, his face intent. "What are we seeing? What is the range of normal personality?"

LAYER

5

CONCLUSIONS

17

The Necessity of Love

As I worked on this book, I kept returning to the image of the Zen master at the Japanese tea ceremony. The pouring of the tea is ritual, strictly codified in an elaborate ceremony whose mastery requires years of dedicated practice. At the same time, in a paradox that is at the very core of Zen, every gesture is spontaneous and utterly free. I asked psychiatrists how they saw themselves—without revealing this image of my own—and I was given far more prosaic answers.

Michael emphasized a particular quality of toughness. "There are two images of the psychiatrist in pop culture that are really flip sides of the same coin," he smiled. "On one side he's a cold bastard with x-ray vision, and on the other he's the perfect daddy coming to the rescue. The reality is that you're sort of both. You become a psychiatrist because you want to help, you want to rescue, but what you learn is that you must combine concern with steel. You need to be empathic, but you don't ever earn your fee by being soft."

He drummed his fingers on the desk and stared into space reflectively. Then he said, "I'm working now with a twenty-four-year-old man who's had three hospital admissions in the last two years for schizophrenic episodes. He's stabilized now, and living with his parents, and he began working for the first time a month ago, as a messenger. But he's very frightened of going to work, of not knowing what to do, of failing, and he thinks that the other messengers laugh at him. He spends a lot of session time rocking back and forth and weeping."

Michael held my gaze challengingly. "And I offer support and encouragement and tell him it will get easier if he hangs in there. Because he can

do the job, even if it terrifies him, and sticking it out has multiple bene-
fits. He has to get out of bed, wash, comb his hair. He has to plan ahead
so he gets to his office on time. He has to follow instructions and learn
the skills of a real job, and he has to interact with other people. Now we
can talk about how he feels when someone pushes ahead of him at an elevator, about how his not saying hello affects another messenger's behavior
toward him. We have real material to work with." His voice softened.
"He's becoming a part of the human race, facing real issues, like other
people, sharing some of the same concerns, and learning to trust himself
out in the world. If I can help him hang on, he has a chance at a decent
life eventually."

The psychiatrist must squarely face the patient's needs and wants and
possibilities in order to be of any real help. This assessment is crucial to the
work of psychotherapy and something none of us can truly do for ourselves, because all of us have organized our inner lives around self-
protection, creating unconscious barricades and lines of defense that inevitably keep us from seeing with full clarity the lives we have made for
ourselves.

The protective defenses can too easily become rigid traps, creating their
own anxieties, setting us up for failure, and preventing the development of
flexible adult responses. Still, the barricades offer a known degree of safety;
no one by themselves chooses the naked vulnerability of going without. So
as patients we arrive at the therapist's office wanting to feel better, but
seldom initially willing to pay the price.

We come to treatment because our efforts at coping are failing in work,
or love, or life at large, but what we want is to be saved—our wounds
bound up and our problems magically solved. The psychiatrist, however
she might like to oblige, cannot save us. In the end, we must each live our
own lives for ourselves, and that requires facing that life first, facing the reality of the outer world and the fears of the inner. This work is done in
every kind of treatment.

John talked to me about the psychiatrist's "scalpel." "You can save a lot
of time by a bald statement of fact at the right moment." He sat back, his
soft voice at variance with his words. "I've been seeing a twenty-eight-year-
old, rather masochistic woman who was recently married. The marriage
isn't going well, and she's begun to talk about her husband, vaguely at first,

and in the last session with specifics. How he makes her sleep in the living room every night, how he makes fun of her in front of her friends, and so on. And I said, 'He makes you sleep in the living room?' and then I asked her exactly what he said when he made fun of her. And she told me, in great detail, but still trying to defend him, and I said, 'But that's horrible. He is treating you cruelly.' She cried for the rest of the hour, but now we can go on."

Listening to John, I was reminded of another story related to me by a friend with a history of chronic and severe depression. In her second year of treatment, she lost her job. A week later she had a serious automobile accident that was not totally accidental. From the hospital, she despairingly asked her psychiatrist, "Will it ever end?" Without even seeming to think, he answered calmly, "Of course." She was taken aback, she said, by the absoluteness of his tone. And when she asked what he meant, he said, in the same tone, "You'll be well or you'll be dead." She told me she'd burst out laughing, relieved in the oddest way by the stark truthfulness of his response, the sublime clarity he'd placed around her life. The decision was hers to make, terrifying in its simplicity, and at the same time an ultimate simplification. When I told the story to Laura, she smiled in recognition. She, too, called it "using the scalpel."

Several psychiatrists stressed their role as teachers, educating people in the skills of life. "Sometimes the teaching is very specific, very concrete," Laura said. "I've taught one woman how to balance a checkbook. I've role-played job interviews." She frowned, trying to be specific. "I saw a man for two years who had absolutely no idea how to make small talk. Learning a number of opening remarks, learning to ask what someone was studying, or what their work was, or what part of the country they came from, even learning that there was a ritual to all of this rather than total mystery, not only allowed him to begin attending to other people rather than to his anxiety, but helped introduce him to the realization that others also had to learn these rules—that no one was born knowing them, that, basically, he'd missed out on a developmental stage."

Rosemary said softly, "I see a woman, not very ill, in her twenties, whose chief complaint is that she can't meet men. She's attractive, bright, and very successful at work. I'd only seen her a few times when she told me she'd been to a party and was very pleased at herself for how nice she'd been to a man she was sure had come just because he knew she would be there. When I asked, she said she'd spent ten minutes with him before going back to the people she came with. And I said to her, and I put an edge into my voice, 'You spent ten minutes with him, and you think that's nice? You really think he'll call you again?'" Her china blue eyes were as opaque as ever. "I wasn't nasty, but I wanted to get her attention. Because whatever the psychological meaning of her coldness, she's genuinely ignorant of how to behave. She truly thought she was being nice, and one of my jobs is to teach her better social skills."

"I see much of what I do as educative," Gary agreed. "Many of the people I see, for example, can't label their emotions, so we begin by having them describe this puzzling physical experience of nausea, and wet palms, and rapid pulse. And I tell them that this sounds like anxiety or tension." He leaned back and stretched out his legs. "Adolescents will sometimes tell me that they have a strange feeling of nausea along with a peculiar tickling sensation in the groin area, and I tell them this is called arousal, or lust. . . . Then we work on finding events around them that seem connected with these experiences. Because the same tension can be fear or anger or humiliation or lust for different people or at different times." He added, a bit absently, "Almost everyone can learn more about themselves by really paying attention."

He was silent for a moment, apparently trying to decide how specific he'd be. "Regardless of diagnosis, so many of us block what we're feeling or don't connect what we feel to our circumstances. When Freud began working, most of the people he saw had problems with repression. They were torn by conflicting wishes which couldn't be acknowledged." He grinned. "And so you had these flamboyant conversion reactions in which Anna O., say, became blind so as not to have a sexual reaction to the sight of her dying father's penis. And, of course, she couldn't see the connection between her blindness and the unconscious infantile sexuality toward her father. Much of treatment still requires making the unconscious conscious, but it's so often more pedestrian, just a constant noting of what happened next, and how did you feel then, and how do you feel now, telling me this?"

Later Gary told me another story. "One of my patients is a very intelligent woman, a university professor, but she has some very odd thoughts at times, particularly during a depressive episode. She's had serious depressions since childhood, and after they pass, she's very frightened about being insane. The thoughts focus around the notion that other people are really Russian spies, beginning with her parents. And what I've done is compliment her. Her parents are both very peculiar people who abused her sexually, and as a child she found them threatening, incomprehensible, and unlike any other adults she knew. And so I've pointed out that her belief that they were Russian spies was a translation of her experience of them, chosen in part because she was growing up in the McCarthy era among people who were obsessed by him. And I've told her that as a child she had nowhere to go, she was completely at her parents' mercy, and it was safer to explain their behavior by thinking of them as alien spies than to face the inexplicability of their cruelty to her. She did what she could to make sense of her world.

"And what we've worked on is that it's not her underlying perception of them that's crazy. It's that she lost the sense of the translation into metaphor. That she concretized her insight and saw these orthodox Jewish parents from Brooklyn as truly being Russian spies. That we can label the literalness of it as a delusion. And that the larger issue is the extension of her childhood perception of her parents to her adult experience of the entire human race during these depressive episodes. And I've asked her to keep track of what other people actually do and say, compared to her parents, and to keep a diary.

"Three weeks ago, she was very silent for two sessions, and very tense. At the end of the second session I could see her pull herself together, as if she were walking into the lion's den. She looked at me very anxiously and said that she'd been thinking about something for several days and decided that she had to ask me directly. That she was very frightened, but she knew this was very important, something she'd never done in her life. And then in a trembling voice she asked me if I was lying to her all along. Was I really a Russian spy? I knew it was a critical moment. And I laughed and said to her, 'Me? I'm just a bar mitzvah boy from Long Island.' And after a moment she laughed too, with immense relief. A bar mitzvah boy from Long Island she could understand."

I thought about this story for a long time, because so many other comments I'd heard clustered around it. In talking about the central role therapists play in the lives of patients, John was the only person to say it just this way: "I see myself as a witness for someone's life." He spoke slowly and earnestly. "I noticed when I was in analysis, that everything I was doing I would think about telling my analyst, and near the end I realized I wasn't going to have that anymore. I'd be alone." He adjusted his glasses once more, his eyes dark behind the magnifying lenses. "I suppose it's what Kohut would call the mirroring transference, and for so many of us who didn't as children have anyone to register what we did, treatment offers a validation of our lives that we never had." He paused. "It's what I do when my son hits a ball in Little League, and I tell him how terrific that was, or he tells me he's having trouble with arithmetic, and I ask him to talk about it with me."

When I thought about Gary's informing his terrified patient that he was, in all its reassuring essence, someone like herself, or about John's sense of being a witness, I was reminded of something Laura had said: "In spite of its intimacy, it's a totally uneven relationship. You're with the patient as an introject, as my analyst was for me. They carry you with them, inside themselves. That's part of the treatment, to have them borrow aspects of you to modulate what they brought from childhood. But you don't *really* go to the movies with them or see them outside the office. And the borrowing isn't reciprocal. You think about them, and you care about them, but *you* don't carry them inside you when you go to the movies."

In this context, it seemed to me that the therapist-patient relationship is closest to the parent-child one, and the psychiatrists I asked agreed. "I feel total responsibility to do the best work possible with a patient," Laura offered. "And I get tremendous gratification when someone does well. Any therapist would be a liar to say he doesn't. The issue is to recognize it and stay honest.

"But at some point I also have to think, It's their life, not mine, and they have to live it as they choose." Saying that although she had no children, she knew what it was like to be someone's child, she sat back, crossing her legs. "You feel the same sense of responsibility with a baby, and a similar letting go with an adult child." She looked at me closely, and her voice sharpened. "On the other hand, you're never likely to be as able to accept what your children do without judgment. You make judgments all the time when they're growing up, and you try to mold them in ways that you never would with a patient, and you carry your children inside you forever, and maintain a real relationship. You see them, or speak on the phone or write. Because they always remain a part of you, you're likely to be somewhat more selfishly invested in how they turn out, less free to let them be simply themselves."

Then she switched gears and began talking about her treatment of a schizophrenic man, now in its ninth year. "Sometimes I don't know why I see him," she said softly. "He's much better. He doesn't hallucinate anymore, and he has much less thought disorder, but mainly he sits home and watches television. Every so often we talk about his moving out of his parents' home, living in a residential center, or even starting again at a day-treatment center, and he tells me how wonderful I am and how patient I am with him, but he doesn't actually make a move."

When I commented that this sounded like glacially slow treatment, she nodded. "That's why I only see him every month or two now. And sometimes I wonder if he's gotten stuck, and if he needs to see someone else. But yesterday, as he was putting on his coat, I looked at him and I thought, I love him. If he wants to see me for twenty more years, he can. I simply love him."

✍

Much as I am drawn to the image of the Zen master at the tea ceremony, imbued with grace and rhythm and light after his years of study, I don't think this image truly applies to the discipline of psychiatry. Unlike the Zen master, the psychiatrist, I think, plays a role—and it remains a role despite the dancing spontaneity the best psychiatrists bring to it. Although several psychiatrists accepted my formulation that they fulfill a complex role (more in some cases than in others, but always complex), but Gary firmly rejected it.

"I wouldn't call it a role," he insisted. "It's that I pull out different facets of myself. Just as I'm one way with my children, or at a conference, or when I talk to a baby. Those aren't roles. They're parts of me."

Yet I still see it as a role—incredibly subtle, with many facets, obviously dependent on what each therapist can extract from her particular range of experience, but a role painfully learned through years of training, with bits and pieces of new skills and new understanding slowly added and integrated with what is already in place. By the time I spoke to these psychiatrists, they'd been in practice for ten years or more, and their responses were essentially spontaneous, so spontaneous that the idea of calling their experience a role might seem a falsification. Yet I think I'm being fair. The Zen master is fully himself at the tea ceremony, but the psychiatrist in a session is not, because the parameters in the office are defined within the relationship, by the patient's needs at each moment, and not by the therapist's. As the therapist moves back and forth, treading a line between her own perceptions and an empathic sense of what it feels like inside the patient's head, she is always responding in terms of what is best for him—even if she is no longer conscious of making the decision.

To call the psychiatrist's work a role is not to diminish it: It is unique. This is the only room in the world where we are accepted exactly as we are, where the other person in the room is always on our side, without judgment. Listening to therapists, I heard their voices soften when they spoke of patients, and if they answered a call in my presence, their voices were so nurturant I wanted to crawl into their laps. Yet at the same time they see patients clearly, all their strengths and weaknesses. Their voices may have sounded like those of doting grandparents when they talked of their patients, but they weren't doting grandparents because they could also demonstrate dispassionate objectivity. What I heard was total and absolute acceptance. We might be frightened of our thoughts, but they aren't. We might condemn ourselves, but they don't. We might be afraid of our failure, but they are not. Unafraid of his patient's delusion about Russian spies, Gary could in all honesty reassure her, empathically choosing a response that resounded at all levels of her being.

If I sit in the therapist's office, mourning, "Am I just a patient?" I totally miss the point. I am never *just* a patient, or even *a* patient. I am always unforgettably and uniquely myself in all my manifestations, appreciated and cared for as nowhere else in my life.

EPILOGUE

What to Look for in Good Treatment

This book is an exploration of a world unknown to most of us. It is also meant to guide anyone in psychiatric treatment or psychotherapy and anyone considering treatment for themselves or someone they care for.

Since at least a third of us will have a psychiatric disorder at some time in our lives, we ought to know what our standards of care ought to be. We should know what the *best* care is—not the average, and not the minimum—so that we can have a gauge against which to measure. Then we can make our choices.

I thought this book would be easy to write. It was not, and I kept working on it only because I believed it would be of unique value. The psychiatrists I interviewed were telling me what good treatment really *sounded* like, and I hope the reader can now say, "Oh yes, my therapist sounds like that," or, "My therapist never sounds like that"—and act accordingly.

This book is not a cookbook, but it *is* a guide to what you can expect to find in good therapy. In the paragraphs below, I have listed a number of crucial points in regard to the therapeutic relationship and what you can expect from treatment. I have also made some suggestions for finding a therapist.

The Healing Bond

1. Your relationship with your therapist is crucial. Although it may have its ups and downs over the course of treatment, you should feel the therapist is really listening to you, with total concentration. Therapists should not be distracted, uninterested, or hurried.

2. Even if some subjects embarrass or frighten you, you should feel that they don't embarrass or frighten your therapist. During therapy sessions, you should be able to talk about anything that matters to you.

3. The therapist should *never* initiate or accept a sexual relationship with you.

4. In a general way, you should feel that the therapist has compassion for you. The therapist should not seem to be judgmental or dismissive of your pain, or unfeeling, and certainly not sarcastic.

5. You should feel that the therapist understands you, at least most of the time, and often seems in tune with your feeling in a gut way, as if from the inside. Indeed, you may never have had an experience quite like this before.

6. You should feel that the therapist sees you clearly, and not through some distorting lenses, including rose-colored ones. While you must not feel that the therapist sees you as worse than you are, you also must not feel that he or she gives you meaningless praise or cheerleading. You need to be able to trust in your therapist's perception of you and your capabilities.

7. You should feel that the therapist is working actively with you in the course of sessions. This is a collaboration in which you are seeking the help of an expert. Both you and your therapist should be working hard. You shouldn't be left to flounder on your own, but you shouldn't feel ordered around either.

8. You should feel that the therapist is your ally, on your side, and not the ally instead of your family or anyone else.

Changes
1. Intellectual insight is never enough. Expect to feel better and behave differently, even if the changes are initially small. Remember, you came into treatment because you wanted your life to be better.

2. You may have some specific target areas in mind: you want to end the relationship you're in, or start a new one, or get a better job. These goals should be talked about and kept seriously in mind as treatment proceeds.

3. You should begin to show some kind of change rapidly, whether it's feeling less distressed or more able to concentrate. The first signs are likely to appear in a few weeks, six at the most, although continuing change is going to be stepwise or apparent only after looking backward.

4. If *nothing* in your life changes after six months, or if you feel at any time that treatment isn't going as it should, talk with your therapist about a consultation. If your therapist consistently opposes a consultation, interpret this as a very bad sign. And get a consultation.

Finding a Therapist

If you don't know of a good therapist, try to find out who among your friends or family has had a particularly fine psychotherapy experience, or find out if anyone knows someone who has. If you succeed, call that therapist. If that course doesn't work, ask a doctor you like and respect for a recommendation. Some local hospitals offer a referral service. It may be worth trying. At the least, the person you call will be licensed.

Remember: You must feel you can work with the person you see. If the match between you doesn't feel right after two sessions, try someone else. Initial interviews are difficult, but the stakes are too high for you to settle for second best. It's your life and no one else's.

NOTES

Introduction: The Healing Bond

1. There are three ways of computing an average: taking the mean score (as in computing a grade point average or a batting average), which is the sum of all scores divided by the number of scores; taking the mode, which is the single most common score; or taking the median, which is the middle score of a distribution, with half the scores falling above this middle and half below. I've assumed the average to be the median.

Of course, the median can still be very good, depending on the sample being evaluated. For example, those Olympic skaters who score below the median for all Olympic skaters are very, very good skaters. Those physicists in the bottom half of their class at MIT are still likely to very good at math, etc. But I do not believe that the least good psychiatrists are indeed very good.

2. There are three professions that provide specific training in doing psychotherapy and that commonly involve seeing patients in a private practice setting: Psychiatry is one, clinical psychology the second, and clinical social work the third. (A fourth profession is psychiatric nursing, which requires master-level training and certification as a nurse, but very few such professionals are in private practice.) The psychiatrist has an M.D. degree, the psychologist a Ph.D. or Psy.D., and the social worker an M.S.W. or D.S.W. Any of them may also obtain additional training in psychoanalytic theory and technique at a specialized psychoanalytic institute. In the United States, such psychoanalytic training is generally available only to those who have already completed, or are in the midst of, specialized graduate work in one of these three fields.

Anyone can call himself a therapist without fear of legal reprisal. But no one can legally call himself by the title of psychiatrist or psychologist until he receives a license from his state (or a temporary permit, pending licensure). In psychiatry, to become licensed one must earn an M.D. degree, serve a year-long internship, and pass an examination in general medicine. In psychology, licensure generally requires a doctoral degree, two years of supervised experience as a psychologist, of which at least one year involves direct patient care, and passing an examination in general psychology. Until recently, clinical social workers (CSW) did not necessarily require state licensure, but the rules have been changing in recent years. Licensure generally requires an M.S.W., nine hundred hours of field work, and passing an examination in social work.

Training in the three professions is very different. Psychiatrists are medical doctors with additional specialized training in treating mental disorders. As physicians, they tend to be relatively pragmatic, interested in *what* works even if they do not have an adequate theory of *why*. Clinical psychologists come from the parent field of general psychology, a research science that studies both normal and abnormal mental functioning. Psychologists learn about memory, learning, perception, and social behavior as well as personality development and theory. Generally trained to do research, psychologists are likely to be a bit more concerned than are psychiatrists with underlying theory. Social work training stresses expertise in coordinating services from various social agencies, and is particularly oriented to working with families who have multiple economic, social, and psychiatric problems. Social workers are often trained in group, family, or couple treatment more than in individual psychotherapy, for the field emphasizes the client's role within a shifting family and community structure more than individual psychology.

Each of the professions has its own strengths and weaknesses. People within these fields often comment that experienced practitioners who are good share many similarities.

3. After wrestling with the question of the generic use of "he," I have either used "they" or alternated the use of "he" and "she" from one chapter to the next. Because many psychiatrists are women, alternation seemed particularly appropriate. The patient will always be the opposite sex of the therapist so as to avoid ambiguity.

4. Since 1990, a pilot program of the Department of Defense has been training a few psychologists to prescribe medication within the armed forces. "DOD Expands Program to Train Psychologists to Prescribe Drugs," *Psychiatric News,* 18 November 1994, 1.

5. About one-third of all Americans have had or will have a psychiatric disorder. Anxiety is most common, followed by depression and alcohol or other substance abuse. In any given year, more than 10 percent of the adult population appear to show substantial impairment from mental disorders—not including substance abuse—and over the course of a lifetime the prevalence is closer to 20 percent. Medication is an appropriate part of the treatment for most of these disorders. See H. I. Kaplan and B. J. Sadock, *Synopsis of Psychiatry,* 6th ed. (Baltimore: Williams & Wilkins, 1991), chap. 4.

6. I have used the word "patient"—rather than "client"—throughout this

book because that is how psychiatrists themselves refer to the people they treat.

7. The psychiatrists who were interviewed for this book told me that they generally expected to see something change in the person's life within four to six weeks of beginning treatment. (Actually they told me four weeks, but when I refused to believe them, a few went grudgingly to six.) Not that the person was cured, or his life entirely changed, but *something* happened. And these psychiatrists stressed that the main goal of treatment is always change—not self-understanding or insight.

8. Upon completing a yearlong internship, physicians take a three-part licensing exam given by the National Board of Medical Examiners. After passing this exam, they are entitled to call themselves medical doctors and can see patients in private practice. (A separate examination process for medical licensure for graduates of foreign medical schools is administered by the Educational Commission for Foreign Medical Graduates. Many states require such graduates to take an additional licensing exam administered through individual state medical licensing agencies.) Most physicians, however, get further training in a particular specialty as a resident in a hospital training program. After specialty training is completed (in psychiatry this takes three years), the graduate can sit for an examination given by the national medical board for that specialty; the whole procedure is called board certification. In psychiatry, the exams are given by the American Board of Psychiatry and Neurology and can be taken no sooner than one year after completion of specialty training. Prior to October 1, 1994, certification was for a lifetime; currently, certification is for ten years at a time.

The percentage of psychiatrists who are board certified has risen dramatically in the last decade, up to about 70 percent, about the same as for physicians in general. See J. H. Shore, "Order and Chaos: Subspecialization and American Psychiatry," *Academic Psychiatry* 17 (1993): 12–20.

9. The first psychoanalysts were simply disciples of Freud, studying his work and undergoing analysis with him. As the number of those wanting to become psychoanalysts grew, special training institutes were created, first in Berlin, Vienna, and London and later in the United States. The requirements at these institutes, even now, include classes in theory, control cases (supervised psychoanalyses of patients applying for analysis and screened by the psychoanalytic institute for their suitability for psychoanalysis) and a personal psychoanalysis of the candidate by a psychoanalyst approved by the institute. The entire process generally takes from four to ten years, and is usually done concurrently with other training and sometimes after other training is completed.

Freud himself did not believe that psychoanalysts need have medical degrees. See S. Freud, "The Question of Lay Analysis: Conversations with an Impartial Person," in *The Standard Edition of the Complete Psychological Works of Sigmund*

Freud, vol. 20 (London: The Hogarth Press and the Institute of Psycho-Analysis, 1955); hereafter abbreviated as *S.E.*

However, some institutes have been restricted to physicians, and some institutes follow psychoanalytic theories other than Freud's (e.g., Carl Jung's).

Chapter One: Background

1. Freud spent eight years in medical school because he worked five of those years in the laboratory of Ernst Brücke, a major leader of the reductionist movement, and one of Europe's most famous physiologists. He reluctantly left Brücke's lab in 1882, one year after graduation, to begin the practice of general medicine (because he felt he needed to earn more to support a wife), but soon he moved (from the surgical service of the General Hospital in Vienna) to the associated Psychiatric Clinic of Theodore Meynert, who was the finest brain anatomist of the time. Learning from Meynert, and using his laboratory for anatomical studies of the neonate brain, Freud decided to become a neurologist. In 1885 he won a coveted traveling grant and left for Paris to study for nineteen weeks under the brilliant French neurologist Jean-Martin Charcot. Charcot was the first to take seriously the phenomenon of hysteria, in which patients demonstrated a variety of apparently physical disorders, particularly paralyses and loss of sensation for no apparent physical reason. Charcot treated hysteria as neither malingering (which was the commonest view of the disorder) nor the product of the patient's imagination but as the result of congenital degeneration of the brain. Freud was fascinated by Charcot's work, particularly by the doctor's ability to induce hysterical symptoms through hypnosis. Eventually Freud's own studies of hysteria went in an entirely different direction and became the foundation of his theories of psychoanalysis. See Freud, "An Autobiographical Study," *S.E.,* vol. 20 (1925 [1924]).

2. Freud, "Project for a Scientific Psychology," *S.E.,* vol. 1 (1950 [1895]).

3. Americans have misrepresented Freud in attributing to him the idea that each of us starts life with a clean slate, our eventual personalities determined solely by our environment. Like his contemporaries, Freud was certain that inborn factors made some people more vulnerable than others to mental disorders:

> In the pathogenesis of the major neuroses, then, heredity fulfills the role of a precondition, powerful in every case and even indispensable in most cases. It could not do without the collaboration of the specific psychological causes; but the importance of hereditary disposition is proved by the fact that the same specific causes acting on a healthy individual produce no manifest pathological effect, whereas in a predisposed person their action causes the neurosis to come to light, whose development will be proportionate in intensity and extent to the degree of the hereditary precondition" (Freud, "Heredity and the Aetiology of the Neuroses," *S.E.,* vol. 3 [1896], 147).

4. See T. B. Karasu, "Psychotherapy and Pharmacotherapy: Toward an Integrative Model," *Am. J. Psychiatry* 139: 1102–12. The quotation from Freud appears on page 1103: "The future may teach us to exercise a direct influence, by means of particular chemical substances, on the amounts of energy and their distribution in the mental apparatus. It may be that there are other still undreamt-of possibilities of therapy" ("An Outline of Psychoanalysis," *S.E.,* vol. 23).

5. Freud, "An Autobiographical Study," *S.E.,* vol. 20: 16.

6. A. M. Freedman and H. I. Kaplan, eds., *Comprehensive Textbook of Psychiatry* (Baltimore: Williams & Wilkins, 1967), 272.

7. Mesmer had pioneered the use of hypnotism in the eighteenth century to alleviate patients' (probably hysterical) symptoms through the use of suggestion. In 1889 Freud spent some weeks at the clinic run by A. A. Liébault in Nancy, France, observing Liébault's use of hypnotism to alleviate symptoms of hysteria as well as watching the Frenchman's colleague, Hyppolyte Bernheim, using hypnotism among French peasants to treat symptoms of other disorders as well. And he himself began his work with hysterics by using hypnotism. But psychoanalysis was the first technique that attempted to achieve cure, not merely symptom alleviation, by psychological means. See Freud, "Autobiographical Study," *S.E.,* vol. 20.

8. N. Dain, "Reflections on Antipsychiatry and Stigma in the History of American Psychiatry," *Hospital and Community Psychiatry* 45 (1994): 10, 1010–14.

9. Z. J. Lipowski, "Holistic-Medical Foundations of American Psychiatry: A Bicentennial," *Am. J. Psychiatry* 138 (1981): 888–95; the quotation derives from page 889.

10. Ibid., 889.

11. H. R. Lamb, "A Century and a Half of Psychiatric Rehabilitation in the United States," *Hospital and Community Psychiatry* 45 (1994): 1015–20.

12. See G. Mora in Freedman and Kaplan, *Comprehensive Textbook of Psychiatry,* 363–66.

13. Ibid., 1018.

14. A. M. Brandt, "The Syphilis Epidemic and Its Relation to AIDS," *Science* 239 (1988): 375–80. Paul Ehrlich announced the discovery of Salvarsan in 1909 and called it a "magic bullet."

15. See E. W. Busse in Freedman and Kaplan, *Comprehensive Textbook of Psychiatry,* 731–32.

16. See M. E. Chafetz in Freedman and Kaplan, *Comprehensive Textbook of Psychiatry,* 1018.

17. Lipowski, "Holistic-Medical Foundations."

18. G. N. Grob, "Origins of DSM-I: A Study in Appearance and Reality," *Am J. Psychiatry* 148 (1991): 421–31.

19. Also by the eminent psychologist and educator Stanley Hall, who as president of Clark University introduced Freud to the United States when he invited

him to lecture in 1909; J. J. Putnam, a Harvard University neurologist who lectured brilliantly about psychoanalysis; E. S. Jelliffe, cofounder of the *Psychoanalytic Review;* A. A. Brill and Ernest Jones, both disciples of Freud's, by their writings and lectures; and Karl Abraham, a disciple of Freud and gifted psychoanalytic theorist in his own right.

20. The holistic views of Meyer and White and their connection with Benjamin Rush have been reemphasized in recent review articles as history is reassessed in terms of the current drive toward integrating medicine and psychoanalysis, but in the heyday of psychoanalysis it was not their medical orientation but their enthusiasm for psychological explanations and Freudian beliefs that were emphasized. See Lipowski, "Holistic-Medical Foundations."

21. Grob, "Origins of DSM-I."

22. However, anyone reading Freud's papers quickly realizes that only some of his patients had the degree of ego strength that psychoanalysts usually expect today in office practice. Freud's patients were often totally incapacitated by illness, unable to function in any area of life, and in need of constant nursing care. Paradoxical as it may seem, many of Freud's theories of neurosis seem to have derived from the treatment of patients we would now classify as much sicker.

23. See R. R. Greenson, *The Technique and Practice of Psychoanalysis* (New York: International Universities Press, 1967).

24. E.g., Harry Stack Sullivan, Frieda Fromm-Reichmann, and Harold Searles.

25. They might debate the exact dynamics, or the degree of constitutional vulnerability of a patient, or the importance of particular events in his life, but they agreed that not only neurosis but disorders such as schizophrenia, mania, and depression (psychotic and nonpsychotic) could in essence be explained in terms of experiences of childhood and the specific psychological effects these experiences engendered. For example, see F. Fromm-Reichmann, *Psychoanalysis and Psychotherapy* (Chicago: University of Chicago Press, 1959).

26. Karl Menninger was singularly influential in converting American psychiatry to this view, arguing for a single unitary concept of mental illness and stressing the importance of the symptom's meaning. His book *The Vital Balance* was particularly famous. For example, see M. Wilson, "DSM-III and the Transformation of American Psychiatry: A History," *Am. J. Psychiatry* 150 (1993): 399–410.

27. Wilson, "DSM-III and the Transformation of American Psychiatry."

28. Although different medications may be used to treat the same disorder, the chemical structures of the drugs may be widely different or very similar. When the structures are very different, their mode of operation in the brain is also likely to be different, even if we don't know how; the drugs are also likely to have somewhat different effectiveness and different side effects. Imipramine, for example, belongs to a class of antidepressants known as tricyclics; while another class entirely is the monoamine oxidase inhibitor; and a third class, inhibitors of sero-

tonin receptors, includes Prozac. New classes, as well as variations within a class, continue to be found for many psychiatric disorders. In the last few years, for example, we have seen the use of Clozaril in schizophrenia, the first of an entirely new class of medication, and it has been followed by others such as Risperdal (or risperidone).

29. S. H. Snyder, *Biological Aspects of Mental Disorder* (New York: Oxford University Press, 1980).

30. Between 1946 and 1955, the mental hospital population rose from 462,000 to 560,000. From 1955 to 1966, with the rise in the use of chlorpromazine (or Thorazine), the population fell by one-fourth to 426,000. Ibid., 63.

31. Kaplan and Sadock, *Synopsis of Psychiatry,* 137.

Chapter Two: Learning to Listen

1. D. G. Langsley and J. Yager, "What's a Psychiatrist?" In *The Future of Psychiatry as a Medical Specialty* (Washington D.C.: American Psychiatric Press, 1989).

2. Teaching hospitals are connected with medical schools and teach medical students. Much of the hospital's staffing consists of doctors still in training as interns or residents; in turn they are taught and receive supervision from doctors who have completed training. Some of these doctors are themselves on the paid staff of the hospital; more of them are volunteers on what is known as the unpaid attending staff: they donate teaching and supervision in return for an affiliation with the hospital. In general, teaching hospitals offer more state-of-the-art medicine than nonteaching hospitals. See also D. G. Langsley and M. H. Hollender, "The Definition of a Psychiatrist," *Am. J. Psychiatry* 139 (1982): 81–85.

3. A few medical schools, such as Johns Hopkins, are noted for treating students more humanely; most are not.

4. The average intern spends up to eighty hours a week with patients. Since the infamous Libby Zion case, in which part of the blame for Libby Zion's death at New York Hospital was placed on the practice of having interns work as much as a hundred or more hours a week, the law, at least in New York State, limits the workweek for interns to eighty hours.

5. Although it may still be legal, this is essentially impossible in practice. No hospital would grant such a doctor admitting privileges for his patients, nor would colleagues make referrals, nor would insurance companies provide coverage for patients. Also the physician would not be protected by malpractice insurance.

6. In 1966, for example, 20 percent of nonpsychiatry interns and residents surveyed considered psychiatry the worst-taught subject in medical school; in 1986 21 percent thought it was the worst-taught. In 1966 37 percent had been indifferent to or disliked psychiatry; in 1986 the comparable figure was 41 percent. D. G. Daniel, C. L. Clopton, and P. Castelnuovo-Tedesco, "How Much Psychiatry Are Medical Students Really Learning?" *Academic Psychiatry* 14 (1990): 9–16.

7. W. Sledge, P. Leaf, and M. Sacks, "Applicants' Choice of Residency Training Programs," *Am. J. Psychiatry* 144 (1987): 501–3.

8. Daniel, Clopton, and Castelnuovo-Tedesco, "How Much Psychiatry."

9. See Sledge, Leaf, and Sacks, "Applicants' Choice of Residency Training." Also, psychiatrists are, on average, older than other physicians. Even though psychiatry continues to grow at essentially the same rate as primary care medicine, for example, only 11 percent of psychiatrists were under thirty-four in 1993 as compared to 20 percent of all physicians. See, "AMA Study Shows Psychiatry Grew by 5.2 Percent in 3 Years," *Psychiatric Times,* Feb. 1995, 62.

10. Research substantiates his statement. For example, one study found that 50 to 80 percent of outpatients in a general medicine setting have considerable emotional distress or psychiatric symptoms. Almost 70 percent of one thousand consecutive patients seen in a general medicine clinic had no apparent physical problem. In J. Shemo et al., "A Conjoint Psychiatry-Internal Medicine Program: Development of a Teaching and Clinical Model," *Am. J. Psychiatry* 139 (1982): 1437–42.

11. In the course of the 1960s, the free-standing internship disappeared in internal medicine, becoming fused with residency training. For seven years, from 1969 to 1976, the American Board of Psychiatry and Neurology dropped the internship requirement entirely, although many psychiatrists in training took one anyway. In 1977 internship and residency in psychiatry was fused into a four-year program. M. K. Crowder and H. B. Roback, "The Internship Year in Psychiatry: A Status Report," *Am. J. Psychiatry* 138 (1981): 964–66.

The former internship is now known as P(ost)G(raduate)Y(ear)-1. As of 1991, approximately half the nation's psychiatry training programs surveyed required four months of internal medicine or pediatric training, one-third required five months to six months, and one-tenth required more. Two months of neurology are now required as well. The average amount of time in psychiatry is about five and a half months.

Although the purely medical experience now takes up less than a full year, it does not seem to have changed the essential nature of the training. In addition, many psychiatrists still take a full year of medical internship and transfer into the psychiatry residency in the second year, or PGY-II. The second year, or PGY-II, is what used to be the first year of residency, and it is still largely spent on an inpatient service. The third year is generally with outpatients, and the fourth year has a number of clinical elective options, clinical or research, as well as teaching and continuing follow-up with outpatients.

In a general way, about twenty hours a week is set aside for didactic experience: rounds, conferences, seminars, and supervision. The remaining half or more of the week is spent in direct clinical work. See J. Kay, ed., *Handbook of Psychiatry Residency Training* (Washington, D.C.: American Psychiatric Association, 1991).

12. Until the 1980s, many hospitals had long-term inpatient units for psychiatric patients, where patients might stay for a year or more, receiving intensive psychotherapy as well as medication. A few particularly well-thought-of hospitals were known to keep patients for as many years as necessary while continuing to provide psychotherapy many times a week, with or without medication. This kind of treatment tended to be limited to the very well-to-do and was quite different from the type of custodial or medication-only care the chronically mentally ill received in state hospitals.

As medication has become the treatment of choice for the most serious mental illnesses, inpatient stays have become shorter and shorter. Few hospitals offer any sort of long-term psychiatric care nowadays, and certainly not as part of a package of intensive psychotherapy. The only people likely to be long-term inpatients are those who are simply unresponsive to medication and cannot be released from state hospitals; many are also suffering from dementia or are mentally retarded. By 1989 the average length of stay for psychiatric inpatients had dropped to 14.1 days in psychiatric hospitals and to 10.7 days for psychiatric patients in general hospitals without dedicated psychiatric units. Cited in *Hospital and Community Psychiatry* 43 (1992): 1065; from *Business and Health,* 1 May 1991.

13. H. S. Sullivan, *Conceptions of Modern Psychiatry.* Reprinted from *Psychiatry,* 3: 1–117, 1940; 8: 177–205, 1945 (Washington, D.C.: William Alanson White Psychiatric Foundation, 1947).

Chapter Three: Empathy

1. Hannah Green, *I Never Promised You a Rose Garden* (New York: Holt, Rinehart and Winston, 1964).

2. E. L. Thorndike and C. L. Barnhart, eds., *Scott Foresman Advanced Dictionary* (Glenview, Illinois: Scott Foresman and Co., 1988).

3. R. Greenson, "Empathy and Its Vicissitudes," *Int. J. Psychoanal* 41 (1960): 418–24.

4. H. Kohut, "Introspection, Empathy and Psychoanalysis: An Examination of the Relationship Between Modes of Observation and Theory," *J. Am. Psychoanal Assoc.* (1959); 7: 459–83.

5. From Freud, "Group Psychology and the Analysis of the Ego," *S.E.,* vol. 18 (1921), 108, 110. Cited in M. F. Basch, "Empathic Understanding: A Review of the Concept and Some Theoretical Considerations," *J. Am. Psychoanal. Assoc.* 31 (1983): 101–26.

6. In a much-quoted study, Spitz observed ninety-one infants in a foundling home from birth. For the first three months of life, the babies were breast-fed by their mothers, or by one of the other mothers if their own mother was not available. The mothers left after three months, and from then on the babies received good physical care but no mothering or affection. Although they had shown nor-

mal development in the first three months, at this point they went into a decline, becoming more and more passive, inactive, and seemingly retarded. Thirty percent died by the end of the first year, and more than another 7 percent died by the end of the second. Of those who survived that long, developmental levels were only 45 percent of normal. See R. A. Spitz, in collaboration with W. G. Cobliner, *The First Year of Life: A Psychoanalytic Study of Normal and Deviant Development of Object Relations* (New York: International Universities Press, 1965), 278–81.

7. A major part of medical training involves the formal presentation of cases to an audience of more senior colleagues for their comments and critiques. Such training begins in medical school and continues through internship and residency, and often beyond.

8. Sechehaye believed that it was necessary for the schizophrenic patient to have the therapist act out the role of the good mother, even nursing the patient. See M. A. Sechehaye, *A New Psychotherapy in Schizophrenia* (New York: Grune & Stratton, 1956).

9. For example, see S. A. Arieti, *Interpretation of Schizophrenia* (New York: Basic Books, 1974); F. Fromm-Reichmann, *Principles of Intensive Psychotherapy* (Chicago: University of Chicago, 1950); J. G. Gunderson and L. R. Mosher, *Psychotherapy of Schizophrenia* (New York: Jason Aronson, 1975); most of the writings of H. F. Searles, particularly *Countertransference and Related Subjects* (New York: International Universities Press, 1979); and H. S. Sullivan, particularly *Schizophrenia as a Human Process* (New York: Norton, 1962).

10. D. Light, *Becoming Psychiatrists* (New York: Norton, 1980), 24. This book is an intensive study of the recruitment and training process in psychiatry. In the particular example just preceding Light's comment, he cites a resident apologetically explaining that he was simply unable to empathically follow (into the murder scene) a patient who had drowned her two little children in the bath.

11. H. Searles, *The Nonhuman Environment* (New York: International Universities Press, 1960).

12. Freud compares the analyst to the surgeon, "who puts aside all his feelings, even his human sympathy, and concentrates his mental forces on the single aim of performing the operation as skillfully as possible." In Freud, "Recommendations to Physicians Practicing Psychoanalysis," *S.E.*, vol. 12 (1912), 115.

Chapter Four: Identification

1. Freud, "Civilization and Its Discontents," *S.E.*, vol. 21 (1930), 59–145.

2. In the 1950s, a number of researchers suggested that it was useful to look beyond the individual patient to the family in which he or she was imbedded. Using the new computer approach as a base, they suggested that the whole family operated as a system with multiple feedback loops that acted to maintain the status quo and resist change. Moreover, each member of the family played certain

roles as part of this feedback process. One such role, often played by the patient, was that of victim or scapegoat. See M. M. Berger, ed., *Beyond the Double Bind: Communication and Family Systems, Theories, and Techniques with Schizophrenics,* (New York: Brunner/Mazel, 1978).

3. In 1956 a seminal paper on family systems in schizophrenia stressed certain kinds of maladaptive communication patterns within the family unit. See G. Bateson et al., "Toward a Theory of Schizophrenia," *Behav. Sci.* 1 (1956): 251–64.

But in stressing the mother's role in particular, the theory all too readily sanctioned the assignment of blame, as if mothers of schizophrenic patients were disease agents or "schizophrenogenic."

4. At that time, many more residents went into psychoanalytic treatment or intensive psychotherapy than do now. But there are no statistics available for then or now.

Chapter Five: Hearing the Unsaid Meaning

1. Freud, "A Difficulty in the Path of Psycho-Analysis," *S.E.,* vol. 17 (1917).

2. Freud, "On the History of the Psychoanalytic Movement," *S.E.,* vol. 14 (1914): 17–19.

In the last decade, childhood sexual abuse has taken center stage as a societal problem, but the question still remains as to how reliable memory of abuse is (or lack of memory). In fact, the whole question is part of the larger issue of the nature of memory. A vast body of research suggests that much of autobiographical memory is less like a computer record and more like a construction, the making of a coherent story based on limited data. For an excellent review of the issues see E. F. Loftus, "The Reality of Repressed Memories," *American Psychologist* 48 (1993): 518–37; also see S. J. Lynn and J. W. Rhue, eds., *Dissociation: Clinical and Theoretical Perspectives* (New York: The Guilford Press, 1994).

3. Freud, "Three Essays on the Theory of Sexuality," *S.E.,* vol. 7 (1905).

4. Freud, "The Psychopathology of Everyday Life," *S.E.,* vol. 6 (1901); Freud, "The Interpretation of Dreams," *S.E.,* 4, 5 (1900–1).

5. Freud, "Introductory Lectures on Psychoanalysis," *S.E.,* vols. 15, 16 (1916–17) [1915–17]. See particularly Lecture 23, "The Paths to the Formation of Symptoms," *S.E.,* vol. 16: 358–77. See also Freud, "Inhibitions, Symptoms and Anxiety," *S.E.,* vol. 20 (1926 [1925]).

In Freud's basic conflict theory, the psyche had three masters jockeying for control: the ego, which is the voice of realism; the id, which is the source of our most primitive impulses and feelings; and the superego, which represents both a punishing conscience and idealized self-images. Id impulses are repressed or channeled into acceptable modes of expression and cause anxiety when they threaten to erupt undisguised. The superego acts as a moral force but is frequently too rigid, unreasonable, and childish, and it creates its own brand of anxiety. In the treatment of a classic neurotic, both id and superego must be tamed by transferring as much unconscious material as possible to the domain of awareness and the rational ego. But in many people seen nowadays, the problem has changed. It is no longer a matter of the balance of power among these three imagos but some sort of failure in their initial development, leading to quite different psychological problems and therapeutic needs.

6. Freud, "Remembering, Repeating and Working-Through (Further Recommendations on the Technique of Psycho-Analysis, II)," *S.E.*, vol. 12 (1914).

7. The incidence of particular disorders changes with time. Just as tuberculosis, Parkinson's disease, and different varieties of cancer have waxed and waned this century, some psychiatric conditions have become rare and others more common. The rigidly repressed neurotic of Freud's time is far rarer in our culture, and problems of sexual acting out, aggression, and violence are more common. Presumably the differences could be traced to changed childrearing practices as well as global changes in parental attitudes and behavior. The culture, too, is different—far more violent and more sexually permissive.

8. For the clearest statement of these ideas see Freud, "The Disposition to Obsessional Neurosis: A Contribution to the Problem of Choice of Neurosis," *S.E.*, 12 (1913). See particularly Editor's Note, 313–16.

9. For a clear introduction to Kohut, see H. S. Baker and M. N. Baker, "Heinz Kohut's Self Psychology: An Overview," *Am. J. Psychiatry* 144 (1987): 1–9.

10. For a clear introduction to the issues, see G. N. Grob, "Origins of DSM-I: A Study in Appearance and Reality," *Am. J. Psychiatry* 148 (1991): 421–31; and M. Wilson, "DSM-III and the Transformation of American Psychiatry: A History," *Am. J. Psychiatry* 150 (1993): 399–410.

Chapter Six: The Therapist as Patient

1. T. Reik, *Listening with the Third Ear* (New York: Farrar, Straus, 1948).

2. The *Handbook of Residency Training* outlines the debate and states that current requirements are that residents must spend "at least one year (or its full-time-equivalent if done on a part-time basis) in an organized and well-supervised outpatient program which includes experience with a wide variety of disorders, patients, and treatment modalities with experience in both brief and long-term care of patients utilizing both psychodynamic and biological approach to outpatient treatment" (J. Kay, ed., *Handbook of Residency Training* [Washington, D.C.: American Psychiatric Association, 1991], 66).

Nonetheless, this requirement leaves considerable room for variation. In 1990 a joint task force of the Association for Academic Psychiatry and the American Association of Directors of Psychiatry Residency Training published a model curriculum for teaching the core skill of long-term psychodynamic psychotherapy that is very specific. What will happen next is yet to be seen. See P. C. Mohl et al.,

"Psychotherapy Training for the Psychiatrist of the Future," *Am. J. Psychiatry* 147 (1990): 7–13.

3. Freud, "Analysis Terminable and Interminable," *S.E.*, vol. 23 (1937), 248. While Freud is referring specifically to the psychoanalyst, the understanding he refers to applies to the psychiatrist (and other psychotherapists) as well. For a more complete discussion, see Fromm-Reichmann, "Notes on Personal and Professional Requirements of a Psychotherapist," chap. 5, *Psychoanalysis and Psychotherapy*.

4. Freud, "Analysis Terminable and Interminable," *S.E.*, vol. 23, 249. He recommended reanalysis every five years or so in addition to constant self-examination.

5. "It has accomplished its purpose if it gives the learner a firm conviction of the existence of the unconscious, if it enables him, when repressed material emerges, to perceive in himself things which would otherwise be incredible to him" (Ibid., 248).

6. Fromm-Reichmann, *Psychoanalysis and Psychotherapy,* 102.

7. Even if the candidate was in successful psychotherapy, or in psychoanalysis with an analyst not on the list, he now had to begin anew with an analyst assigned by the institute—whether or not he wanted to. Moreover, the approved analyst was the one to decide whether the candidate would be allowed to graduate. So the analyst wore two hats, functioning as empathic analyst while also acting as the clinic's watchdog. Since anything learned in the treatment could be used to judge whether a candidate would be permitted to graduate, many candidates experienced their analysis as a juggling act in which they tried to watch their tongues for fear of losing standing within the institute. Many graduates simply went on to a second or even a third analysis after graduation. In recent years, however, the system has changed to preserve the confidentiality of the session, and the candidate's analyst now plays no part in deciding whether he graduates.

8. In the United States, the dominant school is Freudian, with a strong admixture of later theorists such as Anna Freud, Heinz Hartmann, D.W. Winnicott, Heinz Kohut, and Otto Kernberg (although in the Baltimore-Washington network, Sullivanians are influential). It is also possible to see a follower of Carl Jung or Melanie Klein, or disciples of the neo-Freudians Karen Horney or Alfred Adler or Erich Fromm. See any standard psychiatry text for more.

9. But Freudian-based psychotherapy doesn't predominate everywhere. In England, for example, an analyst is likely to follow Melanie Klein; in Switzerland, Carl Jung.

10. From the 1988–89 Professional Activities Survey of the American Psychiatric Association. R. A. Dorwart et al., "A National Study of Psychiatrists' Professional Activities," *Am. J. Psychiatry* 149 (1992): 1499–1505.

11. Indeed, it has been impossible to make a hard and fast distinction between the two at the borderline. See Freedman and Kaplan, *Comprehensive Textbook of Psychiatry*.

12. The concept was developed by Franz Alexander (1891–1964), an early disciple of Freud, a major force in American psychoanalysis, and the founder of the Chicago Institute of Psychoanalysis. See Kaplan and Sadock, *Synopsis of Psychiatry*, 186.

13. See A. Beck, *Cognitive Therapy and the Emotional Disorders* (New York: International Universities Press, 1976); or A. Beck et al., *Cognitive Therapy of Depression* (New York: Guilford Press, 1979).

Chapter Seven: The Healing Bond and the Psychiatrist's Own Baggage

1. D. Light in *Becoming Psychiatrists* provides the most recent major compilation of information, but most of the studies he cites are themselves rather old. We know the demographics of psychiatry have changed even since the 1980s when Light's book was written. In particular, the percentage of women in training between 1977 and 1988 increased from 32 percent to 41 percent. In general medicine, by comparison, the percentage of women in training went from 19 to 28 percent. See T. H. Dial et al., "Sex Differences in Psychiatrists' Practice Patterns and Incomes," *Am. J. Psychiatry* 151 (1994): 96–101.

The other known demographic factor is the number of graduates of foreign medical schools. According to Light, about 40 percent of all psychiatry residents were graduates of foreign medical schools in 1975, as part of what was then a rising trend; immigration laws cut them out for a time, but the percentage has been rising again and is now about 25 percent ("Psychiatry's Match Results Continue to Decline," *Psychiatric News*, 1 April 1994, 1).

For what it is worth, however, the earlier studies were fascinating. They include W. E. Henry, J. H. Sims, and S. L. Spray, *The Fifth Profession* (San Francisco: Jossey-Bass, 1971); A. A. Rogow, *The Psychiatrists* (New York: G. P. Putnam's Sons, 1970); R. R. Holt and L. Luborsky, *Personality Patterns of Psychiatrists* (New York: Basic Books, 1958); W. E. Henry, J. H. Sims, and S. L. Spray, *Public and Private Lives of Psychotherapists* (San Francisco: Jossey-Bass, 1973).

2. P. H. Ornstein, "Sorcerer's Apprentice: The Initial Phase of Training and Education in Psychiatry," *Comprehensive Psychiatry* 9 (1968): 293–315.

3. See, for example, M. R. Sharaf and D. J. Levinson, "The Quest for Omnipotence in Professional Training," *Psychiatry* 27 (1964): 135–39.

4. P. Livingston and C. N. Zimet, "Death Anxiety, Authoritarianism and Choice of Specialty in Medical Students," *Journal of Nervous and Mental Diseases* 140 (1965): 222–30.

5. The sex typing is in the original psychoanalytic literature, part of the view of human beings as profoundly bisexual, having incorporated aspects of the self

from each parent separately. Women do most of the nurturing (even now), and men are generally more aggressive.

6. R. N. Zabarenko, L. Zabarenko, and R. A. Pittenger, "The Psychodynamics of Physicianhood," *Psychiatry* (1969): 102–118; and K. A. Menninger, "Psychological Factors in the Choice of Medicine as a Profession," *Bull. Menninger Clinic* 21 (1957): 51–58, 99–106.

Chapter Eight: Peculiar Rules and Lopsided Intimacy

1. When I told Laura's story to another psychiatrist, he added a new dimension to my understanding of why the patient must reveal her thoughts. "I'd really sink my teeth in that," he said. "I'd want to know why she so much wanted to hurt me." It took me months to understand him, because I thought at first he meant that she shouldn't have spoken. Finally, one day, I realized he didn't mean that at all. He meant just what Laura had: Her thoughts were important and to be revealed to the therapist because they were keys to her unconscious life. In fact, although she had no conscious awareness of it, she was angry at her analyst. She was jealous of his daughter, and she wanted to hurt him. (The only question I was left with was whether her analyst had missed an opportunity. After her dream they'd examined her jealousy—not before, when she'd first told him that his daughter was homely. They never used this opportunity to examine her wish to hurt him as a distinct component of her inner life, potentially independent of her jealousy.)

2. See A. B. Hollingshead and F. C. Redlich, *Social Class and Mental Illness* (New York: Wiley, 1958). Also, R. F. Mollica and F. C. Redlich, "Equity and Changing Patient Characteristics—1950–1975," *Arch. Gen. Psychiatry* 37 (1980): 1257–63.

3. The introspectionists of the late nineteenth and early twentieth centuries pioneered rigorous self-observation in a variety of experimental conditions as a means of understanding cognitive processes. What they found, ultimately, was that much of cognitive activity appeared to operate outside of consciousness.

4. "Consciousness . . . does not appear to itself chopped up in bits. . . . A 'river' or a 'stream' are the metaphors by which it is most naturally described. In talking of it hereafter, let us call it the stream of thought, of consciousness, or of subjective life." W. James, *The Principles of Psychology* (New York: Dover, 1950), 239. Originally printed (New York: Holt, 1890).

5. For a detailed description of Freud's office, see P. Gay, *Freud, A Life for Our Time* (New York: Norton, 1988). For a discussion of the ways in which Freud sometimes ignored his own dictums on technique, see P. Roazen, *Freud and His Followers* (New York: Knopf, 1975). On page 127, Roazen comments that "American analysts in particular tended to be more orthodox than Freud, since European analysts were likely to have more regular contact with him."

Chapter Nine: Ghosts from the Past

1. Like certain other patients Freud defined as neurotic, she seems too sick to fit the very category he invented for her. I always think it one of the ironies of psychoanalytic history that many of the same cases on which Freud erected his theory of neuroses hardly fit the concept of neurotic in common use today.

2. Freud, "An Autobiographical Study," *S.E.*, vol. 20, 19–23.

3. While sitting anxiously at her father's bedside, Anna had fallen into a dream state in which she saw a threatening black snake moving toward her father from the wall, and in this state she had been unable to move her arm in defense. See J. Breuer and S. Freud, "Studies on Hysteria II: Case Histories," *S.E.*, vol. 2 (1893–95).

4. [Breuer and Freud, "Studies on Hysteria:] I. On the Psychical Mechanism of Hysterical Phenomena: Preliminary Communication."

5. [Breuer and Freud, "Studies on Hysteria:] III. Hysterical Conversion."

6. Ibid., 6.

7. For a modern account of Janet's work see B. A. van der Kolk and O. van der Hart, "Pierre Janet and the Breakdown of Adaptation in Psychological Trauma," *Am. J. Psychiatry* 146 (1989): 1530–40.

8. "Thus a psychical force, aversion on the part of the ego, had originally driven the pathogenic idea out of association and was now opposing its return to memory. The hysterical patient's 'not knowing' was in fact a 'not wanting to know'—a not wanting which might be to a greater or less extent conscious. The task of the therapist, therefore, lies in overcoming by his psychical work this resistance to association." Breuer and Freud, "Studies on Hysteria: IV. The Psychotherapy of Hysteria," *S.E.*, vol. 2, 269–70.

9. J. Malcolm, *Psychoanalysis: The Impossible Profession* (New York: Knopf, 1981), 14. In a footnote (165), Malcolm says recent research finds that some parts of this story (which I have left out) are wrong. But the fantasied pregnancy and sexual attachment to Breuer, and Breuer's assumption that Anna's passion for him was personal rather than a transference phenomenon are apparently true. See Freud, "An Autobiographical Study," and "Studies on Hysteria," 41n.

10. Breuer and Freud, "Studies on Hysteria," 302. In this paper, in which Freud introduces the concept of transference, he has not as yet developed his belief in the pervasive and crucial role of sexual feeling in all neurosis, whether hysteria or some other kind—and indeed, in all of human life. Breuer did not accept this view, and it was Freud's work on sexual theories (primarily) that led to the discontinuance of their collaboration. Also see S. Freud, "Autobiographical Study," *S.E.*, vol. 20.

11. Breuer and Freud, "Studies on Hysteria," *S.E.*, vol. 2, 302.

12. Freud, "The Dynamics of Transference," *S.E.*, vol. 12 (1912). Also consider the following: "Transference is merely uncovered and isolated by analysis. It is a

universal phenomenon of the human mind, it decides the success of all medical influence, and in fact dominates the whole of each person's relations to his human environment" (Freud, "Autobiographical Study," *S.E.*, vol. 20, 42).

13. S. Freud, "New Introductory Lectures on Psycho-Analysis," *S.E.*, vol. 22 (1933 [1932]), 106–7.

14. E. Berne, *Games People Play: The Psychology of Human Relationships* (Grove Press: New York, 1964).

15. The perception, indeed, is often acutely accurate. It is the interpretation the patient then makes, as to the therapist's dislike or boredom, for example, that indicates the distortions of transference.

16. Freud actually gave two reasons. The first was a personal one: "I cannot put up with being stared at by other people for eight hours a day (or more)." The other was an issue of treatment; that "I do not wish my expressions of face to give the patient material for interpretation or to influence him in what he tells me" (both are in Freud, "On Beginning the Treatment: Further Recommendations on Technique in Psychoanalysis (I)" *S.E.*, vol. 12 (1913), 134.

Chapter Ten: The Psychiatrist's Strange Loneliness

1. Rogow, *The Psychiatrists,* refer to notes of chap. 7, above.

2. About thirty-four thousand were members of the American Psychiatric Association; those ten thousand who were not members were physicians in the American Medical Association who identified themselves as psychiatrists. From the 1988–89 Professional Activities Survey of the American Psychiatric Association. M. Olfson, H. A. Pincus, and T. H. Dial, "Professional Practice Patterns of U.S. Psychiatrists," *Am. J. Psychiatry* 151 (1994): 89–95.

3. Dorwart, "National Study of Psychiatrists'"; see note 10 of chap. 6 above.

4. Sledge, Leaf, and Sacks, "Applicants' Perceptions of Psychiatric Training Programs," *Academic Psychiatry* 13 (1989): 24–30.

5. Psychiatrists in full-time practice were the oldest group and constituted only about ten percent of the total; psychiatrists primarily working in private psychiatric or general hospitals were the youngest group. Olfson, Pincus, and Dial, "Professional Practice Patterns."

6. Paid jobs are labeled "full-time" at thirty hours per week, or "half-time" at fifteen hours per week; but the jobs often call for more than that in reality, while salaries are usually lower than private practice fees. These paid jobs form the backbone of hospital psychiatry departments and include such posts as director of residency training or chief of a service, as in running an inpatient ward.

7. Dorwart, "National Study of Psychiatrists.'" Hospitals staff their training programs (in all specialties) with volunteers. Unlike colleges or universities, they don't pay most of their teaching faculty, offering instead limited rank in the academic hierarchy. Usually hospitals offer admitting privileges too; in any case,

some work in the hospital is seen by the psychiatrist as necessary to his own mental health.

8. See note 14 of chap. 9 above.

9. The average workweek is forty-eight hours—over forty-nine hours for men, and forty-three for women—but the proportion of time with patients remains the same. T. H. Dial et al., "Sex Differences in Psychiatrists' Practice Patterns and Incomes," *Am. J. Psychiatry* 151 (1994): 96–101.

10. The code of ethics for psychiatry derives from principles codified for medicine in general by the American Medical Association, first in 1847. The current code is a revision by the American Psychiatric Association dating from 1989. The code covers issues that revolve around clinical documentation, confidentiality, informed consent, and the psychiatrist's obligations and duties in a range of circumstances. Kay, *Handbook of Residency Training.*

A specific major focus of the code is on violations of the boundary between psychiatrist and patient, particularly on issues of intimacy and sex. Sex with a current patient is unequivocally forbidden; there is still debate as to whether it is ever allowable with a former patient.

Local chapters of psychiatric societies have ethics boards whose psychiatrists hold hearings on complaints of ethics violations. A guilty finding, particularly in regard to sexual transgressions, results in suspension or expulsion. But only 113 members of the APA were suspended or expelled between 1981 and 1991, primarily for sexual violations. See Editorial, "Sex with Former Patients Almost Always Unethical," *Am. J. Psychiatry* 149 (1992): 855–57. For a general discussion, see P. S. Appelbaum and L. Jorgenson, "Psychotherapist-Patient Sexual Contact after Termination of Treatment: An Analysis and a Proposal," *Am. J. Psychiatry* 148 (1991): 1466–73.

11. Refer to note 1 of this chapter, above.

Chapter Eleven: Passivity and the Surrender of Control

1. See Kaplan and Sadock, *Synopsis of Psychiatry,* 834.

The possibility of a malpractice suit has added another component to the doctor's caretaking, but the psychological issues cannot be underestimated.

2. "The doctor should be opaque to his patients and, like a mirror, should show them nothing but what is shown to him" (Freud, "Recommendations to Physicians," *S.E.,* vol. 12, 118).

3. See note 16 of chap. 9 above.

4. Suicide watch generally meant confining the patient to a small, bare room where he or she was watched by a staff member around the clock.

5. See Kaplan and Sadock, *Synopsis of Psychiatry,* 614.

6. Depression includes much more than sadness. Irritability, even rages, are common, as well as a wide variety of physiological changes, including changes in sleep patterns, sexual responsiveness, appetite, and memory. Delusions may also be seen.

7. There are two major types of mood disorders. One is depression, of various degrees of intensity and chronicity, and the other is called mania, or in its milder forms, hypomania. In current understanding, hypomania or mania is part of a manic-depressive cycle found with depression, although one may initially see only depression. Just as depression involves a slowing down, hypomania is a kind of speeding up, with increased energy and flow of ideas and speech. Hypomania can go with creative work and great achievement but as it shades into mania, one sees impulsiveness, impaired judgment, and a great deal of irritability. At its worst, mania involves major disorganization of thought and action, delusions, profound paranoia, and assaultiveness, and it can look like schizophrenia.

8. Freud, "Recommendations to Physicians," *S.E.*, vol. 12, 114.

Chapter Twelve: The Real Relationship

1. Freud, "Dynamics of Transference," *S.E.*, vol. 12.

2. Freud, "Recommendations to Physicians," *S.E.*, vol. 12, 115.

3. Ibid., 118. See also note 2 of chap. 11 above.

4. See, for example, A. Freud, "The Widening Scope of Indications for Psychoanalysis: Discussion," *J. Amer. Psychoanal. Assn.* 2 (1954): 607–20; A. Freud, *Normality and Pathology in Childhood: Assessments of Development* (New York: International Universities Press, 1965); L. Stone, *The Psychoanalytic Situation* (New York: International Universities Press, 1961).

5. Greenson, *Technique and Practice of Psychoanalysis*, 219–20.

6. Ibid.

7. "The first problem confronting an analyst who is treating more than one patient in the day will seem to him the hardest. It is the task of keeping in mind all the innumerable names, dates, detailed memories and pathological products which each patient communicates in the course of months and years of treatment, and of not confusing them with similar material produced by other patients under treatment simultaneously or previously. . . . The technique, however, is a very simple one. . . . It consists simply in not directing one's notice to anything in particular and in maintaining the same 'evenly suspended attention' . . . in the face of all that one hears" (Freud, "Recommendations to Physicians," *S.E.*, vol. 12, 111–12).

8. I didn't ask Gary if he'd bottle-feed Maureen today. It didn't even occur to me.

9. Over 6 percent of psychiatrists appear to have engaged in some kind of sexual relationship, usually including intercourse, with one or more patient(s), usually less than six months before termination. The number seems to be about the same for psychologists. N. Gartrell et al., "Psychiatrist-Patient Sexual Contact: Results of a National Survey, I: Prevalence," *Am. J. Psychiatry* 143 (1986): 1126–31.

Chapter Thirteen: Feelings for the Patient

1. See Greenson, *Technique and Practice of Psychoanalysis,* particularly pp. 388–92, for wonderfully clear commentary on Freud's thought and for further references.

2. Ibid., particularly pp. 358–411.

3. Even after one is out in private practice, it is easy to get supervision on a case by paying a colleague, usually a senior colleague, for his time. Sometimes therapists organize weekly group meetings instead, in which a few colleagues provide supervision for each other on a regular basis, either on difficult cases or on special problems as they arise with patients.

4. In H. F. Searles, *Countertransference and Related Subjects* (New York: International Universities Press, 1979), 73. The whole book is of interest.

5. In addition to Searles, *Countertransference,* see, for example, J. J. Maltsberger and D. H. Buie, "Countertransference Hate in the Treatment of Suicidal Patients," *Arch. Gen. Psychiatry* 30 (1974): 625–33; or G. Adler, "Helplessness in the Helpers," *Brit. J. Med. Psychol.* 45 (1972): 315–26.

Chapter Fourteen: Medicines

1. ECT is valuable in the treatment of depression, mania, and some episodes of schizophrenia. For a general discussion, see Kaplan and Sadock, *Synopsis of Psychiatry,* 669–73. Also see "Efficacy of ECT: A Meta-Analysis," *Am. J. Psychiatry* 142 (1985): 297–302; and S. Mukherjee, H. A. Sackeim, and D. B. Schnur, "Electroconvulsive Therapy of Acute Manic Episodes: A Review of 50 Years' Experience," *Am. J. Psychiatry* 151 (1994): 169–76.

However, it does seem that some patients develop enormous fear of the procedure even when it is effective and without side effects. The reason is as yet unknown. See H. A. Fox, "Patients' Fear of and Objection to Electroconvulsive Therapy," *Hospital and Community Psychiatry* 44 (1993): 357–60.

2. Through a 1982 state referendum. Fox, "Patients' Fear," 358.

3. See L. Kalinowsky in Freedman and Kaplan, *Comprehensive Textbook of Psychiatry,* 1285–89. I was told that wards that frequently used insulin coma therapy needed twenty or more staff members in order to monitor patients carefully enough, and the team stayed together as a working unit for years at a time.

4. See M. Greenblatt in Freedman and Kaplan, *Comprehensive Textbook of Psychiatry,* 1291–95.

5. As stated in Chapter 1, different drugs and different classes of drugs have been found. Tegretol (carbamazepine), for example, is an anticonvulsant used to treat acute mania and to prevent relapse in manic-depressive disorder.

6. L. L. Bachrach, "What We Know about Homelessness among Mentally Ill Persons: An Analytical Review and Commentary," *Hospital and Community Psychiatry* 43 (1992): 453–64.

7. E. F. Torrey, *Nowhere to Go: The Tragic Odyssey of the Homeless Mentally Ill* (New York: Harper and Row, 1988).

8. *Newsweek*, 9 November 1987, 48.

9. Bachrach, "What We Know about Homelessness."

10. Training programs were fragmented. The already floundering resident was totally at a loss as to what he was actually supposed to know, and unable to create a solid professional identity because he had no one to model himself on. While some modalities, such as hypnosis, were more often taught in residency programs late in the 1970s, biofeedback and behavioral conditioning were generally returned to the realm of the psychologist, along with most administration of community mental health centers.

For a very funny and sophisticated presentation, see J. Yager, "A Survival Guide for Psychiatric Residents," *Arch. Gen. Psychiatry* 30 (1974): 494–99.

11. Freud, *S.E.*, vol. 1 (1950 [1895]).

Chapter Fifteen: Remedicalization and the Healing Bond

1. Freud, "On Psychotherapy," *S.E.*, vol. 7 (1905), 263.

2. Freud, "Recommendations to Physicians," *S.E.*, vol. 12, 119.

3. Freud, "An Autobiographical Study," *S.E.*, vol. 20. Also see S. Freud, "Beyond the Pleasure Principle," *S.E.*, vol. 18.

4. Schizophrenia is most commonly characterized by the presence of such symptoms as hallucinations (almost always auditory), delusions (often peculiar or bizarre); peculiarities of appearance and social behavior, inappropriate emotion or flatness, concreteness of thought, difficulties with logical thought, apathy, and lack of ability to initiate activity. Before the use of lithium in the United States, schizophrenia was often given as a diagnosis whenever hallucinations were present, but hallucinations alone are insufficient for making a diagnosis because a variety of conditions, including drug intoxication, may produce hallucinations in the absence of schizophrenia. The common image of schizophrenia as a "split personality" has nothing to do with schizophrenia but with what are called "dissociative disorders" which are related to the hysteria of Freud's early patients.

Schizophrenia was first described as a specific disorder by the great German psychiatrist Emil Kraepelin. In his 1896 textbook he considered the condition to be a progressive deteriorating disease of unknown origin, usually seen in young adults, and called it dementia praecox. In 1911 the French psychiatrist Eugen Bleuler put dementia praecox on a new footing. Observing that some patients recovered, Bleuler, who was influenced by Freud, wrote that the disorder had both organic and psychological components. He stressed the splitting of the personality as the central feature of the disease, referring to specific disturbances of affect, association, and volition. "Split personality" has been confused since with the kind of splitting seen in multiple personality (à la Dr. Jekyll and Mr. Hyde) and other dissociative disorders.

5. See. H. E. Lehmann in Freedman and Kaplan, *Comprehensive Textbook of Psychiatry*, 641. Also see a landmark study by R. E. Kendall et al., "The Diagnostic Criteria of American and British Psychiatrists," *Arch. Gen. Psychiatry* 25 (1971): 123–30.

6. See, for example, R. Keisling, "Underdiagnosis of Manic-Depressive Illness in a Hospital Unit," *Amer. J. Psychiatry* 138 (1981): 672–3. The main thrust of this study was rediagnosis, and Keisling found that when a cohort of patients were rediagnosed in 1980, the ratio of schizophrenic to manic-depressive illness was approximately 1:1; whereas the ratio for the entire hospital in 1979, using the old criteria, was 12:1.

7. "Bipolar Patients Suffer from Long-term Misdiagnosis," *Psychiatric News*, 16 September 1994, 1.

8. There's a small but important literature on misdiagnosis, specifically of African-American patients. See, for example, S. Mukherjee et al., "Misdiagnosis of Schizophrenia in Bipolar Patients: A Multiethnic Comparison," *Am. J. Psychiatry* 140 (1983): 1571–74; or C. Lehmann, "Racism Often at Root of Misdiagnosing Minority Patients," *Psychiatric News*, 16 December 1994, 9.

9. E. F. Torrey, *Surviving Schizophrenia: A Family Manual*, rev. ed. (New York: Harper and Row, 1988).

10. Kaplan and Sadock, *Synopsis of Psychiatry*, 137.

11. Ibid.

12. Ibid., 136.

13. P. R. Breggin, *Toxic Psychiatry* (New York: St. Martin's, 1991).

14. Kaplan and Sadock, *Synopsis of Psychiatry*, 136.

15. See, for example, M. A. Fauman, "Psychiatric Components of Medical and Surgical Practice, II: Referral and Treatment of Psychiatric Disorders," *Am. J. Psychiatry* 140 (1983): 760–63.

16. For example, a 1987 survey found that only 38 percent of internists would send a depressed patient for ongoing treatment, and only about 25 percent would refer a patient with anxiety attacks. C. Lehmann, "Working with Primary Docs Brings MH Care to More People," *Psychiatric News*, 7 October 1994, 5.

Chapter Sixteen: Where Do We Go from Here?

1. See note 7 for chap. 11 above.

2. In DSM-III diagnosis is divided into two main categories: Axis I involves relatively clear-cut syndromes that we are likely to experience in terms of discrete symptoms, such as depression, panic disorder, or substance abuse; Axis II involves more global disorders of overall personality, such as paranoid personality disorder, or borderline, or passive-aggressive, or antisocial. (Between 5 and 10 percent of the population seems to have these personality disorders.) Patients may have difficulties in both areas, but the primary diagnosis is usually the one

that is the main focus of treatment. Axis I diagnoses are often more striking or florid as well.

Personality disorder is more pervasive and ever present; depressions, panics, phobias, and other Axis I diagnoses often have a peculiar on-off quality. We often tend to think these diagnoses more serious than personality disorders because the symptoms are so dramatic, but when they're gone, they're gone.

Reliability measurements on Axis I diagnoses are very high; the areas of most dispute lie on Axis II.

For an introduction to the subject, see Kaplan and Sadock, *Synopsis of Psychiatry*, chap. 3. See also Grob, "Origins of DSM-I"; and Wilson, "DSM-III and the Transformation of American Psychiatry."

3. That is, other anxiety-produced conditions such as phobic disorders, with or without panic attacks; panic disorder; generalized anxiety disorder; post-traumatic stress disorder; or obsessive-compulsive disorder.

4. A kind of amphetamine, Ritalin and its analogues are an effective treatment in 70 to 80 percent of patients with attention-deficit disorder. See Kaplan and Sadock, *Synopsis Psychiatry*.

5. A large group of depressed patients is particularly sensitive to changes in ambient light and demonstrate what is called a "seasonal affective disorder" (SAD) usually in winter. This specific syndrome, which can be treated by exposure to full-spectrum light at high intensities, may also interact with other depressive disorders. It may have to do with some abnormality of melatonin regulation by the pineal gland. Ibid.